ROUTLEDGE LIBRARY EDITIONS:
ANXIETY

Volume 4

ANXIETY AND SELF-FOCUSED ATTENTION

ANXIETY AND SELF-FOCUSED ATTENTION

Edited by
RALF SCHWARZER AND
ROBERT A. WICKLUND

Routledge
Taylor & Francis Group
LONDON AND NEW YORK

First published in 1991 by Harwood Academic Publishers

This edition first published in 2016
by Routledge
2 Park Square, Milton Park, Abingdon, Oxon OX14 4RN

and by Routledge
711 Third Avenue, New York, NY 10017

Routledge is an imprint of the Taylor & Francis Group, an informa business

British Library Cataloguing in Publication Data
A catalogue record for this book is available from the British Library

ISBN: 978-1-138-92488-8 (Set)
ISBN: 978-1-315-67294-6 (Set) (ebk)
ISBN: 978-1-138-93763-5 (Volume 4) (hbk)
ISBN: 978-1-138-93972-1 (Volume 4) (pbk)
ISBN: 978-1-315-67476-6 (Volume 4) (ebk)

Anxiety and Self-Focused Attention

Edited by

Ralf Schwarzer
Freie Universität Berlin, FRG

and

Robert A. Wicklund
Universität Bielefeld, FRG

harwood academic publishers
chur • london • paris • new york • melbourne

Harwood Academic Publishers

Post Office Box 197
London WC2E 9PX
United Kingdom

58, rue Lhomond
75005 Paris
France

Post Office Box 786
Cooper Station
New York, New York 10276
United States of America

Private Bag 8
Camberwell, Victoria 3124
Australia

The articles appearing in this book were first published in the journai
Anxiety Research in Volume 1 Nos 1, 2 and 3
2 Nos 2 and 3
3 No 2

Library of Congress Cataloging-in-Publication Data

Anxiety and self-focused attention / edited by Ralf Schwarzer and Robert A. Wicklund.
p. cm.
Includes bibliographical references and index.
ISBN 3-7186-5068-1
1. Anxiety. 2. Self-perception. 3. Self psychology.
I. Schwarzer, Ralf. II. Wicklund, Robert A.
BF575.A6A576 1991
152.4'6 – dc20 90-21313
CIP

 Printed in The United States of America by Braun-Brumfield, Inc.

CONTENTS

PREFACE

Theoretical perspectives in the field of anxiety research have broadened considerably in recent years and innovative empirical works have increased in number. Particularly notable among these developments is a certain cognitive direction, including not only analyses of information processing *vis à vis* anxiety, but also the variable of self-focused attention. The idea underlying this volume is that of integrating a number of conceptual approaches to anxiety, most of which bear directly on the self-focus notion, and all of which touch the notion at least indirectly. These chapters stem from diverse sources, including psychologists in the areas of social, clinical and personality psychology. Their common ground is the overriding idea that anxiety, as a state of distress, has a strong determinant or accompaniment in self-directed attention. Thus, the book poses a theoretical challenge to more traditional anxiety research and theory, where psychometric issues, clinical case studies and classical personality constructs have dominated.

The chapters have appeared as journal articles in the first three volumes of *Anxiety Research, An International Journal.* The widespread interest in many of these articles encouraged us to think in terms of bringing a select number of them together in integrated form.

This volume is not only designed for researchers in the fields of anxiety and self-theory, but is also pertinent to clinical, personality, social and educational psychologists.

Ralf Schwarzer
Robert A. Wicklund

INTRODUCTION

ROBERT A. WICKLUND
Universität Bielefeld, FRG

The present volume comes to grips with a psychological process that is characteristically associated with manifestations of anxiety. The core of this process is self-focused attention, or "self-related cognitions," a concept frequently referred to in addressing the relation between anxiety arousal and disfunctioning (Sarason, 1960, 1978, 1988; Wine, 1971). Among the chapters included here, the reader will find that self-focused attention is related to symptoms of anxiety arousal, to information-processing associated with anxiety, and in some chapters, to classic measurement of anxiety. However, several of the chapters do not discuss anxiety as such: Rather, beginning with the self-focus concept, a number of phenomena are examined that traditionally have a close relation to effects observed in classical anxiety research. What are some of these effects?

Self-awareness and distress. In 1932 Wolff published a series of studies in which subjects' attention was steered toward physical aspects of themselves. They were shown photos of their own hands, they examined their own profiles, and they heard playbacks of their own voices. Wolff's interest was in subjects' readiness or ability to recognize these photos, profiles, and voices, given that a number of photos of different hands were shown, and several different voices were played back. Particularly interesting among his findings was an apparent avoidance phenomenon: Subjects were unlikely to identify their own voices correctly, relative to their success in identifying acquaintances' voices. According to Wolff, the spontaneous recognition rate for one's own voice was only 10.5%; for the recognition of acquaintances' voices, it was 37%.

Why should these effects be theoretically interesting? As Wolff observed, hearing one's own voice evidently sets off an affective state, resulting in a certain refusal to acknowledge that the present sound indeed belongs to oneself. It is possible to extend this observation a step further, and to talk about the induction of self-awareness (no matter how that induction comes about) as generating entire arrays of unpleasant psychological states. An integral part of such a line of thought is that hearing one's own voice, seeing one's self in a mirror, or finding oneself to be stranded outside an ongoing group can bring the person to focus on still further facets of the self. It is here that we begin to arrive at the subject matter of the present papers.

For instance: A thoroughgoing assumption of these contributions is that self-directed attention can quickly bring the person to sense, and become preoccupied with, existing *discrepancies*. These discrepancies are particularly interesting insofar as they involve (a) societal standards, and (b) behaviors of the individual. Thus the discrepancy, as recognized by the person, involves a clash between societal rules (perhaps internalized rules, but in any case standards felt by the person) and the behavior or thought tendencies of the individual. In more common language, such discrepancies are labelled as immoral behavior, hypocrisy, conducting oneself in an inconsistent manner, or failing to live up to achievement standards.

If we begin with a person whose actions or motivations fall short of internalized standards, the occurrence of self-focused attention is said to steer the person's attention especially to those personal lacks. And the result, in the language of the papers to follow, is distress, depression, anxiety, loneliness, a drop in self-esteem, and frequently the attempt to depart from that state of self-focused attention. The routes taken to these effects vary from author to author, as the reader will find, but the core idea is the instigation of self-focused attention – however it may come about – as basic to the individual's distress and tendency to flight. Such reactions are based theoretically in the person's coming to cognize a given shortcoming.

Self-awareness: A civilizing influence. In 1934 a number of ideas were set down by Mead that are commonly referred to as symbolic interactionism. One of the principles was a societal controlling mechanism – the generalized other – coming to have a general impact on the individual's behavior. A frequently overlooked insight of Mead's, later spelled out in some detail by Shibutani (1961), was the relation between self-consciousness and the workings of the generalized other. Insofar as the person's attention is self-directed, the generalized other as "self", i.e., the depository of shared societal standards, comes to exert control on behavior.

One can discuss this principle in still more simplified language. If the person has come to internalize the views, values, standards, or opinions of a segment of society, those internalized elements will come to be realized in behavior only to the extent that the person is self-focused. This means that the self-directed attention of the individual serves the group's need to control the individual. Once the person becomes self-reflexive, consistency with one's internalized moral standards increases, strivings toward achievement standards are accelerated, and the commission of hypocrisies diminishes. A host of pro-social effects can also come into play, such as perspective-taking, helping, and even conformity to the values of dominant groups of individuals.

Plagued and controlled. At this midpoint in the discussion we may try placing the two broad sets of phenomena into a juxtaposition: On the one hand, the self-aware person is said to become increasingly sensitive to inner-self discrepancies – to suffer a variety of psychological maladies that can variously be depicted as anxiety, depression, sadness, fright, or lowered self-esteem. At the same time, this same self-focused person has a decided readiness to excel; there is not only a sensitivity to discrepancies, but a simultaneous striving to eliminate such discrepancies, striving in the direction of socially-set goals. Such striving, perhaps needless to say, can have the effect of eliminating potential discrepancies, or the opposite: If unsuccessful, the self-awareness will lead to the potpourri of affects and discomforts.

It should now be clear that self-awareness is not regarded simply as a cognitive fact, i.e., as direction of attention *per se*. Rather, self-awareness can be shown to be a basis of society's control over the individual. Whether this control device in fact results in the person's coming to be more consistent and more successful depends on whether the extent of self-focus turns into a debilitating factor. And to be sure, the chapters to follow point to both kinds of effects – the civilizing "superego" effect of self-focused attention as well as the direct detrimental consequences of self-awareness on various forms of functioning.

The border between individual and group. But there is still another side to the self-awareness processes examined here. In a classic analysis of suicide (and for that matter, homicide), Durkheim (1951) drew attention to the condition of individuation ("egoism" in his language) brought about through a lack of the individual's being surrounded by the props of a steady stream of cultural influence. By Durkheim's analysis, the person who has to shoulder the responsibility for decisions, particularly decisions in the moral and achievement spheres, comes to suffer as a result of not being surrounded by an *integrated* security-engendering social system, a system of social rules that prevents the individual from having to decide in a social vacuum.

While Durkheim did not refer to this individuation as self-awareness, aspects to the present volume pick up where he left off. It may be argued that the self-aware person is simultaneously cut off from a system of immediate social support and guidance, and is left to try to cope with the world on the basis of a handful of presumably internalized values. Hence the loneliness of the self-aware condition. To be sure, the sense of being separated from others, or standing out as a minority, has traditionally been regarded as going hand-in-hand with self-focused attention (Shibutani, 1961), and it should also follow that the self-aware person would have an interest in moving back to the group, toward a clear system of standards, and even toward the non-self-aware condition of deindividuation.

On theorizing about anxiety. Are we talking here about anxiety? This question will occur and recur to the reader, and the question is best answered now, as a prologue to all of what follows: (a) If we continue with the direction set by Wolff's (1932) experimentation and add a bit of theoretical elaboration, we come to the picture of the self-aware human as someone who is potentially in a state of distress, experiences negative affect, is prone to self-blame, and is susceptible to the injurious implications of reality; (b) If we add Mead (1934) and the elaborations of Shibutani (1961), we push the picture a step further, toward the person who is preoccupied with doing right by societal rules. The person becomes controllable from the outside, predictable for the group, and potentially susceptible to the woes associated with not living up to internalized standards; (c) The final element in the picture is added by the direction hinted at by Durkheim (1951) – The self-aware individual may be regarded as alone, as having to cope with whatever is internalized, and as being psychologically set off from the immediate group.

Is this triad of phenomena, closely tied to the self-reflexive potential of the human, anything resembling anxiety? The approach taken here answers the question with a very open question mark. Numerous phenomena studied under the rubric of self-awareness overlap with manifestations observed within classic anxiety-research settings. The sense of not living up to standards, of anticipating failure, of being cut off from others (Baumeister & Tice, in press) and of preoccupation with one's own internalized values are all to be found in such classic paradigms. However, many of the present chapters *do not* begin with a cluster of manifestations labelled anxiety, but instead, follow the human through the course of adopting and internalizing values, through the discrepancies that in turn result, and through the diverse arrays of effects that then stem out of the individual's direction of attention – toward or away from the self. Thus the central focus is on antecedent variables, i.e., theoretical variables that indicate when self-focus will increase or decline, variables that refer to the extent of a discrepancy and to its salience in the person's perceptual field, and variables that steer the individual forward, to satisfy those standards, or backward, to flee from a distress-laden state of affairs.

In the course of such an approach, the question of whether any given outcome ("symptom") constitutes an instance of anxiety is not of paramount significance. Rather, one's attention is on the combination of theoretically-specified, antecedent variables and their workings on a qualitatively heterogeneous set of outcomes. These outcomes will overlap with what has traditionally been called anxiety, but still more important, they will also involve effects that would seldom be included among lists of anxiety symptoms. But this is enough prologue. We will now turn to the individual contributions, to see how each of them addresses the issues just raised.

References

Baumeister, R.F. & Tice, D.T. (in press). Anxiety and social exclusion. *Journal of Social and Clinical Psychology.*
Durkheim, E. (1951). *Suicide.* New York: The Free Press. (Originally published 1897).
Mead, G.H. (1934). *Mind, self and society.* Chicago: University of Chicago Press.
Sarason, I.G. (1960). Empirical findings and theoretical problems in the use of anxiety scales. *Psychological Bulletin,* **57**, 403–415.
Sarason, I.G. (1978). The test anxiety scale: Concept and research. In C.D. Spielberger & I.G. Sarason (Eds.), *Stress and anxiety* (Vol. **5**, pp.193–216). New York: Wiley.
Sarason, I.G. (1988). Anxiety, self-preoccupation and attention. *Anxiety Research: An International Journal,* **1**, 3–7.
Shibutani, T. (1961). *Society and personality: An interactionist approach to social psychology.* Englewood Cliffs, N.J.: Prentice-Hall.
Wine, J. (1971). Test anxiety and direction of attention. *Psychological Bulletin,* **76**, 92–104.
Wolff, W. (1932). Selbstbeurteilung und Fremdbeurteilung im wissentlichen und unwissentlichen Versuch. *Psychologische Forschung,* **16**, 251–328.

Part 1: SELF-FOCUS AND NEGATIVE AFFECT

A CONTROL-PROCESS PERSPECTIVE ON ANXIETY

CHARLES S. CARVER*

University of Miami, Florida, USA

and

MICHAEL F. SCHEIER

Carnegie-Mellon University, Pennsylvania, USA

A view of certain consequences of anxiety is presented in which anxiety causes an interruption in ongoing self-regulation, leading to an assessment of outcome or coping expectancy. In this theory, people with favorable expectancies return to the interrupted activity, whereas people with unfavorable expectancies experience an impulse to disengage from further efforts. Our view differs from other attentional theories of anxiety in the following way: we argue, with the support of research evidence, that *both* the renewed effort and the disengagement (and its consequent performance impairment) are exaggerated by subsequent self-focused attention.

KEY WORDS: Anxiety, attention, self-focus, confidence, doubt.

Our work over the past dozen years has focused on certain processes in the self-regulation of human behavior. In doing this work—constructing and testing a theoretical model of how we think self-regulation proceeds—we have several times examined the effects of anxiety on behavior (e.g. Carver, Blaney and Scheier, 1979; Carver, Peterson, Follansbee and Scheier, 1983; Carver and Scheier, 1984; Carver, Scheier and Klahr, 1987). Based on this work, we think we can point to several principles that serve to further our understanding of anxiety and its effects on behavior.

We believe that human behavior is regulated in a system of feedback control (see, e.g. Carver and Scheier, 1981, 1986, for broader statements). In this view, people continually establish goals, standards and intentions for themselves (both very short-term and much longer-term goals), which they then use as reference points. As people act, they self-attentively monitor their actions with regard to those reference points. When necessary, they make adjustments to bring their actions into closer conformity with the intended or desired actions. Such discrepancy reductions are basic to self-regulation via feedback control.

Although these processes are often executed smoothly and easily, problems in the smooth flow of self-regulation do arise occasionally. Sometimes difficulties occur in the form of environmental impediments. Sometimes, however, difficulties involve conflict between competing reference values. We tend to regard anxiety as reflecting the existence of such a conflict. In particular, anxiety arises when people find themselves in situations where attempting to behave in line with one reference value threatens to enlarge discrepancies with respect to another reference value such as physical safety, acceptance from other people, personal comfort, or holistic personal integration (cf. Rogers, 1980). This rising anxiety, in effect, serves as a warning signal

* Address correspondence to: Charles S. Carver, Department of Psychology, P.O. Box 248185, University of Miami, Coral Gables, Florida 33124, USA.

to the person that he or she should consider a change in behavioral priorities (Simon, 1967).

Our view of the nature of anxiety is similar in many ways to contemporary approaches that emphasize the role of cognitive and attentional processes. We would agree, for example, with Hamilton (1983) that anxiety, as information in the nervous system, takes up space in working memory and, for that reason, can potentially interfere with other cognitive activity. We would also agree with Simon (1967) that anxiety represents an interruptor of action and a call for reconsideration of which goals deserve one's most immediate attention and efforts. The aspect of anxiety that we are most inclined to emphasize, however, is its impact on behavior.

CONSEQUENCES OF ANXIETY

One curious thing about the effect of anxiety is that it does not automatically impair performance. In some circumstances, anxiety has only an energizing and focusing effect on the person experiencing it. Another curious thing is that the physiological aspect of anxiety is apparently not what influences behavior. For example, several recent studies have found that physiological arousal reactions before and during evaluative examinations do not distinguish people who are high in test anxiety from those who are low in test anxiety (Deffenbacher and Hazaleus, 1985; Hollandsworth, Glazeski, Kirkland, Jones and Van Norman, 1979; Holroyd, Westbrook, Wolf and Badhorn, 1978). People of both groups become aroused, and they do so to equivalent degrees. Yet the eventual impact on behavior differs greatly between groups.

Why is this so? The effect of anxiety arousal on performance depends not on physiological change, but instead on how the person orients and responds to the anxiety and to the situation more broadly. We share this view with many contemporary theorists. It is widely accepted, for instance, that the dysfunctional effects of test anxiety are produced not by emotional arousal *per se*, but by a cognitive "worry" factor (Deffenbacher, 1980; Morris and Ponath, 1986). We differ somewhat from other theorists, however, in our view of how these cognitive processes lead to impairment or disruption in behavior. In our view, there is one particularly critical variable, which causes a fundamental variation in response, which in turn has multiple manifestations.

The critical variable in our view is the person's expectancy (favorable versus unfavorable) of being able to cope with the anxiety being experienced and being able to complete the action that is being attempted (see Figure 1). The person who expects to be able to cope, who is sufficiently confident of being able to complete the action, responds to anxiety arousal with renewed effort. When this person's attention is self-directed, the result is enhanced persistence and even enhanced performance.

The person who has serious doubts about being able to cope, who has the expectation of a bad outcome, is likely not to persist in the face of anxiety arousal. This person is more likely to experience an impulse to disengage. Consistent with this, Galassi, Frierson and Sharer (1981) have reported that the most frequent thought intrusion among test-anxious students during a test is the desire to escape. This impulse sometimes results in overt withdrawal from the behavioral setting. It is sometimes expressed more subtly as disengagement of effort toward goal attainment. These responses, in turn, can result in impaired performances when attention is self-directed (Carver *et al.*, 1979, 1983; Rich and Woolever, in press).

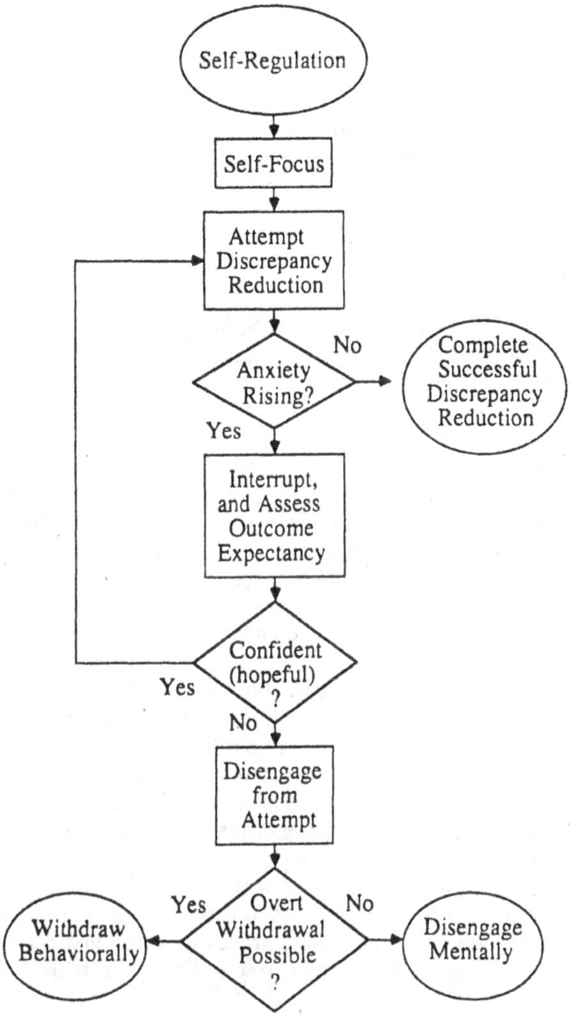

Figure 1 Flow-chart diagram of the various consequences that can follow from the attempt to match one's behavior to a standard of comparison in a situation that is anxiety provoking. As indicated here, behavior may be interrupted if anxiety rises noticably (or if difficulties or impediments are encountered). What follows this interruption is determined by the person's expectations about whether or not continued efforts will promote a good outcome.

Social or other constraints often prevent overt manifestations of this impulse. In such cases it may be expressed covertly, through self-distraction or off-task thinking. Many situations in which people become anxious, however, do not permit even this psychological disengagement to be sustained for long. Rather, the person typically re-emerges into the behavioral situation, becomes aware of the anxiety again, and promptly reconfronts the doubts that had prompted the initial disengagement.

Over a period of time, this cycle of doubt, disengagement, reconfrontation and renewed doubt often produces a phenomenology of self-deprecatory rumination under conditions of high anxiety. This self-deprecatory rumination has been given the label "self-focus" by such theorists as Wine (1971, 1982) and Sarason (1975). This view of highly test-anxious people as being highly self-focused has further come to be known as the cognitive-attentional theory of test anxiety, a theory that by extrapolation also applies to other sorts of anxiety.

THE ROLE OF SELF-FOCUS

We agree that theorists such as Wine and Sarason have accurately described the phenomenology experienced by test-anxious people in test settings. In our view, however, using the label "self-focus" to characterize this phenomenology is an oversimplification, one that is potentially quite misleading.

That is, our theoretical analysis assumes that self-focused attention is involved *both* in task engagement *and* in this dysfunctional response to anxiety. Consistent with this assumption, there is much experimental evidence that self-focus can enhance persistence and task performance, provided the person in whom self-focus is induced has a relatively favorable expectancy for successful goal attainment (see Carver and Scheier, 1986, for a review). Indeed, facilitation due to self-focus when expectancies are favorable occurs even among people who are very susceptible to anxiety arousal—for example, people high in test anxiety (Slapion and Carver, 1981; Rich and Woolever, in press). Such facilitation seems not to be easy to reconcile with a theory in which the concept of self-focused attention is inextricably linked to behavioral dysfunction.

In our view, the difference between facilitation and dysfunction depends not on presence or absence of self-focus *per se*, but on a difference in the processes taking place in the person. The person with favorable expectancies remains task engaged, even when highly anxious and highly self-focused. As a result, the phenomenology of this person is likely to be construed by the theorist observer as "task"-focus rather than as "self"-focus. Yet, from the control-process viewpoint, one *cannot* be task-focused without being simultaneously focused on an aspect of the self. In particular, the task-focused person will remain focused on the comparison between the intended behavioral goal and his or her present state, in the attempt to move the latter steadily toward the former (see Carver *et al.*, 1979, and Scheier and Carver, 1983, for research evidence on this point).

The person whose performance is deteriorating under the pressure of anxiety may be self-focused, but in this case the focus is simply on a different aspect of self. This person's attention is focused specifically on perceived deficits of the self, salient self-doubts, and the possible larger ramifications of being unable to proceed toward his or her goal. It is precisely this sort of cognitive content that should follow from an impulse to disengage, when that impulse is not being expressed behaviorally (Figure 1).

SUMMARY

To sum up the essence of our position, our view is that the impact of anxiety on performance depends on the person's expectancy of being able to cope, of being able to carry out the action as intended. Favorable expectancies are associated with continued or repeatedly renewed efforts, and ultimately with little performance impairment (unless task demands on attention are so high that the presence of anxiety creates a bottleneck in processing).

Unfavorable expectancies are associated with an impulse to disengage. This results in decreased effort, physical withdrawal or psychological disengagement, and ultimately in impairment of the behavior the person is attempting. Unfavorable expectancies under some circumstances also give rise to a phenomenology of self-deprecatory rumination. It is worth re-emphasizing that we view both the performance impairment and the self-deprecatory (so-called self-focused) phenomenology as being products of a more fundamental impulse to disengage, which in turn is based on unfavorable coping expectancies.

Finally, high levels of self-focused attention can be expected to exaggerate each of these consequences—resulting in facilitation in some circumstances and disruption in others.

We believe that these principles are consistent with a great deal of what is known about anxiety and human behavior. We also believe that they account somewhat better for dysfunctional responses to anxiety than do alternative models, by treating these dysfunctional responses as manifestations of a series of underlying processes. At the same time, this theory also addresses disruptions for reasons other than anxiety, as well as aspects of behavior in which there is no dysfunction.

We think that this model can be useful to many people as an organizing framework for understanding the dynamics of anxiety. If it is inadequate to the task, it will eventually be proven so. By posing the model and encouraging its empirical evaluation, we hope to contribute to a better—and ultimately broader—understanding of the processes and consequences of anxiety.

Acknowledgement

Preparation of this article was facilitated by support from the National Science Foundation (BNS 84-14601, BNS 84-06235, BNS 87-06271 and BNS 87-17783).

References

Carver, C.S. and Scheier, M.F. (1981) *Attention and Self-Regulation: A Control-Theory Approach to Human Behavior*. New York: Springer-Verlag

Carver, C.S. and Scheier, M.F. (1984) Self-focused attention in test anxiety: A general theory applied to a specific phenomenon. In *Advances in Test Anxiety Research*, Vol. 3, edited by H.M. van der Ploeg, R. Schwarzer and C.D. Spielberger, pp. 3–20. Lisse/Hillsdale, NJ: Swets and Zeitlinger/Erlbaum

Carver, C.S. and Scheier, M.F. (1986) Functional and dysfunctional responses to anxiety: The interaction between expectancies and self-focused attention. In *Self-related Cognitions in Anxiety and Motivation*, edited by R. Schwarzer, pp. 111–141. Hillsdale, NJ: Erlbaum

Carver, C.S., Blaney, P.H. and Scheier, M.F. (1979) Focus of attention, chronic expectancy, and responses to a feared stimulus. *Journal of Personality and Social Psychology*, **37**, 1186–1195

Carver, C.S., Peterson, L.M., Follansbee, D.J. and Scheier, M.F. (1983) Effects of self-directed attention on performance and persistence among persons high and low in test anxiety. *Cognitive Therapy and Research*, **7**, 333–354

Carver, C.S., Scheier, M.F. and Klahr, D. (1987) Further explorations of a control-process model of test anxiety. In *Advances in Test Anxiety Research*, Vol. 5, edited by R. Schwarzer, H.M. van der Ploeg and C.D. Spielberger, pp. 15–22. Lisse: Swets and Zeitlinger

Deffenbacher, J.L. (1980) Worry and emotionality in test anxiety. In *Test Anxiety: Theory, Research, and Application*, edited by I.G. Sarason, pp. 111–128. Hillsdale, NJ: Erlbaum

Deffenbacher, J.L. and Hazaleus, S.L. (1985) Cognitive, emotional, and physiological components of test anxiety. *Cognitive Therapy and Research*, **9**, 169–180

Galassi, J.P., Frierson, H.T. Jr and Sharer, R. (1981) Behavior of high, moderate, and low test anxious students during an actual test situation. *Journal of Consulting and Clinical Psychology*, **49**, 51–62

Hamilton, V. (1983) *The Cognitive Structures and Processes of Human Motivation and Personality*. Chicester, England: Wiley

Hollandsworth, J.G. Jr, Glazeski, R.C., Kirkland, K., Jones, G.E. and Van Norman, L.R. (1979) An analysis of the nature and effects of test anxiety: cognitive, behavioral, and physiological components. *Cognitive Therapy and Research*, **3**, 165–180

Holroyd, K.A., Westbrook, T., Wolf, M. and Badhorn, E. (1978) Performance, cognition, and physiological responding in test anxiety. *Journal of Abnormal Psychology*, **87**, 442–451

Morris, L.W. and Ponath, P.M. (1986) Differences in anxiety among androgynous women: relation to achievement motivation variables. In *Self-Related Cognitions in Anxiety and Motivation*, edited by R. Schwarzer, pp. 55–64. Hillsdale, NJ: Erlbaum

Rich, A.R. and Woolever, D.K. (in press) Expectancy and self-focused attention: experimental support for the self-regulation model of test anxiety. *Journal of Social and Clinical Psychology*

Rogers, C.R. (1980) *A Way of Being*. Boston: Houghton Mifflin

Sarason, I.G. (1975) Anxiety and self-preoccupation. In *Stress and Anxiety*, Vol. 2, edited by I.G. Sarason and C.D. Spielberger, pp. 27–44. New York: Wiley

Scheier, M.F. and Carver, C.S. (1983) Self-directed attention and the comparison of self with standards. *Journal of Experimental Social Psychology*, **19**, 205–222

Simon, H.A. (1967) Motivational and emotional controls of cognition. *Psychological Review*, **74**, 29–39

Slapion, M.J. and Carver, C.S. (1981) Self-directed attention and facilitation of intellectual performance among persons high in test anxiety. *Cognitive Therapy and Research*, **5**, 115–121

Wine, J.D. (1971) Test anxiety and direction of attention. *Psychological Bulletin*, **76**, 902–104

Wine, J.D. (1982) Evaluation anxiety: a cognitive-attentional construct. In *Achievement, Stress, and Anxiety*, edited by H.W. Krohne and L.C. Laux, pp. 207–219. Washington, DC: Hemisphere

ANXIETY, SELF-PREOCCUPATION AND ATTENTION

IRWIN G. SARASON*

University of Washington, Seattle, USA

A cognitive view of anxiety is outlined that emphasizes the role self-preoccupation plays in attention and information processing. Two applications of this theoretical approach are given, one in the area of test anxiety and the other relating to cognitive therapies for anxiety.

KEY WORDS: Anxiety, test anxiety, self-preoccupation, self-related cognitions, attention, information processing.

Cognitive, behavioral and physiological factors play important roles in anxiety. While there is general agreement about the need to incorporate these factors in any comprehensive anxiety construct, there are differences among existing theories in the emphasis given to each of them. In this article, I describe a cognitive view of anxiety that focuses on the role self-preoccupation plays in behavioral and physiological outcomes. Acording to this view, how well people perform, how anxious they feel in particular situations, and their levels of physiological activation are powerfully influenced by self-related thoughts. Self-related thoughts are significant influences over behavior because they direct attention in idiosyncratic ways. This article discusses the role these thoughts play in adaptation and maladaptation.

The cognitive view of anxiety grows out of the conceptualization that personality can be understood from an information-processing perspective. Cognitive events include the ways in which a person searches the environment for cues, selects cues that are relevant to thought and action, integrates new information with old, and makes decisions that result in observable behavior. Self-preoccupying cognitive events are as much behavior as a muscle twitch or a signature on a piece of paper. However, cognitive events are not directly observable and inferential support for their existence must come from behavior that can be observed.

Self-preoccupation has attentional properties because it leads people to focus on environmental cues to which they are especially sensitive (Strack, Blaney and Ganellen, 1985). The amount and type of self-preoccupation influences the degree to which the person is receptive to the available stimulus information and the amount of physiological arousal. Task-oriented persons who are deeply immersed in their jobs will be especially attentive to cues that might contribute to job completion. Students who are worried about failure will be especially attentive to stimuli suggestive of possible evaluations of their work. Paranoid persons will be especially attentive to cues that relate to their distinctive systems of ideation. To the extent that the self-preoccupied person attends to environmental cues, the cues are dealt with by the person's distinctive information-processing system. A major research challenge is the identification and measurement of individual differences involved in information processing.

A preoccupied individual is engrossed in thought. Illustrative preoccupations include worry over the future of humanity, concern about food shortages throughout

* Address correspondence to: Irwin G. Sarason, Department of Psychology NI-25, University of Washington, Seattle, WA 98195, USA.

the world, fearful thoughts about snakes or failing in school, and anger over perceived slights and insults. The range of self-preoccupations is narrower because it is limited to being involved in thought about oneself. Self-preoccupation may intrude on information processing at three points: attention to environmental cues, encoding and transformation of this information, and selection of an overt response. The cognitive preoccupations of the angry person may interfere with the veridical preception of environmental cues, their interpretation, and decisions about responses to them. Similarly, but probably for different reasons, the person engulfed in sexual fantasies may also experience maladaptive functioning at these stages of information processing. There are many clinical examples of the diversity of cognitions with which persons become self-preoccupied, the degree to which self-preoccupation influences attentiveness to external cues, and the ways in which information from the environment is stored, retrieved and acted upon. Self-preoccupation is not restricted to the domain of worry or anxiety.

ANXIOUS SELF-PREOCCUPATION

Anxious self-preoccupation consists of heightened concern over one's inadequacies and shortcomings. The anxious person is concerned about present or potential dangers, threats, and the inability to cope with them. This does not mean that danger and threat necessarily cause anxious self-preoccupation. Self-preoccupation of any type is a function not only of objective life events but also of the interpretation placed on those events by the individual. Whether self-preoccupation occurs depends on the skills a person has learned in coping with dangers and threats. The anxious person often seems deficient in these skills.

Patterns of self-preoccupying thought function as templates or schemas that direct attention to salient aspects of the environment and interpersonal relationships. However, the person may have articulated neither these templates nor their functional relationship to behavior. Self-preoccupations not only interfere with or otherwise influence performance, but also serve to direct attention to personally salient problems that require solutions. A generalized tendency toward self-preoccupation seems to be a stable personality characteristic that leaves individuals vulnerable to high levels of interfering thought in particular kinds of situations. However, other personal characteristics may serve as protection from high levels of cognitive interference under stress even in otherwise vulnerable individuals. For instance, after a situation in which subjects were asked to recall recent negative events they had experienced, subjects low in perceived social support reported a greater increase in cognitive interference than subjects high in perceived social support (Sarason and Sarason, 1987).

A task confronting anxiety researchers is identification of the operations and transformations individuals perform on information that result in high levels of worry and anticipations of unpleasant outcomes. Accomplishing this task will require empirical inquiry into the assumptions, strategies and expectancies of people falling at different points along the continuum of anxious self-preoccupation, as well as into the rules by which they label and make judgments about whether an environmental event represents a personal threat. It is encouraging that this challenge has been taken up by researchers who are assessing persons' expectations and attributions, and other elements of their cognitive worlds (Kendall and Hollon, 1981; Merluzzi, Glass and Genest, 1981).

TEST ANXIETY, SELF-PREOCCUPATION AND ATTENTION

Because of its delimited content domain and the ubiquitousness of personal concerns about taking tests and being evaluated, test anxiety has been studied widely from a research standpoint (Sarason, 1980). Evidence of a negative correlation between test anxiety and performance in evaluative situations has led to a wide variety of experiments aimed at evaluating hypotheses about the processes that may be involved. Evidence has accrued showing the deleterious influence of high levels of test anxiety on information processing and performance. This negative influence is heightened by evaluational stressors. The more complex, more demanding the task, the stronger the influence.

There usually is more to test anxiety than a history of failure experiences. Test-anxious people process their objective successes and failures in distinctive ways, and their anxiety is related importantly to how they, and significant others in their lives, evaluate their test-taking experience. Every teacher can think of bright, successful students who, contrary to what one would expect, spend inordinate amounts of time worrying about whether they can meet the next academic challenge they must face. Proneness to self-preoccupation and, most specifically, to worry over evaluation is a powerful component of what is referred to as test anxiety.

While both general and test anxieties are usually defined as complex states that include cognitive, emotional, behavioral and bodily components, most anxiety measures yield only one global score. Wine (1982) has pointed out that it is not immediately obvious how to identify the active or most active ingredients in this complex and has suggested that test anxiety might fruitfully be reconceptualized primarily in terms of cognitive and attentional processes aroused in evaluational settings. In order to assess separately several components of a person's reactions to test situations, an instrument, the Reactions to Tests (RTT), has recently been created (Sarason, 1984). It consists of four factor analytically derived scales:

Tension ("I feel distressed and uneasy before tests")
Worry ("During tests, I wonder how the other people are doing")
Test-Irrelevant Thought ("Irrelevant bits of information pop into my head during a test")
Bodily Reactions ("My heart beats faster when the test begins".)

While these scales are positively intercorrelated, the correlations are low enough to justify comparisons among them concerning their predictive value. In one study, the RTT was related to performance on a difficult digit-symbol task under evaluative conditions (Sarason, 1984). The Worry scale was more consistently related to performance and post-performance reports of cognitive interference than were the other scales. The Tension scale approached the Worry scale as a predictor of performance.

The RTT has been related to physiological measures obtained during a test-taking situation. Burchfield, Sarason, Sarason and Beaton (1983) examined the relationship of the RTT to physiological indices gathered while college students worked on tasks of the type found in intelligence tests. Both the Tension and Worry scales were significantly correlated with skin conductance (GSR) and finger-tip temperature changes during performance. There were no significant correlations with EMG changes. Interestingly, the Task-Irrelevant Thinking and Bodily Reactions scales were unrelated to the physiological change measures. More studies dealing with relationships among components of anxiety, performance variables and physiological measures are needed (Deffenbacher, 1986).

Experimental studies have shown test-anxious people to be sensitive to a variety of interventions. Emphasis on the evaluational component of a situation heightens the self-preoccupation of those prone to be test anxious and lowers their performance. Reassuring instructions, modeling and relaxation training often have salutary effects on the performance of test-anxious people (Sarason, 1980).

THERAPEUTIC APPLICATION OF THE COGNITIVE VIEW OF ANXIETY

A major development in research on the cognitive view of anxiety has been its application to therapeutic situations. Beck (1986) has developed one of the most influential cognitive therapies. He believes that the core psychological problem in anxiety disorders is a vulnerability growing out of the individual's tendency to devaluate his or her problem-solving ability as well as to exaggerate the degree of threat in a problematic situation. The anxious individual perceives many threats to social relationships, freedom and self-identity. From this perspective, self-preoccupying thoughts about these perceptions mediate the relationship between eliciting events on the one hand, and behavioral and physiological response patterns on the other.

Three steps are involved in cognitive therapy: (1) Conceptualizing the patient's problem, (2) choosing strategies and tactics to deal with it, and (3) assessing the effectiveness of those strategies and tactics. In cognitive therapy, the therapist encourages the patient to talk openly about his or her fears and concerns, and conveys empathy for the patient's anxiety. The Socratic method is used to help the patient become aware of what his or her thoughts are, examine them for cognitive distortions, and substitute for them more realistic thoughts.

Beck's theory of cognitive therapy argues that each of us has an inner voice. When that voice interferes with our ability to function adequately, the unproductive thoughts must be replaced by productive ones. By correcting thinking errors and having patients work on pertinent homework assignments, they can develop not only improved ways of thinking but also more effective, less anxiety-producing behaviors.

CONCLUSIONS

The study of anxiety from a cognitive perspective has led to productive lines of inquiry with regard to both research and clinical practice. While all people experience self-preoccupation, self-related thoughts become maladaptive when they are excessively preoccupying and when they interfere with task-oriented thinking and attention to situational realities. Further research and theory is needed concerning (1) interactions among cognitive, behavioral, and physiological systems, (2) ways to help people articulate their self-preoccupying thoughts, (3) assessment of profiles of intrusive thoughts, and (4) interventions directed toward modifying the cognitive mediators of maladaptive behavior. Studies of anxiety that involve experimental and therapeutic interventions are in agreement that self-related worries and fears can be influenced. The influence process, in turn, affects observable behavior.

References

Beck, A.T. (1986) Cognitive approaches to anxiety disorders. In *Anxiety Disorders: Psychological and Biological Perspectives*, edited by B.F. Shaw, Z.V. Segal, T.M. Vallis and F.E. Cashman. New York: Plenum Press

Burchfield, S.R., Sarason, I.G., Sarason, B.R. and Beaton, R. (198?) Physiological aspects of test anxiety. Unpublished research, University of Washington, USA

Deffenbacher, J.L. (1986) Cognitive and physiological components of test anxiety in real-life exams. *Cognitive Therapy and Research*, **10**, 635–644

Kendall, P.C. and Hollon, S.D. (1981) Editors. *Assessment Strategies for Cognitive Behavioral Interventions*. NY: Academic Press

Merluzzi, T.V., Glass, C.R. and Genest, M. (1981) Editors. *Cognitive Assessment*. NY: The Guilford Press

Sarason, I.G. (1980) Editor. *Test Anxiety: Theory, Research and Applications*. Hillsdale, NJ: Erlbaum

Sarason, I.G. (1984) Stress, anxiety, and cognitive interference: reactions to tests. *Journal of Personality and Social Psychology*, **46**, 929–938

Sarason, I.G. and Sarason, B.R. (1987) Effects of focus on positive and negative life events on cognitive interference and performance of subjects differing in social support. Unpublished research, University of Washington, USA

Strack, S., Blaney, P.H. and Ganellen, R.J. (1985) Pessimistic self-preoccupation, performance deficits, and depression. *Journal of Personality and Social Psychology*, **49**, 1076–1085

Wine, J.D. (1982) Evaluation anxiety: a cognitive-attentional construct. In *Achievement, Stress, and Anxiety*, edited by H.W. Krohne and L. Laux, pp.207–219. Washington, DC: Hemisphere

SELF-EVALUATION AND SELF-PERCEPTION: THE ROLE OF ATTENTION IN THE EXPERIENCE OF ANXIETY

FREDERICK X. GIBBONS

Iowa State University

Self-awareness promotes the experience of anxiety in two ways. It does so directly, by enhancing awareness of the emotional state itself, and by initiating the self-evaluation process that is necessary for anxiety to occur. It also does so indirectly, by constraining some behaviors and inhibiting others. In particular, it increases accuracy of self-perception, and, in so doing, retards the process of self-delusion. This is important, because the latter process has been shown to have a salutary effect on mental health, acting as a buffer against dysphoric states such as depression and anxiety.

KEYWORDS: Self-evaluation, self-accuracy, illusions, negative affect

In this article I will make the argument that self-awareness promotes the experience of anxiety in two different ways. The first way is facilitative and it is fairly straightforward. Like any other emotion, the experience of anxiety is heightened by self-attention. Unlike many other emotions, however, self-attention is a necessary component of the anxiety experience. As Izard (1972) has suggested, the state of anxiety is actually a complex combination of emotions that includes an element of self-evaluation, as well as the concern and apprehension that self-evaluation produces. Self-evaluation cannot occur unless attention is focused on the self. Thus, self-focus has a direct link to anxiety through its impact on emotional awareness, and through the self-evaluation that it engenders. Both are necessary for anxiety to occur.

The second way in which self-focus affects anxiety is indirect, and, in many respects, more interesting. Self-focus inhibits many behaviors. Among those behaviors are some of the self-protective "strategies" that people engage in that act as a buffer between the ego and the environment in which it functions. Paradoxically, these are strategies — such as deception, denial and fabrication – that appear on the surface to be pathological in nature, but in fact often have a positive effect on mental health. They do so by counteracting the development or limiting the duration of debilitating emotional states such as anxiety and depression. I will describe both types of effects within the context of relevant research, most of it prompted by self-awareness theory.

Self-focused Attention and Affect

One of the most consistent findings to come out of the research prompted by self-awareness theory (Duval & Wicklund, 1972) involves the effect that self-directed attention has on affect or emotion. Beginning with Scheier's (1976) dissertation, this research has demonstrated that awareness of emotional states and reactions to those

Address Correspondence to: Frederick X. Gibbons, Department of Psychology, Iowa State University, Ames, Iowa 50011, USA.

states is heightened significantly when attention is directed toward the self. In Scheier (1976), for example, subjects who had been provoked by another person retaliated more against that person if their attention was self-focused when they were responding. Similar results have been reported in a variety of other empirical situations involving a number of different emotions (see Scheier, Carver, & Matthews, 1982, for a review). The explanation that has been provided for these results is rather straightforward, based more or less strictly on attentional factors. That is, the attention of a self-aware person tends to focus on whatever aspect of self is most salient at the time (Duval & Wicklund, 1972). When that dimension happens to be affect, it attracts attention, and, as a result, awareness of that affect, and the impact of that affect on behavior increases.

In looking back at these self-focus/affect studies an interesting characteristic can be seen in virtually all of them. That is the fact that the affect that was enhanced was almost always negatively toned (e.g., anger, fear, disgust, etc.). The majority of experiments that attempted to enhance positive affect either produced marginal effects (e.g., Scheier & Carver, 1977, Experiment 3), or no differences at all (e.g., Davies, 1982). Perhaps most informative in this regard were the results of a study by Csikszentmihalyi and Figurski (1982) who used a "beeper" technique to randomly assess the mood states of participants at various times throughout the day. What they found was that subjects were most likely to report being self-aware when they were engaged in voluntary activity; *and* they also reported experiencing negative affect during those times that they were self-focused.

This pronounced negative tendency in the self-focus/affect literature is in line with more recent research by Greenberg and Pyzsczynski (e.g., Greenberg & Pyzsczynski, 1986) suggesting that the disposition toward chronic self-focus (as measured by the Self-Consciousness Scale; Fenigstein, Scheier & Buss, 1975) is associated with chronic negative affect, specifically depression. More generally, the negative bias found in the affect studies is quite consistent with earlier research in the area of self-awareness indicating that, when possible, people try to avoid directing attention back on themselves (cf. Duval & Wicklund, 1972; Gibbons & Wicklund, 1976). In short, being the focus of one's own attention usually makes people uncomfortable. Why that is the case has a number of implications for a discussion of self-focused attention and anxiety.

SELF-FOCUS AND SELF-EVALUATION

The primary reason why self-focus causes discomfort was suggested by Duval and Wicklund (1972). They maintained that focusing attention on the self necessarily engages a self-evaluation process whereby the individual compares his or her current status on the salient (self) dimension with an ideal or standard that he or she maintains on that dimension. Duval and Wicklund defined a standard as a "criterion of correctness" or an ideal. In other words, the way the person thinks she or he *should* behave, what they should be, what they should believe, and so forth. This comparison between the actual and "the should" inevitably produces evidence of a discrepancy – the self is seldom seen as being as good as it could be – and it is the awareness of this discrepancy that motivates a response. The person either tries to bring the real self closer to the ideal, by changing one or more behaviors; or if that is not possible, something is done to direct attention off of the self. For example, people who tend dispositionally to be self-focused are more reactive to failure than are persons who are less self-focused, and they are more likely to use alcohol as a means of escaping self-focus after failure (Hull, Young, & Swank, 1982). In any case, the experience of self-focus tends to be phenomenologically aversive *most* of the time.

More than just producing discomfort, however, the state of self-focus also constrains behavior in a number of ways. For example, the self-aware person has relatively little tolerance for intrapersonal inconsistency. Consequently, when attention is directed back toward the self, the desire to reduce cognitive dissonance, usually through attitude change (cf. Innes & Young, 1975), increases. In contrast, persons whose attention has been distracted toward the environment seem to be quite content to accept (and presumably not think about) the inconsistency and the dissonance it produces, even when their behavior is publicly observable. I will discuss in more detail later the ways in which self-focus constrains behavior; but first I will discuss an obvious parallel between the two "states" of anxiety and self-focused attention.

Anxiety and Self-evaluation

The hypothesized self-evaluation process, which is perhaps the most fundamental tenet of self-awareness theory, is also a characteristic of at least one type of anxiety. Sarason (1975) has argued that there are two primary factors that contribute to the decline in performance that is a consequence of test-anxiety. One is a tendency for test anxious persons to become overly concerned with self-evaluation while they are trying to take an exam. The other, of course, is a sense of pessimism about the test outcome. In essence, the test anxious person devotes a considerable amount of the time that should be spent on the exam ruminating about the self and specifically the self's ability or inability to perform well. Essentially the same argument has been proposed to explain the negative effect that excessive self-attention has on sexual performance (Barlow, 1986). These two factors: the increase in self-directed attention, plus the tendency to spend that time self-evaluating, suggest that, at the very least, the test-anxious or sexually dysfunctional person is behaving in a manner that is very similar to that of people who are self-aware. Specifically, it is self-awareness within a performance context.

However, while everyone experiences some self-awareness and therefore self-evaluates when embarking on and during all but the most routine of tasks, certainly not everyone becomes test anxious or overly self-evaluative in the process. The reason has to do with outcome expectancies (cf. Carver, Peterson, Follansbee, & Scheier, 1983; Ellis, 1962). Those with high expectations of performance success will not perseverate in self-assessment. Those with low expectations are likely to become anxious about the outcome and enter into a self-focus/self-evaluative cycle from which it is difficult to exit (cf. Carver & Scheier, 1981; Greenberg & Pyzszczynski, 1986). Test anxious persons appear to be caught in such a cycle of self-preoccupation (Wine, 1982). It would be safe to conclude, then, that within a performance context, (performance) anxiety and self-awareness are virtually identical. That is, people who expect to do poorly on an important task of some kind will become anxious when their attention is self-focused before and during the task. On the other hand, as long as attention is directed externally, little or no anxiety will be experienced. There is more to the state of self-awareness than just self-evaluation, however, and the link between self-focus and anxiety in general rests on a broader foundation.

Self-Focus and Behavioral Constraint

In a recent review and update of self-awareness theory (Gibbons, in press), I suggested that self-awareness has an inhibitory effect on behavior that operates more or less independent of the hypothesized notion of discrepancy reduction. That is, behaviors that are counter to an individual's personal standards (e.g., stealing; Diener, Fraser, Beaman & Kelem, 1976; or aggression; Carver, 1975) are less likely to be performed if attention is focused on the self at the time. In this case there is no discrepancy to reduce, nor an ideal self to be attained. Rather, the concern is keeping the self where it should be; in other words, discrepancy prevention. The motivating force behind this tendency is a desire to avoid the negative affect that would be produced if inappropriate behavior were to occur. I suspect that this type of discrepancy prevention is just as common a consequence of self-awareness as is discrepancy reduction. Prevention versus reduction aside, however, the point is that the self-aware person is performing more or less constantly under the watchful eye of an evaluative audience. And that audience, namely the self, is a tough one. Certain behaviors are inhibited – behaviors that otherwise (in the absence of self-focus) will occur with some frequency – while others, which may be difficult to perform (e.g., becoming a better father or quitting smoking) are encouraged. In either case, there is pressure to do what should be done, and that pressure clearly can be aversive.

Private audiences. One other characteristic about the "audience" involved in the self-evaluation process is worth mentioning. Duval & Wicklund (1972) suggested that the value structure comprising personal standards and ideals, that guides behavior when attention is self-focused reflects an "accumulation of perspectives." In other words, it contains internalized values that have been adopted from a variety of reference groups. The construct resembles Mead's (1934) concept of the "generalized other," but it also is similar in many ways to the super-ego or even the conscience. Recently, work by Baldwin & Holmes (1987) has suggested that self-aware persons may also respond to certain specific or "private" audiences made salient by situational circumstances. In their first study, Baldwin & Holmes made half of their subjects self-aware (by means of a mirror) and then asked them to evaluate some pornographic literature. Before doing so, however, they were told to visualize either older members of their family or else friends from campus. The assumption was that the standards of the former group would be seen by subjects as being less accepting of the pornography, and that these standards would influence the behavior of the subjects toward the literature, but only if they were self-aware at the time. Results confirmed the hypotheses. Those who had been asked to visualize their relatives reported much less enjoyment of the literature than did those visualizing friends, but only if they were self-aware when responding to it.

This image of the scowling matron with the wagging index finger seems particularly appropriate to a discussion of anxiety and self-evaluation. But the increased tendency toward self-criticism is only one of the consequences of the self-evaluation that is activated by self-awareness. Self-evaluation affects behavior in a variety of ways. One of the simplest effects has to do with the impact that self-focus has on self-knowledge, which has been termed the veridicality effect. In its simplest form the effect refers to the fact that directing attention toward the self results in an increase in the knowledge or awareness of the self, in particular, the dimension that happens to be salient at the time. This enhanced self-knowledge is manifested in a variety of ways, but it is most evident in self-reports and attributions for behavior. To relate the discussion back to the topic of anxiety, however, it is best to first consider what might be thought of as the opposite of self-knowledge, and that is self-illusion.

SELF-ILLUSION

The prevailing wisdom for many years in clinical psychology has maintained that self-knowledge, or more specifically accurate self-knowledge, is a prerequisite of mental health. Prime evidence of this can be seen in the popularity of self-confrontation as a technique of psychotherapy. The goal of this therapeutic method is to allow the client to obtain a more objective view of the self from a different perspective, specifically that of other persons. In a review of clinical research examining the efficacy of the technique, Sanborn, Pyke, and Sanborn (1975) concluded that self-confrontation has been very useful clinically because it does increase knowledge of the self and "the more an individual knows about his (or her) behavior, the more he (or she) is in a position to do something about it" (p. 185). A similar belief in the benefit of accurate self-knowledge has been evident in much prominent theoretical work in social psychology over the past four decades. Heider (1958), for example, claimed that a desire to obtain more information about the self is a basic goal of the attribution process. It is also one of the primary reasons why people engage in social comparison (Festinger, 1954).

This accuracy perspective maintained considerable popularity until the mid 1970s when researchers working in several different areas began to question its validity. In fact more than just questioning, what these researchers were suggesting was just the opposite notion – that people oftentimes desire to *avoid* accurate knowledge about the self, and will instead seek inaccuracy. Taking social comparison behavior as an example, it was suggested that people sometimes avoid comparison targets who might provide accurate but threatening information about the self (Brickman & Bulman, 1977). By the same token, it has been demonstrated that accurate information about the causes of one's own behavior is sometimes avoided, especially when the behavior has or may have negative consequences. Under these circumstances causal ambiguity or "attribute ambiguity" is sought (Snyder & Wicklund, 1981). Consistent with this reasoning, research began to emerge in clinical psychology around the same time suggesting that, in some respects, *in*accurate self-perception may be a characteristic of mentally healthy people, and that accuracy is actually associated with some types of pathology. In this regard, Sackeim & Gur (1979) provided evidence suggesting that the tendency to self-deceive, as measured by their self-deception scale, (e.g., answering *no* to such threatening but "universally true" items as "Have you ever doubted your sexual adequacy?" or "Have you ever thought your parents hated you?") is *negatively* correlated with measures of psychopathology, such as neuroticism and depression.

Self-Illusion and Mental Health

A recent review by Taylor & Brown (1988) indicated how pervasive the "inaccuracy phenomenon" actually is. These authors reviewed relevant research of the last 15 years and concluded that much of this research suggests that inaccurate perceptions of the self, of the world and of the future, serve an adaptive function and are, therefore, positively related to mental health. They discuss three different types of illusions. The first is an illusion of *control* over events that are actually uncontrollable. People will often overestimate the extent to which they will be able to influence the outcome of something like a lottery or a dice game (Langer, 1975). After the fact, personal responsibility is exaggerated if the outcome was positive, underestimated if it was negative. The second illusion has to do with perceptions of future events. People generally tend to be "overly optimistic" about the likelihood that good things will happen to them, whereas they tend to underestimate the possibility of negative occurrences, such as accidents or illness (Weinstein, 1984). Moreover, this lack of concern or worry about potential misfortune sometimes translates into less precautionary behaviors. Finally, the third type of illusion has to do with self-perceptions. They generally tend to be overly positive. That is, people tend to view themselves and their own behavior more favorably than do others who are observing them (e.g., Lewinsohn, Mischel, Chaplin & Barton, 1980).

Taylor & Brown (1988) also point out that while most people are guilty of engaging in these different types of illusions, that is certainly not the case for everyone. Specifically, people who are low in self-esteem or depressed are much less likely to show these tendencies. Instead, they tend to be more even-handed in their (self) attributions, as well as more realistic – i.e., pessimistic – about their ability to control uncontrollable events. They are also more accurate in assessing the contingencies between behavior and outcome, and more realistic in their self-assessments. Research by Lewinsohn et al. (1980) is a good case in point. In that study nondepressed subjects provided evaluations of their own social behavior that were significantly more favorable than were evaluations of them provided by others who had been observing them. The self-evaluations of the depressed subjects, on the other hand, were much more in line with those of the observers. Of some importance is the fact that the depressed subjects in this and many similar studies were not simply more negative in their responses, as might be expected (cf. Beck, 1972). Instead they were actually more objective and accurate when it came to assessing themselves and their behavior. It was the nondepressed people who were deluding themselves.

Taylor & Brown (1988) argue that the relation between illusion and mental health is not coincidental. Rather, they believe there is a clear, albeit indirect, link that involves mood states. That is, illusions promote happiness and maintain or boost motivation, which, in turn, facilitate healthy behaviors such as enhanced intellectual functioning and task performance, perseverance, creativity, etc. In short, illusions serve as a buffer between the self and reality, which helps shield the self-deceiver from the threats and accusations of persons and events around him. There is an interesting implication here – if nondepressed persons really knew how bad things were or admitted it they too might become depressed. In fact, research with depressed persons who were in therapy (see Fink, 1979) indicated that as their depression declined they showed an *increase* in (problem) denial and self-deception.

Self-Focus and Self-Perception: Veridicality

The veridicality or veracity hypothesis, mentioned earlier, suggests that depressed persons are not alone in their tendency not to self-deceive. Specifically, the hypothesis consists of two related assumptions: (a) people are more aware of different (salient) dimensions of the self when their attention is self-focused; and (b) people are more likely to report accurately on those dimensions if they are self-focused while responding. In the first study to provide evidence of this effect (Pryor, Gibbons, Wicklund, Fazio & Hood, 1977), college students were asked to report on several self-dimensions, including their social behavior (Experiment I), their SAT scores (Experiment II), and their liking for some puzzles that they had just finished working on (Experiment III). In each case the correlation between these self-reports and a measure of their actual previous behavior was much higher if their attention was self-focused when they made the report. A subsequent study (Gibbons, Smith, Ingram, Pearce, Brehm & Schroeder, 1985) provided evidence of a very similar effect among a very different sample of subjects. Alcoholics, depressed persons, and others with a variety of psychological disorders (e.g., "borderline personality") were asked to report on their psychological problems while they were or were not self-aware. Questions concerned problem duration and severity as well as participation in treatment. We then obtained permission from the subjects to check on the accuracy of those reports by comparing them with the hospital records and with evaluations provided by hospital psychologists. This check revealed that, as expected, the reports of the self-focused group were much more in line with the information we had obtained from the other sources.

In fact, the same tendency toward accurate self-description has been demonstrated on a variety of different dimensions. Self-attention, for example, has been associated with an increase in awareness and accurate report of heightened somatic and affective states (e.g., Scheier, Carver & Gibbons, 1979), as well as the *absence* of affect or arousal (Gibbons, Carver, Scheier & Hormuth, 1979; Hansen, Hansen & Crano, in press). The same applies to the attribution process. Self-focused persons are less likely than those whose attention is not internally directed to overestimate their own contribution to group activity (Stephenson & Wicklund, 1983).

Self-Focus and Self-Illusion

There is an obvious parallel between the self-illusion research discussed by Taylor & Brown (1988) and the research associated with the veridicality hypothesis. That parallel is perhaps best illustrated by the Lewinsohn et al. (1980) and the Pryor et al. (1977) studies mentioned earlier. In both cases subjects were asked to assess their own social behavior, and then those evaluations were compared with similar evaluations provided by observers. In the former case the assessments of the depressed subjects were more accurate, whereas in the latter study it was the evaluations of the self-focused subjects that were more in line with reality. Reality in both cases meant less self-aggrandizing. In short, people whose attention is self-focused tend to behave very much like persons who are depressed.

At first glance it is not clear why simply being accurate in reporting about the self would be at all problematic – and in fact this is the basic paradox of the self-illusion phenomenon. To better understand the "problem" with veridicality, however, it is necessary to examine the behavior of the subjects in the self-awareness studies who were not self-aware when they described themselves or their behavior. In the first veridicality study (Pryor et al. 1977; Experiment II), we found that all subjects tended to embellish their SAT test performance somewhat, which is not surprising given that they did not know that the experimenter had access to, or would even be interested in, their actual scores. Moreover, that tendency was much more pronounced among subjects who did relatively poorly on the test. More important, the tendency was much greater among poor performers who were not self-aware; self-aware subjects exaggerated relatively little, regardless of their level of performance. A similar relationship appeared in the Gibbons et al. (1985) study when we compared the self-reports of the self-focused psychiatric subjects with their non-self focused counterparts. The latter group underestimated the amount of time they had had their problem and how many times they had been hospitalized for it, whereas the former group was quite accurate. Finally, in Gibbons & Gerrard (1986) incarcerated women underestimated the severity of their crimes and the sentence they had received for it, but only if their attention had *not* been self-directed during the self-report.

The pattern in each of these studies is clear: The non-self focused persons were embellishing their self reports somewhat, thereby presenting a more favorable and more accepting image of themselves. Interestingly, these subjects showed virtually no evidence of guilt or compunction about their misrepresentation. In fact, just the opposite occurred. We assessed the mood states of both the psychiatric patients and the prisoners and found that those whose attention had been internally directed reported experiencing more negative moods at the same time that they were self-reporting more accurately. The point here is not so much that accuracy in and of itself is depressing. Rather, it is the fact that accuracy, especially self-accuracy, is constraining. The ability to delude or deceive the self, on the other hand, helps to relieve some of the burdens of a stressful environment. Although there is certainly something to be said for veridicality and self-knowledge, the fact is that it oftentimes "gets in the way," and constrains behavior in ways that can promote or at least maintain anxiety, worry and depression.

Impression Management

Looking at the experimental situations in these studies from a slightly different perspective, it can be seen that in virtually all of them subjects were given an opportunity to self-present. And, in fact, impression management does appear to be a logical characterization of their behavior – provided they were not self-focused at the time. Self-awareness, on the other hand, appeared to inhibit or at least reduce the amount of self-presentation subjects were engaging in. More direct evidence of this inhibitory effect can be seen in a recent study by Gibbons & Gaeddert (1984). Subjects in that study were asked to work on a diagnostic math problem set after they had been given a placebo. Instructions indicated that the "drug" would either facilitate or interfere with their performance on the problem set. As expected, subjects who had been told the drug would interfere indicated to the experimenter that they thought it was much more active, but, once again, that was true only for the externally-focused subjects. The self-focused group provided an accurate description of their arousal states (which were elevated, presumably because of the math test), but their assessments of the drug's effects did not vary as a function of its "utility." Consequently, they were not able to benefit from the augmentation principle (Kelley, 1972), in terms of presenting a favorable impression to the experimenter, whereas the other subjects were able to.

Self-deception? The experimental or self-aware subjects in these studies actually acted as a control for the non-self aware subjects in the sense that their responses provided evidence that accurate self-reports were quite possible. Although we have not asked participants in our research directly whether they were aware that their self-descriptions were somewhat embellished, most of the research in this area suggests that this type of impression management is intended as much for the self as it is for external observers. That is, people manage impressions in private as well as public (Greenberg & Pyszczynski, 1985). Moreover, one is seldom aware that she or he is engaging in self-deception (Sackeim, 1983). It would appear, then, that these people really did believe what they were saying; and saying it left them feeling better about themselves and their situation.

One final point about the veridicality studies is worth mentioning. Unlike in Baldwin & Holmes (1987), in none of these studies was a specific "private" audience made salient. This was because we assumed that the value that inhibits misrepresentation or lying about the self is a universal, one that most people would have internalized. Thus, in the absence of a specific source or image (such as the relatives in Baldwin & Holmes, 1987), the value structure that guides behavior resembles the generalized other. It is a nebulous or vague source, to be sure, but it is also very effective. It acts as an internalized monitor of behavior that comes into play only when attention is self-focused.

Inhibition and Interference

The generalized other (as well as many private audiences) is also a very harsh *judge* of behavior, which means, paradoxically, that self-attention sometimes interferes with the outcome that the self wishes to achieve. Such would be the case for the test-anxious person (Sarason, 1975), or, according to Carver & Scheier (1981), virtually anyone who is pessimistic about their chances to successfully perform a task they are engaged in. By the same token, self-focus oftentimes interrupts the "flow" of routine action (cf. Csikszentmihalyi & Figurski, 1982), drawing attention away from the task at hand, thereby interfering with performance. That interference may occur on a range of behaviors, from those that are automatic, such as humor appreciation (Cupchik & Leventhal, 1974), to more involving behavior such as sexual intercourse (Barlow, 1986, calls this "spectatoring", i.e., the interference produced by self-attention during intercourse).

In a similar manner, self-focus also inhibits future behaviors. Specifically, it inhibits behaviors that are inconsistent with the personal value structure, and therefore would create discrepancies of the nature that Duval & Wicklund (1972) talked about. But, they are also behaviors that people frequently choose to engage in in the absence of self-focus. They range from the benign, such as exaggerating reports of one's accomplishments (Pryor et al., 1977), or enjoying pornography (when one's standards suggest that is inappropriate, Gibbons, 1978; cf. Baldwin & Holmes, 1987), to the malicious, such as stealing Halloween candy (Diener et al., 1976), to the destructive, such as the violence associated with the state of deindividuation, especially as manifested in a mob (cf. Diener, 1979).

CONCLUSION

In reviewing these self-awareness studies one almost gets the impression that the self-focused individual is an overly-constrained, depressed, "nervous wreck." That certainly is not an accurate description. There are, of course, many circumstances in which self-focus can promote positive behavior, such as helping others (Duval, Duval, & Neely, 1979), not harming others inappropriately (Carver, 1975), and displaying independence (Froming, Walker, & Lopyan, 1982). By the same token, while having the ability to self-deceive is related to mental health, clearly too much self-deception is pathological (Sackeim, 1983). The same is true for too little self-focus – the example of the sociopathic personality comes to mind here. In this sense, it appears that some level of self-focus, because it is constraining, is necessary to maintain control over behavior. It has a "civilizing" effect on behavior (cf. Wicklund, 1978), that is most noticeable in those situations in which direct societal control is missing (i.e., in the absence of others).

On the other hand, there are clearly some costs associated with that control. Not only does self-focus inhibit some potentially enjoyable activities and interfere with others, but there is also the enhanced awareness of negative affect, which is oftentimes associated with the state and is sometimes created by it (e.g., guilt, disappointment, pessimism). Behavior is relatively unfettered when attention is not internally focused, which means the individual has the freedom to deceive the self, delude others (through self-presentation), and more or less do what he or she likes. But that changes, for most of us anyway, when attention is directed back toward the self. Then the value structure, with its myriad private audiences and ideals and the generalized other comes into play, and issues like morality, integrity and responsibility become salient. As a result, freedom is replaced by constraint, spontaneity with deliberation and (the sense of) impunity with self-evaluation and concern, or worry. Unfortunately, these are costs that must be paid if we are to live in a social structure, especially one that works. Fortunately, the costs are temporary, and the state of self-focus is usually limited. Most of us are adept at distracting attention and lifting the constraints (although some are better than others, of course). Likewise, most of us do experience the discomfort of anxiety from time to time but it, too, is a temporary experience. For some, however, the experience of anxiety and its associated self-evaluation can be prolonged. When that happens, self-focus can be very debilitating.

References

Baldwin, M. W., & Holmes, J. G. (1987). Salient private audiences and awareness of the self. *Journal of Personality and Social Psychology*, **52**, 1087–1098.

Barlow, D. H. (1986). Causes of sexual dysfunction: The role of anxiety and cognitive interference. *Journal of Consulting and Clinical Psychology*, **54**, 14–148.

Beck, A. T. (1972). *Depression causes and treatment*. Philadelphia: University of Pennsylvania Press.

Brickman, P., & Bulman, R. J. (1977). The pain and pleasure of social comparison. In J. Suls & R. Miller (Eds.) *Social comparison processes: Theoretical and empirical perspectives*. (pp. 149–186). Washington, DC: Hemisphere.

Carver, C. S. (1975). Physical aggression as a function of objective self-awareness and attitudes towards punishment. *Journal of Experimental Social Psychology*, **11**, 510–519.

Carver, C. S., Peterson, L. M., Follansbee, D. J. & Scheier, M. F. (1983). Effects of self-directed attention on performance and persistence among persons high and low in fast anxiety. *Cognitive Theory and Research*, 7, 337–354.

Carver, C. S., & Scheier, M. F. (1981). *Attention and self-regulation: A control-theory approach to human behavior*. New York: Springer.

Csikszentimihalyi, M., & Figurski, T. J. (1982). Self-awareness and aversive experience in everyday life. *Journal of Personality*, **50**, 15–28.

Cupchik, G. C. & Leventhal, H. (1974). Consistency between expressive behavior and the evolution of humorous stimuli: The role of sex and self-observation. *Journal of Personality and Social Psychology*, **30**, 429–442.

Davies, M. F. (1982). Self-focused attention and personality validation. *Current Psychological Research*, **2**, 87–93.

Diener, E. (1979). Deindividuation, self-awareness, and disinhibition. *Journal of Personality and Social Psychology*, **37**, 1160–1171.

Diener, E., Fraser, S. C., Beaman, A. L. & Kelem, R. T. (1976). Effects of deindividuating variables on stealing by Halloween trick-or-treaters. *Journal of Personality and Social Psychology*, **33**, 178–183.

Duval, S., Duval, V., & Neely, R. (1979). Self-focus, felt responsibility, and helping behavior. *Journal of Personality and Social Psychology*, **37**, 1769–1778.

Duval, S., & Wicklund, R. A. (1972). *A theory of objective self-awareness*. New York: Academic Press.

Ellis, A. (1962). *Reason and emotion in psychotherapy*. New York: Lyle Stuart.

Fenigstein, A., Scheier, M. F., & Buss, A. H. (1975). Public and private self-consciousness: Assessment and theory. *Journal of Consulting and Clinical Pscyhology*, **43**, 522–527.

Festinger, L. (1954). A theory of social comparison. *Human Relations*, **7**, 117–140.

Fink, M. (1979). *Convulsive therapy: Theory and practice*. New York: Raven.

Froming, W. J., Walker, G. R., & Lopyan, K. J. (1982). Public and private self-awareness: When personal attitudes conflict with societal expectations. *Journal of Experimental Social Psychology*, **18**, 476–487.

Gibbons, F. X. (1978). Sex guilt and reactions to pornography: Enhancing behavioral consistency through self-focused attention. *Journal of Personality and Social Psychology*, **36**, 976–987.

Gibbons, F. X. (in press). Self-attention and behavior: A review and theoretical update. In M. Zanna (Ed.) *Advances in experimental social psychology*, Vol. 23. San Diego: Academic Press.

Gibbons, F. X., Carver, S. C., Scheier, M. F., & Hormuth, S. E. (1979). Self-focused attention and the placebo effect: Fooling some of the people some of the time. *Journal of Experimental Social Psychology*, **15**, 263–274.

Gibbons, F. X., Gaeddert, W. P. (1984). Focus of attention and placebo utility. *Journal of Experimental Social Psychology*, **20**, 159–176.

Gibbons, F. X., & Gerrard, M. (1986). *Self-awareness and the truth-as-standard hypothesis*. Paper presented at the American Psychological Association Convention, Washington, DC.

Gibbons, F. X., Smith, T. W., Ingram, R. E., Pearce, K., Brehm, S. S., & Schroeder, D. J. (1985). Self-awareness and self-confrontation: Effects of self-focused attention on members of a clinical population. *Journal of Personality and Social Psychology*, **48**, 662–675.

Gibbons, F. X., & Wicklund, R. A. (1976). Selective exposure to self. *Journal of Research in Personality*, **10**, 98–106.

Greenberg, J., & Pyszczynski, T. (1985). Compulsatory self-inflation: A response to the threat to self-regard of public failure. *Journal of Personality and Social Psychology*, **49**, 273–280.

Greenberg, J., & Pyszczynski, T. (1986). Persistent high self-focus after failure and low self-focus after success: The depressive self-focusing style. *Journal of Personality and Social Psychology*, **50**, 1039–1044.
Hansen, R. D., Hansen, C. H., & Crano, W. D. (in press). Sympathetic arousal and self attention: The accessibility of interoceptive and exteroceptive arousal cues. *Journal of Experimental Social Psychology*.
Heider, F. (1958). *The psychology of interpersonal relations*. New York: Wiley.
Hull, J. G., Young, R. D., & Swank, L. E. (1982). Self-consciousness, self-esteem, and success-failure as determinants of alcohol consumption in male social drinkers. *Journal of Personality and Social Psychology*, **44**, 1097–1109.
Innes, J. M., & Young, R. F. (1975). The effects of presence of an audience, evaluation apprehension and objective self-awareness on learning. *Journal of Experimental Social Psychology*, **11**, 35–42.
Izard, C. (1972). *Patterns of emotion: A new analysis of anxiety and depression*. New York: Academic Press.
Kelley, H. H. (1972). The process of causal attribution. *American Psychologist*, **27**, 107–128.
Langer, E. J. (1975). The illusion of control. *Journal of Personality and Social Psychology*, **32**, 311–328.
Lewinsohn, P. M., Mischel, W., Chaplin, W., & Barton, R. (1980). Social competence and depression: The role of illusory self perceptions. *Journal of Abnormal Psychology*, **89**, 203–212.
Mead, G. H. (1934). *Mind, self, and society*. Chicago: University of Chicago Press.
Pryor, J. B., Gibbons, F. X., Wicklund, R. A., Fazio, R., & Hood, R. (1977). Self-focused attention and self-report validity. *Journal of Personality*, **45**, 513–527.
Sackheim, H. A. (1983). Self-deception, self-esteem, and depression: The adaptive value of lying to oneself. In J. Masling (Ed.), *Empirical studies of psychoanalytic theories* (Vol. 1, pp. 101–157). Hillsdale, NJ: Analytic Press.
Sackheim, H. A., & Gur, R. C. (1979). Self-deception, other-deception, and self-reported psychopathology. *Journal of Consulting and Clinical Psychology*, **47**, 213–215.
Sanborn, D. E., Pyke, H. F., & Sanborn, C. J. (1975). Videotape playbook and psychotherapy. A review. *Psychotherapy: Theory, research and practice*, **12**, 179–186.
Sarason, I. G. (1975). Anxiety and self-pre-occupation. In I. G. Sarason & C. D. Spielberger (Eds.). *Stress and anxiety* (Vol. 2, pp. 27–44). New York: Wiley.
Scheier, M. F. (1976). Self-awareness, self-consciousness, and angry aggression. *Journal of Personality*, **44**, 627–644.
Scheier, M. F., & Carver, C. S. (1977). Self-focused attention and the experience of emotion: Attraction, repulsion, elation, and depression. *Journal of Personality and Social Psychology*, **35**, 625–636.
Scheier, M. F., Carver, C. S., & Gibbons, F. X. (1979). Self-directed attention, awareness of bodily states, and suggestibility. *Journal of Personality and Social Psychology*, **37**, 1576–1588.
Scheier, M. F., Carver, C. S., & Matthews, K. A. (1982). Attentional factors in the perception of bodily states. In J. Caccioppo & R. Petty (Eds.), *Social psychophysiology*, (pp. 520–542), New York: Guilford Press.
Snyder, M. L., & Wicklund, R. A. (1981). Attribute ambiguity. In J. H. Harvey, W. Ickes, & R. F. Kidd (Eds.), *New directions in attribution research*, (Vol. 3, pp. 197–221). Hillsdale, NJ: Erlbaum.
Stephenson, B., & Wicklund, R. A. (1983). Self-directed attention and taking the other's perspective. *Journal of Experimental Social Psychology*, **19**, 58–77.
Taylor, S. E., & Brown, J. D. (1988). Illusion and well-being: A social psychological perspective on mental health. *Psychological Bulletin*, **103**, 193–210.
Weinstein, N. D. (1984). Why it won't happen to me: Perceptions of risk factors and susceptibility. *Health Psychology*, **3**, 431–457.
Wicklund, R. A. (1978). Three years later. In L. Berkowitz (Ed.) *Cognitive theories in social psychology*. (pp. 509–521). New York: Academic Press.
Wine, J. D. (1982). Evaluation anxiety: A cognitive-attentional construct. In H. W. Krohne & L. C. Laux (Eds.). *Achievement, stress, and anxiety*, (pp. 207–222). Washington, DC: Hemisphere.

SELF-CONSCIOUSNESS, ROLE DISCREPANCY, AND DEPRESSIVE AFFECT

JAY G. HULL,‡ NORA P. REILLY, and LOUIS C. ENNIS

Dartmouth College, Washington State University, Dartmouth College

Two studies were conducted to test the hypothesis that depressive affect is a joint function of private self-consciousness and the extent to which an individual's self-concept is discrepant from the requirements of a significant role. In the first study, the role of college student was empirically defined using a technique developed by Burke and Tully (1977). As predicted, the discrepancy between this role definition and subjects' self-ratings was a more significant predictor of depressive affect among high than low private self-conscious individuals. In the second study, measurements were taken at two time periods that were spaced six weeks apart. In a replication of the results of Study 1, the discrepancy between the role definition and subjects' self-ratings was a more significant predictor of depressive affect at Time 1 among high than low self-conscious individuals. In addition, discrepancy at Time 1 was a significant predictor of depression at Time 2 among high but not low self-conscious individuals. On the other hand, depression at Time 1 was unrelated to discrepancy at Time 2 among high self-conscious subjects. On the basis of these results, it is concluded that high private self-consciousness combined with role-identity discrepancy is associated with increased risk of depression. Finally, additional analyses suggested that depression may itself function to increase subsequent self-consciousness.

KEYWORDS: Role-discrepancy, self-consciousness, depression

According to all major theories of self-awareness, individuals are more sensitive to success and failure feedback when in the self-aware state (Buss, 1980; Carver & Scheier, 1981; Duval & Wicklund, 1972; Hull & Levy, 1979). Furthermore, as a consequence of this greater sensitivity, highly self-aware individuals are postulated to experience greater negative affect following failure and positive affect following success than low self-aware individuals. As a consequence of this greater sensitivity, self-aware individuals are predicted to try to avoid self-awareness eliciting conditions following failure and approach such conditions following success.

Numerous studies have supported such predictions across a variety of situations. Ickes, Wicklund, and Ferris (1973) found that self-awareness stimuli result in lower self-esteem following negative feedback and a tendency toward higher self-esteem following positive feedback. Similarly, Fenigstein (1979) found that self-awareness increased negative responses to negative evaluation and tended to increase positive responses to positive evaluations. Finally, Hull, Van Treuren, Ashford, Propsom, and Andrus (1988) found that private self-consciousness was associated with increased negative mood following failure feedback and this effect appeared to be mediated by the greater propensity of these subjects to encode information according to its self-relevance.

Whereas these studies demonstrated that self-awareness is associated with greater sensitivity and affective response to success and failure, other studies have investigated the corollary prediction that individuals will tend to avoid the self-aware state following failure and approach it following success. Thus, Gibbons and Wicklund

‡Requests for reprints should be sent to Jay G. Hull, Department of Psychology, Dartmouth College, Hanover, NH 03755, USA.

(1976) found that subjects approach or avoid a self-awareness eliciting stimulus as a consequence of receiving positive or negative feedback from another. Similarly, Greenberg and Musham (1981) found that subjects who engage in attitudinally discrepant behavior avoid self-focusing stimuli, whereas those who engaged in attitudinally consistent behavior approached self-focusing stimuli. Finally, Steenbarger and Aderman (1979) found that such aversive reactions and avoidance behaviors occur only when the individual feels that the failure feedback reflects an aspect of self that cannot be readily altered.

This general pattern of results and theoretical reasoning has been extrapolated to explain a number of other phenomena related to self-awareness. Thus, the notion of motivated self-awareness avoidance following failure has been used to explain the fact that private self-conscious individuals seek performance norms following success and avoid such norms following failure (Carver & Scheier, 1985), persist following favorable feedback, but quit following unfavorable feedback (Scheier & Carver, 1982), and drink more alcohol following failure than following success (Hull & Young, 1983; Hull, Young, & Jouriles, 1986). In each instance, individuals low in private self-consciousness showed relatively few behavioral consequences of success and failure.

Self-Consciousness and Depression

Given the amount and variety of research on the general thesis that self-awareness is associated with greater sensitivity and affective response to negative feedback, it is somewhat surprising that it has not been posited as a mechanism in the genesis of depression. To be sure, self-awareness has been associated with depression in a number of different ways. But none of these build on the general thesis that self-awareness coupled with life failures makes one more susceptible to depression.

Some studies have found that a variety of mood inductions (including manipulations of depression) are more effective among situationally self-aware or dispositionally private self-conscious individuals (e.g., Scheier & Carver, 1977). This is theorized to be a consequence of the fact that self-aware individuals are more aware of their internal states. Thus, given that an individual is in a depressed state, manipulations of self-awareness appear to increase the magnitude of the self-reported depression and the accuracy of individuals' self-descriptions of their problems (Gibbons, Smith, Ingram, Pearce, Brehm, & Schroeder, 1985).

Other research has found a simple positive correlation between private self-consciousness and depression (e.g., Ingram & Smith, 1984; Smith & Greenberg, 1981). Such a finding is consistent with the argument by Lewinsohn, Hoberman, Teri, and Hautzinger (1985) that extreme negative affect and disruption of daily activities result in increased self-focus. Similarly, Pyszczynski and Greenberg (1987) argue that depression results in a particular self-focusing style. According to these authors, depression is associated with a significant loss. The result of such a loss is a discrepancy between actual and desired states that can neither be reduced (given the definition of a "loss") nor avoided (because of its significance in the individual's life). As a consequence the individual becomes stuck in a self-regulatory cycle. This leads to virtually constant self-focus, intensified negative affect, and a depressive self-focusing style in which the individual focuses on negative outcomes but not positive outcomes (Greenberg & Pyszczynski, 1986; Pyszczynski & Greenberg, 1985, 1986).[1]

1. Although Pyszczynski and Greenberg (1987) predict that depressives are *less* self-conscious after success (and more self-conscious after failure) and hence one might expect no general correlation between self-consciousness and depression, they also theorize that positive outcomes are relatively infrequent for depressed individuals, the ultimate result being a constant state of negative self-focus.

Although we do not disagree with either of these theses (i.e., that self-awareness in already depressed individuals leads to an excerbation of negative mood and that depression results in increased self-focus and self-consciousness), it is also possible that self-consciousness is implicated in the *origin* of depression. Thus, we propose that self-consciousness and the experience of self-relevant life failures is associated with increased risk of subsequent depression whereas self-consciousness and the experience of self-relevant life success is associated with decreased risk of subsequent depression.

A Formal Model of Self-Consciousness and Depression

The difficulty with such an analysis lies in quantifying life successes and failures. For our purposes, we have adopted a role-theoretic approach that has its roots in symbolic interactionism. The basic principles of this approach can be specified as follows:

(1) Roles exist within social systems. Such roles are defined in terms of a set of behavioral requirements in a specified context.

(2) Individuals have identities that arise within but exist apart from the roles that they occupy.

(3) To the extent that the individual's identity is not well-suited to the definitional requirements of a particular role, the individual will perform in a manner inconsistent with the role. Such performances are indicative of a role-identity discrepancy.

(4) Role-identity discrepancies can be distinguished into those associated with performances ill-suited to one's own definition of the role (a "self-defined" discrepancy) and performances ill-suited to existing social definitions of the role (a "consensually-defined" discrepancy).

(5) To the extent that the individual processes feedback about the performance according to its self-relevance (i.e., to the extent that the person is self-aware), the feedback will be perceived to reflect on the aspect of the individual's identity associated with the role. When performances fail to conform with the requirements of the role, the result is a perceived role-identity discrepancy (self-defined, consensually-defined, or both).

(6) To the extent that individuals value this aspect of their identities, perception of a role-identity discrepancy will result in distress. The more they value this aspect of their identity, the more the distress.

(7) The fewer role-identities individuals possess, the more value they will place in each individual role-identity and the more distress they will experience in response to a given role-identity discrepancy.

(8) Distress will be evidenced in both physical and psychological well-being. For current purposes, we will consider the psychological distress of depression.

(9) Such psychological distress will motivate individuals to (a) alter their identities in the direction of the role definition, (b) decrease the prominence of this aspect of their identity by either moving out of the role or devaluing it in relation to alternative role-identities, (c) adopt a unique definition of the role and develop a social support group for that "deviant identity," and/or (d) attempt to avoid self-awareness. The length of time the individual experiences distress will be a function of their success in adopting such strategies.

These ideas certainly have very identifiable roots within social psychology: from role theory and symbolic interactionistic thought (Mead, 1934; Stryker, 1968) and the relation of role-discrepancies to depression (Oatley & Bolton, 1985), to Duval and Wicklund's (1972) self-awareness theory emphasis on real-ideal self-discrepancies, to our own emphasis that self-awareness involves sensitivity to self-relevant information (Hull & Levy, 1979), Higgins' (1989) notions of self-concept discrepancies and depression, and Linville's notions of self-complexity, depression, and illness (Linville, 1987). For present purposes, however, they offer a solid framework within which to operationalize self-relevant success and failure: Individuals can be regarded as succeeding at life to the extent that they minimize valued role-identity discrepancies.

The Measurement of Role-Identity Discrepancies

There are many ways in which to measure role-identity discrepancies. Most such techniques rely on individuals' reports on their own conceptions of their identities and relevant roles. From the current perspective, the result can be considered a "self-defined" discrepancy. However, a technique developed by Burke and Tully (1977) allows the calculation of both "self-defined" and what we have termed "consensually-defined" discrepancies (Burke, 1980; Burke & Reitzes, 1981).

In the Burke-Tully method, subjects rate a minimum of two roles on a series of semantic differentials. For example, in the experiments to be reported, subjects rated both the high school student role and the college student role on a series of 24 semantic differentials (e.g., studious-nonstudious, social-asocial, etc.). A discriminant function analysis is then performed on these ratings. The purpose of this analysis is to determine which items (studious-nonstudious, social-asocial, etc.) maximally distinguish between the two roles. The result of the analysis is a series of weights or coefficients: The higher the weight, the more useful that item is in distinguishing between the roles. Using all of the coefficients, it is possible to create a mathematical equation that maximally distinguishes between the two roles.

In a sense, the discriminant coefficients can be considered as weights of how important particular semantic differential dimensions are in distinguishing between the roles. Proceeding with the Burke-Tully technique, subjects also rate themselves on the same semantic differentials. By multiplying the subjects' ratings of themselves by the discriminant function coefficients obtained earlier, one effectively places that subject's self in mathematical space along a dimension that extends from one role definition to the other. As a consequence, it is possible to measure the extent to which an individual's identity fits a role definition without ever asking that individual about his or her conception of the role (e.g., see Experiment 2).

EXPERIMENT 1

In Experiment 1, we separately measured subjects' definitions of the high school student role, the college student role, and themselves. Using the Burke-Tully technique, we were then able to order subjects' self-definitions along the dimension of semantic space that extends from one role definition to the other. Given that all subjects objectively occupied the college student role, we predicted that the less a subject's identity fit with the college student role, the greater depressive affect that subject would report.

As stated earlier, we predicted that distress as a consequence of role-identity discrepancy would be a function of the extent to which the individual was sensitive to the self-relevance of feedback indicating poor performance of the role. Based on earlier research, we considered individuals high in private self-consciousness as more sensitive to the self-relevance of such feedback than individuals low in private self-consciousness. Self-consciousness was measured using the scale developed by Fenigstein, Scheier, and Buss (1975).

METHOD

Subjects

Subjects were 43 male and 43 female undergraduates who participated in exchange for course credit. Subjects completed the experimental materials in small groups of 5 – 15 members.

Procedures

Each group of subjects was told that the questionnaire booklet contained a series of scales related to a variety of research projects within the Psychology Department. They were informed that all information would be kept in strictest confidentiality and used only for research and statistical purposes. Subjects were not asked to put their names on the booklets and were told to respond as truthfully as possible. They were told to work straight through the booklet as quickly and accurately as possible and to avoid flipping back through the individual questionnaires.

The first page of each booklet repeated the oral instructions given to each group. The second page requested biographical information including the subject's age, sex, and pre-college institution (either public or private school).

Scales. Each booklet contained a series of questionnaires placed in a variety of orders to negate order effects. Of particular importance, half of the booklets had the Beck Depression Inventory placed before the Self-Consciousness Scale, and half had the questionnaires in reverse order. The specific questionnaires included for the present project were: the Beck Depression Inventory (Beck, 1967), the Self-Consciousness Scale (Fenigstein et al., 1975), and a series of four role scales that asked subjects to rate "themselves in the role of college student," "the typical pre-college 'prep school' student," "the typical pre-college public high school student," and "the typical Dartmouth student" on twenty-four semantic differentials (Burke & Reitzes, 1981).

When finished, each student read and signed a debriefing sheet that explained the purpose of the questionnaire and the expected pattern of results.

RESULTS

Role Definitions

Role definitions were created by conducting a discriminant function analysis comparing subjects' pre-Dartmouth education role scales to their Dartmouth role scales. Thus, if a student attended a private preparatory school before going to college, the "typical prep student" role ratings were selected for that subject's pre-college role. Similarly, if a subject had attended a public high school, the "typical public high school student" role ratings were selected for that subject's pre-college role. These pre-college role ratings were then contrasted with the subjects' own ratings of the "typical Dartmouth student" role using discriminant function analysis. In this case, the discriminant coefficients reflect the unique contribution of each adjective pair toward maximal distinction of the pre-college and college roles. The discriminant coefficients are reported in Table 1. In addition, population means and standard deviations were calculated for each adjective pair in order to create a separate "consensual definition" of the college role.

Table 1 Standardized Classification Coefficients for Adjective Pairs from the Discriminant Analysis of the Pre-College and College Roles

Item		*Coefficient*
Pressured	(Not Pressured)	.27
Competitive	(Non-competitive)	−.15
Studious	(Non-studious)	−.06
Ambitious	(Non-ambitious)	−.08
Motivated	(Non-motivated)	.58
Dedicated	(Undedicated)	.22
Hardworking	(Lazy)	−.34
Responsible	(Irresponsible)	.09
Critical	(Accepting)	−.13
Social	(Antisocial)	−.03
Apathetic	(Interested)	.05
Involved	(Uninvolved)	−.07
Friendly	(Unfriendly)	.28
Concerned	(Unconcerned)	.02
Aggressive	(Non-aggressive)	−.08
Sensitive	(Insensitive)	−.30
Dependent	(Independent)	−.19
Open-minded	(Close-minded)	−.37
Mature	(Immature)	.14
Realistic	(Idealistic)	.27
Individualistic	(Group Oriented)	−.14
Inquisitive	(Bored)	.40
Optimistic	(Pessimistic)	−.22
Creative	(Dull)	.31

Role-Identity Discrepancies

Analysis of subjects' role-identity discrepancies was done in three different ways. First, the Burke-Tully method (1977) of analysis was used. This technique weights each subject's semantic differential ratings of "themselves in the role of college student" with the discriminant function coefficients. These weighted self-ratings are then summed. The discriminant function technique maximally distinguishes the pre-college role ratings from the college role ratings. By using these discriminant function coefficients to weight ratings of self in the college student role, each individual's self-descriptions are placed along a continuum that extends from an identity consistent with the pre-college role to an identity consistent with the college role.

In order to more directly contrast self-defined from consensually-defined discrepancies, two additional scores were calculated for each subject. The first involved the calculation of a self-defined discrepancy. In this case, each subject's self-rating was subtracted from his or her *own* rating of the college role. The absolute value of these differences was then calculated (i.e., direction of self vs. role differences were theorized not to matter). These scores were then weighted by the absolute value of the discriminant function coefficients (i.e., these coefficients were treated simply as indicators of the importance of a particular semantic differential in the pre-college versus college role comparisons such that the sign of the coefficient was theorized not to matter). These weighted scores were then summed. The result is a self-defined discrepancy score that is weighted by the relative importance of each semantic differential in distinguishing the relevant roles.

A separate consensually-defined discrepancy was calculated to parallel the self-defined discrepancy. In this case, each subject's rating of self in the college role was subtracted from the *mean rating* of the college role calculated across all subjects. The absolute value of these differences was then calculated (i.e., again, direction of deviance from this consensually-defined role was theorized not to matter); these scores were then weighted by the absolute value of the discriminant function coefficients; and these weighted scores were summed. The result is a consensually defined discrepancy score that parallels the self-defined discrepancy score.

Self-Consciousness Analyses

Subjects were divided into high and low private self-conscious groups on the basis of a median split using the private subscale of the Fenigstein et al. (1975) Self-Consciousness Scale. For each subpopulation, separate correlations were calculated between the Beck Depression Inventory and the three Role-Identity discrepancies. These correlations for both high and low private self-conscious subjects are shown in Table 2.

As can be seen in this table, depression is significantly related to all three definitions of role-identity discrepancy for high private self-conscious individuals. On the other hand, none of the correlations achieved conventional levels of significance for low private self-conscious subjects. The strongest predictor of depression in high private self-conscious subjects involved the consensually-defined role-identity discrepancy. A direct comparison of the size of this correlation with the corresponding correlation obtained for low private self-conscious subjects yielded a significant difference ($t = 1.77$, $p = .038$, one-tailed). Similar comparisons for the Burke-Tully and self-defined discrepancies did not achieve significance.

When all three measures of role-identity discrepancies were included in a multiple regression analysis, the multiple R was significant for high self-conscious individuals, $R = .62$, $F(3,36) = 5.73$, $p < .01$. Furthermore, of the three individual discrepancies, only the consensually-defined measure remained a significant predictor of depression for high self-conscious individuals, $F(1,36) = 4.26$, $p < .05$, indicating that this measure contributed unique variance to the depression score. Although both the Burke-Tully and self-defined discrepancy predictors were associated with significant zero-order correlations for high self-conscious individuals, neither remained significant predictors when included in the multiple regression analysis ($F(1,36) = 2.69$, n.s. and $F(1,36) = 1.30$, n.s., respectively) indicating that they overlapped in the

Table 2 Experiment 1 Correlations of Depression and Role–Identity Discrepancies Within High and Low Private Self-Conscious Groups

	Beck Depression Inventory
Low Private Self-Conscious Subjects (n=46)	
Burke-Tully Role-Identity Discrepancy	.25
Self-Defined Discrepancy	.29
Consensually-Defined Discrepancy	.23
High Private Self-Conscious Subjects (n=41)	
Burke-Tully Role-Identity Discrepancy	.43**
Self-Defined Discrepancy	.46**
Consensually-Defined Discrepancy	.56***

**$p<.01$; ***$p<.001$

variance they explained. None of the parallel analyses for low self-conscious individuals achieved significance.

Finally, the simple correlation between self-consciousness and depression was calculated. Consistent with earlier studies (e.g., Ingram & Smith, 1984; Smith & Greenberg, 1981), this correlation was positive, but modest in size, $r(86) = .20$, $p = .058$.

DISCUSSION

In support of predictions, role-identity discrepancies were significantly related to depression among individuals high in private self-consciousness, but not among those low in private self-consciousness. Furthermore, among high private self-conscious individuals, all three calculations of discrepancies were related to depressive affect. At the same time, the best single predictor of depression (and the only one associated with unique variance) for these subjects involved discrepancies calculated as differences between ratings of self and the mean ratings of the role by all subjects (i.e., the "consensually-defined" discrepancy). This suggests that depression among high private self-conscious subjects may not simply involve self-defined discrepancies, but rather may be in part a function of feedback from others indicating that they are failing to behave in a manner consistent with a socially prescribed role.

EXPERIMENT 2

In addition to providing initial support for predictions, the results of Experiment 1 also provide a set of mathematical weights (the discriminant function coefficients) that serve to identify individual semantic differential items in terms of their ability to distinguish between the pre-college and college roles for this population. As a consequence, it was possible to apply these weights to the identity ratings of a second set of individuals who were in role transition (i.e., individuals who were just leaving the high school student role and entering the college student role). Because one's identity has its origins in one's past roles, to the extent that a new role has requirements distinct from past roles, the resulting role-identity discrepancy should result in distress. Thus, without asking for subjects' conceptions of these roles, it should be possible to predict depression as a function of identity incongruence with a consensually defined role using the weights and means obtained in Experiment 1.

Subjects were first term freshmen making the transition from high school to college student who completed questionnaire booklets during their first week of classes. In this booklet, subjects completed ratings of themselves "in the role of college student" on the same semantic differentials used in Experiment 1, the Self-Consciousness Scale, and the Beck Depression Inventory. In addition, subjects were recontacted six weeks later and asked to complete the booklet a second time in order to provide longitudinal data of value in distinguishing associations due to spurious correlation from those potentially due to causal influence (Kenny, 1975).

METHOD

Subjects

Half of the Dartmouth freshman class were randomly selected to receive an initial questionnaire booklet during the first week of classes. Of these 536 potential subjects, approximately 40% returned completed questionnaires. All individuals who completed initial questionnaires were mailed a second questionnaire during the seventh week of classes. Of these individuals, approximately 35% returned completed questionnaires. This resulted in a total of 75 subjects who completed usable questionnaires at both Time 1 and Time 2.

Procedures

Instructions for completion of the questionnaire were similar to those used in Experiment 1. The specific questionnaires included for the present project were: the Beck Depression Inventory (Beck, 1967), the Self-Consciousness Scale (Fenigstein et al., 1975), and a scale that asked subjects to rate "themselves in the role of college student" on twenty-four semantic differentials (Burke & Reitzes, 1981). Unlike Experiment 1, subjects were not asked to rate "the typical pre-college 'prep school' student," "the typical pre-college public high school student," or "the typical Dartmouth student." Instead, the discriminate function coefficients and group mean ratings from Experiment 1 were applied to self-ratings in Experiment 2.

RESULTS AND DISCUSSION

Role-Identity Discrepancies

Analysis of role-identity discrepancies was done in two ways that corresponded to techniques used in Experiment 1. First, the Burke-Tully method (1977) of analysis was used: discriminant function coefficients computed in Experiment 1 were used to weight ratings of self in the college student role. As a consequence, each individual's self-descriptions were placed along a continuum that extended from an identity consistent with the pre-college role to an identity consistent with the college role. This was done separately for Time 1 and Time 2 ratings of self.

In addition, consensually-defined role-identity discrepancies were calculated by subtracting each subject's rating of self in the college role from the mean rating of the college role calculated across all subjects in Experiment 1. The absolute value of these differences was then weighted by the absolute value of the discriminant function coefficients from Experiment 1, and these weighted scores were summed. The result is a discrepancy score that represents the deviation of one's ratings of self from a consensual definition of the role.

Self-Consciousness Analyses

Time 1 analyses. Subjects were divided into high and low private self-conscious groups on the basis of a median split using the private subscale of the Fenigstein et al. (1975) Self-Consciousness Scale. For each subpopulation, separate correlations were calculated between the Beck Depression Inventory and the two Role-Identity discrepancies. These correlations at Time 1 for both high and low private self-conscious subjects are shown in Table 3.

As can be seen in this table, depression is significantly related to both definitions of role-identity discrepancy for high private self-conscious individuals. On the other hand, neither of the correlations achieve conventional levels of significance for low private self-conscious subjects. As in Experiment 1, the strongest predictor of depression in high private self-conscious subjects involved the consensually-defined

Table 3 Experiment 2 Time 1 Correlations of Depression and Role–Identity Discrepancies Within High and Low Private Self-Conscious Groups

	Beck Depression Inventory
Low Private Self-Conscious Subjects (n=43)	
Burke-Tully Role-Identity Discrepancy	.18
Consensually-Defined Discrepancy	.08
High Private Self-Conscious Subjects (n=32)	
Burke-Tully Role-Identity Discrepancy	.34*
Consensually-Defined Discrepancy	.48**

*$p<.06$; **$p<.01$

role-identity discrepancy. A direct comparison of the size of this correlation with the corresponding correlation obtained for low private self-conscious subjects yielded a significant difference (t = 1.85, p = .032, one-tailed). Similar comparisons for the Burke-Tully discrepancy did not achieve significance.

The Time 1 results are remarkably similar to those obtained in Experiment 1. In both cases, role-identity discrepancies were significantly related to depression for high but not low private self-conscious individuals and in both cases the strongest relationship existed among high self-conscious individuals for consensually defined discrepancies and depression.

Longitudinal analyses. Both high and low private self-conscious subjects showed similar high correlations between depression at Time 1 and depression at Time 2 (high privates, $r = .63, p < .001$; low privates, $r = .77, p < .001$) and similar low correlations between the Burke-Tully role-identity discrepancy at Time 1 and Time 2 (high privates, r = .22, n.s.; low privates, r = .28, n.s.). Low privates, but not high privates showed stability in consensually-defined role-identity discrepancy from Time 1 to Time 2 (high privates, r = .26, n.s.; low privates, $r = .54, p < .001$).

These statistics are interesting in a number of respects. First, high private self-conscious individuals show similar or slightly lower test-retest reliability over the six-week interval than do low private self-conscious individuals. Such effects argue against an alternative explanation of previous results as due to less accurate self-reports on the part of low private self-conscious subjects (i.e., that low privates show weaker relationships between depression and role-identity discrepancy by virtue of giving less reliable self-reports). In addition, they suggest that the identities of high private self-conscious individuals may be less stable over time because they are in greater flux as a consequence of adjustments to the college environment during the first seven weeks of school (although additional analyses did not show differential *reduction* in role-identity discrepancies for high and low self-conscious subjects).

Finally, the relatively high stability of the measures of depression and the corresponding low stability of the measures of role-identity discrepancy violate the assumptions necessary to conduct cross-lagged panel analyses (Kenny, 1975; Rogasa, 1980). Although a formal test for nonspuriousness was therefore not possible, it is interesting to note that the cross-lagged correlations were at least consistent with the predictions that among high private self-conscious individuals role-identity discrepancy influences subsequent depression rather than vice-versa. Thus, for high private self-conscious subjects, consensually-defined role-identity discrepancy at Time 1 was significantly and positively related to depression at Time 2, $r = .43, p = .01$, whereas depression at Time 1 was unrelated to discrepancy at Time 2, $r = -.10$, n.s. On the other hand, the reverse is actually the case among low private self-conscious individuals with role-identity discrepancy at Time 1 unrelated to depression at Time 2, $r = .01$, n.s., but depression at Time 1 significantly and positively related to discrepancy at Time 2, $r = .43, p = .01$. If anything, such a pattern would suggest that depression *increases* role-identity discrepancies among low private self-conscious subjects. Possibly as a consequence, consensually-defined role-identity discrepancy at Time 2 is now related to depression at Time 2 for low self-conscious subjects, $r = .57$, $p < .01$, although a similar effect was not obtained among high private self-conscious subjects, $r = .08$, n.s.[2]

Finally, as in Experiment 1, it was possible to calculate the simple correlations between self-consciousness and depression. In this case, self-consciousness was positively associated with depression at both Time 1, $r = .31, p < .01$, and Time 2, $r = .24, p < .04$. These correlations are similar in magnitude to those reported by Smith and Greenberg (1981), Ingram and Smith (1984), and in Experiment 1 of the present paper. In addition, given that the correlations between self-consciousness and depression are similar in size at Time 1 and Time 2, (i.e., they do not differ by the Pearson-Filon test; $z = .64$), the assumption of stationarity required for cross-lagged panel anaysis is met (cf. Kenny, 1975). The further assumption of synchronicity is met by virtue of the fact that the measures were collected at the same points in time (cf. Kenny, 1975). Finally, the assumption of equal stabilities (cf. Cook & Campbell, 1979; Rogasa, 1980) is met by virtue of the fact that the autocorrelations for self-consciousness and depression do not differ (Pearson-Filon test, $z = 1.74$). Thus, unlike the role-identity discrepancy data, the data for the simple relationship between self-consciousness and depression do conform to the assumptions necessary for conducting a cross-lagged panel analysis.[3]

Given that the necessary assumptions were met, we next conducted the test for spuriousness. In this case, depression at Time 1 was positively and significantly associated with self-consciousness at Time 2, $r(75) = .33, p < .01$, but self-consciousness at Time 1 was not related to depression at Time 2, $r(75) = .08$, n.s. Furthermore, the cross-lagged differential of depression and self-consciousness was significant (Pearson-Filon test; $z = 2.26, p < .025$). The null hypothesis for spuriousness was therefore rejected. The direction of the difference indicated that depression may be a cause of subsequent increases in self-consciousness rather than the reverse.

GENERAL DISCUSSION

The results of these two experiments support two distinct models of self-consciousness and depression. First, self-consciousness in combination with role-identity discrepancies appears to make one more susceptible to depression. And second, depression appears to have the reciprocal effect of increasing self-consciousness.

The first effect is consistent with the model offered in the introduction of the present paper. Thus, the general predictions that role-identity discrepancies would be associated with increased depressive affect and that this effect would be moderated by the individual's level of private self-consciousness were supported. Although grounded

2. In each case, similar, but weaker results were obtained using the Burke-Tully calculation of role-identity discrepancy.

3. Although cross-lagged panel correlation techniques have been criticized (e.g., Rogasa, 1980), the criticisms principally involve the fact that the data often fail to meet all three assumptions of stationarity, synchronicity, and stability. The current data do meet these assumptions.

in a prediction common to all of the major theories of self-awareness (that self-awareness is associated with increased sensitivity and affective reactivity to success-failure feedback), this research would appear to be the first to demonstrate that self-awareness is associated with depression in this manner.

The second effect, that depression increases subsequent self-consciousness, is consistent with the arguments of Pyszczynski and Greenberg (1987) and Lewinsohn, et al. (1985). According to Pyszczynski and Greenberg (1987), depression occurs as a result of a significant loss. As a consequence of the nature of significant losses, the individual becomes "stuck in a self-regulatory cycle" and "falls into a pattern of virtually constant self-focus" (p. 122). Similarly, according to Lewinsohn et al. (1985) extreme negative affect and the disruption of daily activities result in an increase in self-focus. Although supporting the notion that depression leads to increases in self-consciousness, the present results do not support the converse notion that self-consciousness *per se* (i.e., independent of role-identity discrepancies) leads to increased depression.

Self-Discrepancy Models

In addition to being relevant to the Pyszczynski and Greenberg (1987) and Lewinsohn et al. (1985) models, the present analysis is also relevant to the self-discrepancy model proposed by Higgins (1989). According to Higgins, discrepancies between the way individuals conceive their actual selves and what they see as an ideal self are associated with depressive affect. While related to our approach, the current notion of self-consciousness and role-identity discrepancies differs from Higgins' model in several respects. A primary difference involves our emphasis on role-based standards for performance as opposed to Higgin's attribute-based standards. Whereas Higgins' model is couched in terms of the kinds of attributes one possesses, versus idealizes, versus feels one ought to possess, the present analysis emphasizes that such standards are themselves grounded within specific roles. Thus, the attributes in terms of which the actual, ideal, and ought selves are conceived may differ markedly depending on the reference role (daughter, mother, spouse, professional, etc.). For example, parents may idealize one set of attributes in their child as "a professional" (independence and assertion) and precisely the opposite set of attributes in their child as "their son" (dependence and deference).

A second difference between these two models involves our emphasis on the central role of self-consciousness processes in moderating the relationship between role-identity discrepancies and depression. Although Higgins does not discuss self-consciousness, such processes are easily incorporated within his model if it is assumed that self-consciousness is associated with the activation of knowledge about self (Hull et al., 1988).

A final difference between these two models involves the nature of other-based discrepancies. According to Higgins, deviation from *one's own* conception of the ideals of others leads to depression. According to the present model, deviations from *others' conceptions* of the role requirements leads to feedback which, when encoded as self-relevant, leads to the perception of a role-identity discrepancy and depression. Although, on the surface, these analyses appear very similar, they may differ in their predictions regarding a very common situation: the case where one is forced to guess about others' ideals.

Much of everyday life is characterized by general feedback that the other is satisfied or dissatisfied with one's actions, but a lack of explicit feedback regarding the actual attributes the other values (i.e., his or her ideals). Thus it is possible for one to match one's *own conception* of the specific ideal attributes of others and yet not match *their conception* of their ideals. From the present perspective, feedback from others in the form of their general dissatisfaction with one's performance would still result in a role-identity discrepancy and depression when perceived as self-relevant.

CONCLUSION

The present analysis attempts to characterize one way in which individuals may lapse into depression. Obviously, we make no claim that this is the only source of depression. Nevertheless, we do feel that self-consciousness with respect to a valued role-identity discrepancy does have as one of its consequences susceptibility to depression.

Author's Note

Special thanks to Terris Lustik for her assistance in conducting Experiment 2.

References

Beck, A.T. (1967). *Depression: Clinical, experimental and theoretical aspects.* New York: Harper & Row.

Burke, P.J. (1980). The self: Measurement requirements from an interactionist perspective. *Social Psychology Quarterly*, **43**, 18–29.

Burke, P.J., & Reitzes, D.C. (1981). The link between identity and role performance. *Social Psychology Quarterly*, **44**, 83–92.

Burke, P.J., & Tully, J.C. (1977). The measurement of role identity. *Social Forces*, **55**, 881–897.

Buss, A.H. (1980). *Self-consciousness and social anxiety.* San Francisco: Freeman.

Carver, C.S., & Scheier, M.F. (1981). *Attention and self-regulation: A control theory approach to human behavior.* New York: Springer-Verlag.

Carver, C.S., & Scheier, M.F. (1985). Self-consciousness and self-assessment. *Journal of Personality and Social Psychology*, **48**, 117–124.

Cook, T.D., & Campbell, D.T. (1979). *The design and analysis of quasi-experiments in field settings.* Chicago: Rand McNally.

Duval, S., & Wicklund, R.A. (1972). *A theory of objective self-awareness.* New York: Academic Press.

Fenigstein, A. (1979). Self-consciousness, self-attention, and social interaction. *Journal of Personality and Social Psychology*, **37**, 75–86.

Fenigstein, A., Scheier, M.F., & Buss, A.H. (1975). Public and private self-consciousness: Assessment & theory. *Journal of Consulting and Clinical Psychology*, **43**, 522–527.

Gibbons, F.X., Smith, T.W., Ingram, R.E., Pearce, K., Brehm, S.S., & Schroeder, D.J. (1985). Self-awareness and self-confrontation: Effects of self-focused attention on members of a clinical population. *Journal of Personality and Social Psychology*, **48**, 662–675.

Gibbons, F.X., & Wicklund, R.A. (1976). Selective exposure to self. *Journal of Research in Personality*, **10**, 98–106.

Greenberg, J., & Musham, C. (1981). Avoiding and seeking self-focused attention. *Journal of Research in Personality*, **15**, 191–200.

Greenberg, J., & Pyszczynski, T. (1986). Persistent high self-focus after failure and low self-focus after success: The depressive self-focusing style. *Journal of Personality and Social Psychology*, **50**, 1039–1044.

Higgins, E.T. (1989). Self-discrepancy theory: What patterns of self-beliefs cause people to suffer? In L. Berkowitz (Ed.) *Advances in experimental social psychology.* (Vol. 22, pp. 93–136). New York: Academic Press.

Hull, J.G., & Levy, A.S. (1979). The organizational functions of the self: An alternative to the Duval and Wicklund model of self-awareness. *Journal of Personality and Social Psychology*, **37**, 756–768.

Hull, J.G., Van Treuren, R.R., Ashford, S.J., Propsom, P., & Andrus, B. (1988). Self-consciousness and the processing of self-relevant information. *Journal of Personality and Social Psychology*, **54**, 452–456.

Hull, J.G., & Young, R.D. (1983). Self-consciousness, self-esteem, and success-failure as determinants of alcohol consumption in male social drinkers. *Journal of Personality and Social Psychology*, **44**, 1097–1109.

Hull, J.G., Young, R.D., & Jouriles, E. (1986). Applications of the self-awareness model of alcohol consumption: Predicting patterns of use and abuse. *Journal of Personality and Social Psychology*, **51**, 790–796.

Ickes, W.J., Wicklund, R.A., & Ferris, C.B. (1973). Objective self-awareness and self-esteem. *Journal of Experimental Social Psychology*, **9**, 202–219.

Ingram, R.E., & Smith, T.W. (1984). Depression and internal versus external focus of attention. *Cognitive Therapy and Research*, **8**, 139–151.

Kenny, D.A. (1975). Cross-lagged panel correlations: A test for spuriousness. *Psychological Bulletin*, **82**, 887–903.

Lewinsohn, P.M., Hoberman, H., Teri, L., & Hautzinger, M. (1985). An integrative theory of depression. In S. Reiss & R. Bootzin (Eds.), *Theoretical issues in behavior therapy* (pp. 331–359). New York: Academic Press.

Linville, P.W. (1987). Self-complexity as a cognitive buffer against stress-related illness and depression. *Journal of Personality and Social Psychology*, **52**, 663–676.

Mead, G.H. (1934). *Mind. self, and society*. Chicago: University of Chicago Press.

Oatley, K. & Bolton, W. (1985). A social-cognitive theory of depression in reaction to life events. *Psychological Review*, **92**, 372–388.

Pyszczynski, T., & Greenberg, J. (1985). Depression and preference for self-focusing stimuli after success and failure. *Journal of Personality and Social Psychology*, **49**, 1066–1075.

Pyszczynski, T., & Greenberg, J. (1986). Evidence for a depressive self-focusing style. *Journal of Research in Personality*, **20**, 95–106.

Pyszczynski, T. & Greenberg, J. (1987). Self-regulatory perseveration and the depressive self-focusing style: A self-awareness theory of reactive depression. *Psychological Bulletin*, **102**, 122–138.

Rogasa, D.A. (1980). A critique of cross-lagged correlation. *Psychological Bulletin*, **88**, 245–258.

Scheier, M.F., & Carver, C.S. (1982). Self-consciousness, outcome expectancy, and persistence. *Journal of Research in Personality*, **16**, 409–418.

Scheier, M.F., & Carver, C.S. (1977). Self-focused attention and the experience of emotion: Attraction, repulsion, elation, and depression. *Journal of Personality and Social Psychology*, **35**, 625–636.

Smith, T.W., & Greenberg, J. (1981). Depression and self-focused attention. *Motivation and Emotion*, **5**, 323–331.

Steenbarger, B.N., & Aderman, D. (1979). Objective self-awareness as a nonaversive state: Effect of anticipating discrepancy reduction. *Journal of Personality*, **47**, 330–339.

Stryker, S. (1968). Identity salience and role performance. *Journal of Marriage and the Family*, **4**, 558–564.

ANXIETY AND DEPRESSION: AN INFORMATION PROCESSING PERSPECTIVE

AARON T. BECK

University of Pennsylvania, Philadelphia, USA

and

DAVID A. CLARK*

University of New Brunswick, Fredericton, New Brunswick, Canada

Beck's cognitive theory (CT) of anxiety and depression is briefly described. It is proposed that each psychopathological state has a specific cognitive profile. In anxiety states, this profile involves the theme of perceived physical or psychological threat to one's personal domain, while in depression the ideational content emphasizes loss or deprivation. Moreover, CT postulates differentiation between affective states based on the specific cognitive content evident with each disorder. The empirical literature bearing on the cognitive profile and content-specificity hypotheses is reviewed, and recommendations for further research are discussed.

KEY WORDS: Cognitive theory, anxiety, depression.

In recent years cognitive concepts have become prominent in experimental, social and clinical models of emotion. This shift towards a more cognitive perspective is particularly pronounced in contemporary approaches to affective disorders such as anxiety and depression. This trend has spawned a flurry of experimental activity aimed at investigating the cognitive antecedents of both normal and abnormal emotional responding.

A fundamental assumption of all cognitive-clinical models is that cognitive processes mediate all emotional and behavioral responses. Consequently, cognitive factors are viewed as necessary but not sufficient in the production of affective states. Moreover, cognitive processes are considered crucial in precipitating and maintaining certain maladaptive psychological states (see Beck, 1967, p. 270). However, cognitive theories do recognize a causal role for genetic, biological, environmental and developmental factors in the etiology of affective disorders (Beck, 1967, 1976, 1987).

Currently, there is no generally accepted theory within the cognitive-clinical perspective. A variety of cognitive constructs have been proposed aimed at varying analytic levels. Furthermore, several different cognitive models for affective disorders have been advanced (e.g. Bandura, 1977; Beck, 1967; Beck, Rush, Shaw and Emery, 1979; Beck and Emery, 1985; Ellis, 1962; Peterson and Seligman, 1985). These models differ in the cognitive concepts emphasized, their view on how these constructs interrelate, and how they may mediate emotional arousal.

* Address correspondence to: David A. Clark, Department of Psychology, Univeristy of New Brunswick, Bag Service 45444, Fredericton, New Brunswick, Canada E3B 6E4.

Recently, Ingram and Kendall (1986) proposed a taxonomic system for categorizing the various constructs employed in cognitive-clinical models. Most cognitive variables refer either to cognitive structure, proposition, operation or product, although some variables may fall into more than one category. Cognitive structure refers to the manner in which information is internally organized, while cognitive propositions are the stored contents of these structures. Cognitive operations refer to the processes by which the components of the information processing system interact. Finally, cognitive products are viewed as output resulting from the functioning of the information processing system.

Using Ingram and Kendall's (1986) classificatory scheme as a framework, below we present an information processing model of anxiety and depression. After a brief description of the model, we discuss two concepts crucial to this cognitive theory of affective disorders: the question of cognitive profiles and the content-specificity hypothesis. Finally, we conclude by considering possible directions for future research.

A COGNITIVE THEORY OF ANXIETY AND DEPRESSION

Basic Assumptions

To ensure survival, human beings have evolved an elaborate system for processing information from the environment. We actively construct our reality by selecting, transforming, encoding, storing and retrieving information (Beck, 1967, p. 283; Kelly, 1955). In psychopathological states, however, a systematic bias is introduced into the system so that a shift in the information processing apparatus is evident. For example, the perception of danger and subsequent appraisal of one's capability in dealing with this danger has obvious survival value. However, anxious individuals incorrectly overestimate the degree of threat associated with situations and underestimate their ability to cope (Beck and Rush, in press). Likewise, it is postulated that survival value is involved in the normal withdrawal and conservation of energy triggered by loss and failure events. In depression, however, one finds an exaggerated appraisal of the loss or deprivation with subsequent persistent withdrawal (Beck, 1987). This faulty information processing is evident at all levels of the system.

Cognitive Structure and Propositions

Schemas are functional structures of relatively enduring representations of prior knowledge and experience (Beck, 1967, p. 283; 1987; Greenberg and Beck, in press). These cognitive structures guide the screening, encoding, organizing, storing and retrieving of information (Beck *et al.*, 1979). Stimuli consistent with existing schemas are elaborated and encoded, while inconsistent or irrelevant information is ignored or forgotten (Greenberg, Vazquez and Alloy, in press).

In psychopathological states, maladaptive idiosyncratic schemas dominate the information processing system. These schemas are rigid, impermeable, overinclusive and concrete (Beck, 1967; Clark and Beck, in preparation). The maladaptive schemas remain dormant until triggered by appropriate environmental events. Once activated they frequently override more functional schemas and give rise to faulty information processing. By possessing latent maladaptive schemas, some individuals evidence a cognitive vulnerability for developing anxiety or depression (Beck, 1987; Clark and

Beck, in preparation). Thus, cognitive theory (CT) endorses an interactional model in which relevant life stressors interact with cognitively vulnerable individuals to precipitate a psychopathological state (Greenberg and Beck, in press).

Cognitive Operations

Once activated, maladaptive schemas give rise to systematic distortions in the processing of information. Moreover, these distortions operate in a reciprocal manner, such that maladaptive schemas are confirmed and strengthened, while more adaptive schemas inconsistent with these distortions are suppressed.

Several cognitive errors evident in psychological disorders have been identified (Beck, 1967, 1976; Beck *et al.*, 1979). These include: *arbitrary inference* (formulating a conclusion in the absence of sufficient evidence); *selective abstraction* (taking a detail out of its context while ignoring more important features); *overgeneralization* (basing a conclusion on isolated events and then applying this across diverse situations); *magnification and minimization* (distorting the importance of events); *personalization* (inappropriately attributing external events to one's self); and *dichotomous thinking* (evaluating experiences only in terms of one or two mutually exclusive categories).

As discussed below, each of these cognitive distortions will be present to a greater or lesser degree in all psychopathological states, although differences will be evident in the content or function each plays in the various disorders (Clark and Beck, in preparation).

Cognitive Products

Maladaptive schemas also bias the individual's stream of consciousness. Distressed persons' self-verbalizations or internal dialogue reflect the content of their dysfunctional schemas. The voluntary cognitions and automatic thoughts and images comprising this internal dialogue are transient, state-like phenomena, which are easily accessible to awareness.

THE COGNITIVE PROFILE OF ANXIETY AND DEPRESSION

A major assumption of CT is that each psychological disorder has a specific cognitive profile evident at all levels of cognitive functioning (Beck, 1967, p. 270; Beck and Weishaar, in press). For example, in anxiety we see the theme of perceived physical or psychological danger, with panic disorder a catastrophic misinterpretation of bodily or mental experiences, and in depression loss or deprivation. Moreover, distinct cognitive content can be seen in other psychological disorders such as mania (i.e. an exaggerated view of self, experience and future), hysteria (i.e. a belief in motor or sensory abnormality), obsessional states (i.e. a repetitive warning or doubting about safety), compulsive acts (i.e. rituals to ward off doubts or threat), and paranoid states (i.e. the attribution of negative bias to others).

These distinct cognitive profiles result in the differentiation of emotional states. Table 1 outlines the primary cognitive characteristics of anxiety and depression. In the following sections we discuss the empirical support for a number of these cognitive features.

Table 1 Cognitive differences between anxiety and depression.

Depression	*Anxiety*
Differences in Cognitive Structures	
Negativity toward self, world and future as well as loss within the personal domain.	Physical or psychological threat to one's personal domain and increased sense of vulnerability.
Differences in Cognitive Processing	
Selectivity with enhanced processing of negative self-referent information and minimization of positive material.	Selectivity in processing threat cues with exaggerated estimate of vulnerability.
Negative appraisals are pervasive, global and exclusive.	Negative appraisals are selective and specific to the fear situation.
Negative appraisals are absolute and conclusive.	Negative appraisals are tentative in nature.
Negative events are past-oriented and viewed as predetermined.	Anticipates possible negative events in the future(the "what if" phenomena).
Self-focused attention may reduce responsiveness to external stimuli.[a]	Self-focused attention reflects attempts to gain control over internal or external stimuli.[a]
Differences in cognitive Product	
Thoughts involving loss and failure.	Thought involving threat and danger.
Automatic thoughts usually take the form of negative self-statements.	Automatic thoughts often take the form of questions regarding present danger and future possibilities.[a]

[a] See Kendall and Ingram (1987, pp. 94–98).

Schemas

The schematic organization of the clinically depressed individual is dominated by an overwhelming negativity. A negative cognitive trait is evident in the depressed person's view of the self, world and future (Beck, 1967). As a result of these negative maladaptive schemas, the depressed person views himself as inadequate, deprived and worthless, the world as presenting insurmountable obstacles, and the future as utterly bleak and hopeless (Beck, 1967).

In contrast, the maladaptive schemas in the anxious patient involve perceived physical or psychological threat to one's personal domain as well as an exaggerated sense of vulnerability (Beck, 1967; Beck and Emery, 1985). Moreover, different schematic themes are evident in the various subtypes of anxiety. With generalized anxiety disorder (GAD) a variety of life situations are viewed as threatening to one's self-concept; in panic disorder (PD) bodily or mental experiences are interpreted as catastrophic: with simple phobias danger is attributed to specific avoidable situations; and in agoraphobia panic attacks are associated with external situations and so reinforce avoidance behaviour (Beck and Emery, 1985; Beck and Rush, in press).

Depressive schemas
Recently, a number of empirical studies have investigated the hypothesized negative schemas in depression. To assess these maladaptive structures, the Dysfunctional Attitudes Scale (DAS) (Weissman and Beck, 1978) was developed. The DAS has been validated in a number of clinical studies. It correlates positively with severity of depression (Dobson and Shaw, 1986; Hollon, Kendall and Lumry, 1986) and can distinguish clinically depressed from nondepressed psychiatric controls (Dobson and Shaw, 1986; Hamilton and Abramson, 1983), although contrary results have also been reported (Hollon *et al.*, 1986; Silverman, Silverman and Eardley, 1984).

Numerous experimental studies have investigated the hypothesized negative self-schema in depression by assessing its influence on encoding and retrieval processes. If a negative self-schema dominates, then one would expect a corresponding negative bias in the depressed person's encoding and retrieval (recall or recognition) of relevant information. A number of studies have used a self-referent encoding task (SRET) in which subjects are presented with a list of positive, negative and neutral trait adjectives. An incidental recall and/or recognition task follows presentation of the word list.

Most studies have found that clinically and mildly depressed individuals do rate as self-descriptive more negative and fewer positive words than controls (Bradley and Mathews, 1983; Clifford and Hemsley, 1987; Derry and Kuiper, 1981; Dobson and Shaw, 1987; Greenberg and Alloy, 1987; Roth and Rehm, 1980). In a recent clinical study, Greenberg and Beck (1987) extended these findings to world and future schemas by showing that depressed patients also endorsed more negative world- and future-relevant trait adjectives than anxious and nondepressed-nonanxious psychiatric controls. On the incidental recall or recognition tasks, some have found that depressed subjects do show enhanced recall for the negative material (Bradley and Mathews, 1983; Derry and Kuiper, 1981; Dunbar and Lishman, 1984; Greenberg and Beck, 1987), while others have failed to find such differences (Clifford and Hemsley, 1987; Davis, 1979; Dobson and Shaw, 1987; Hasher, Rose, Zacks, Sanft and Doren, 1985; Pietromonaco and Markus, 1983; Roth and Rehm, 1980). Furthermore, nondepressed subjects exposed to a sad mood induction do show enhanced recall for negative self-referent adjectives (Clark and Teasdale, 1985; Teasdale and Russell, 1983), although Mathews and Bradley (1983) failed to find a close relation between mood shift and self-referent recall bias (see also Clark, Teasdale, Broadbent and Martin, 1983). However, a sad mood does enhance recall of unpleasant memories (Clark and Teasdale, 1982; Teasdale and Taylor, 1981; Teasdale, Taylor and Fogarty, 1980), and accessibility to these memories is related to the severity of depression in clinical patients (Fogarty and Hemsley, 1983).

One of the more consistent findings reported is that nondepressed subjects show a strong bias towards recalling positive self-referent material. However, several researchers have reported mixed results with mildly and, to a lesser extent, clinically depressed subjects, who instead recall an equal amount of positive and negative information (Breslow, Kocsis and Belkin, 1981; Greenberg and Alloy, 1987; Kuiper and Derry, 1982). This has led some to conclude that, in at least mildly depressed states, it is the failure to show a positive self-schema rather than the predominance of negative schemas that is most evident.

Taken together, there is now considerable experimental and questionnaire evidence for the view that negative schemas are activated in both clinical and analogue depressive states. The inconsistent results with the incidental recall experiments may be due to methodological shortcomings. Several researchers have argued that the incidental recall of trait adjectives is an inappropriate measure of schema strength (Dobson and Shaw, 1987; Ferguson, Rule and Carlson, 1983).

Anxious schemas

Fewer studies have examined schematic influences in anxiety states. In studies using the Irrational Beliefs Test (Jones, 1969) as a measure of maladaptive schemas, scores on this instrument were positively correlated with level of anxiety in both clinical and student samples (Sutton-Simon and Goldfried, 1979; Zwemer and Deffenbacher, 1984). Furthermore, Deffenbacher, Zwemer, Whisman, Hill and Sloan (1986) found that a different pattern of irrational beliefs was associated with different subtypes of anxiety within a student population.

In two experiments Nunn, Stevenson and Whalan (1984) reported that agoraphobics showed a biased recall for fear-relevant information on both prose and trait adjective tasks. O'Banion and Arkowitz (1977) found that high socially anxious subjects had better recognition memory for evaluative adjectives. Willner and Neiva (1986) induced a tense mood state in female students by presenting an uncontrollable loud noise during incidental recall of trait adjectives. During the tense mood state, subjects showed a biased recall for negative trait words. In a clinical study, Mogg, Mathews and Weinman (in press) failed to find enhanced recall for threatening self-referent trait words in a group of anxious patients. However, Greenberg and Beck (1987) found that anxious patients did recall more negative than positive anxiety-relevant trait adjectives.

The paucity of research on maladaptive schemas in anxiety precludes any firm conclusions regarding the cognitive profile of anxiety at the schema level. Nevertheless, the preliminary research, for the most part, is consistent with the view that schemas involving physical or psychological threat are activated in anxiety states.

Cognitive Operations

Depression

Several experimental tasks have been employed to investigate the negative information processing bias of depression. Most studies have found that depressed patients do show enhanced processing for negative information but only if it is self-referent in nature. This negativity is not evident when processing neutral or other-referent material. Thus, individuals in a depressed state tend to underestimate positive and overestimate negative feedback after task performance (DeMonbreun and Craighead, 1977; Finkel, Glass and Merluzzi, 1982; Nelson and Craighead, 1977), although contrary results have also been reported (Craighead, Hickey and DeMonbreun, 1979). Other studies have shown that depressives tend to underestimate the success of their performance (Buchwald, 1977; Loeb, Beck and Diggory, 1971). Roth and Rehm (1980) found that depressed patients monitored fewer positive and more negative interpersonal behaviors when viewing a videotape of their role-play performance.

Recently, several studies have investigated whether a depressive-like state enhances perception of mood-congruent (i.e. negative) stimuli. Employing a lexical decision paradigm, Macleod, Tata and Mathews (1987) did not find quicker perception of negative words by depressed patients. This replicates Clark *et al.*'s (1983) earlier finding of similar lexical decision times for pleasant and unpleasant words regardless of the induced mood state. However, Powell and Hemsley (1984) did find a negative perceptual bias when depressed patients were presented with brief tachistoscopic displays of pleasant, unpleasant and neutral words. In addition, Williams and Broadbent (1986) found that for suicide attemptors depression level was significantly correlated with the extent of interference caused by negative words in the Stroop colour-naming task.

At present the experimental literature is inconclusive on whether depressive states are associated with an enhanced processing of negative self-referent material. However, most studies have shown that depressive mood does bias subjects' perception against positive information. The inconsistent results may be due to the varying levels of depression across studies. It may be that the extent of faulty information processing falls along a continuum with depression level. In milder depressive-like states one may find only a blocking of positive information. As one progresses to the more severe clinical forms, an enhanced processing of negative material may also become more apparent. In addition, the negative processing bias in depression may be evident only when there is competition for processing resources, such as when ambiguous stimuli are presented, insufficient time is allowed, or when complex tasks are employed (see Mathews and MacLeod, 1987). Consequently, experimental procedures such as lexical decision may be too elementary to be affected by distorted processing.

Anxiety

Results from a number of studies support the CT view that anxious patients selectively perceive threat and danger. Bulter and Mathews (1983) found that GAD patients reported higher estimates of subjective probability for negative threatening events, a finding replicated by Kent (1985) with dental phobics. Furthermore, GAD patients evidence a significant bias towards interpreting ambiguous stimuli as threatening (Bulter and Mathews, 1983; Eysenck, Mathews and Richards, 1987). On a dichotic listening task, agoraphobics, social phobics and obsessive-compulsives show heightened sensitivity to fear-related words presented in the unattended channel (Burgess, Jones, Robertson, Radcliffe and Emerson, 1981; Foa and McNally, 1986). Foa and McNally found that this bias for fear stimuli was not evident at post-treatment. Mathews and MacLeod (1986) failed to find enhanced recognition for threat words in the unattended channel, although these stimuli did cause more task interference for anxious but not control subjects. These inconsistent results may be due to differences in the instructions given to subjects. Both Burgess *et al.* (1981) and Foa and McNally (1986) told subjects to signal whenever they detected a target word in the unattended channel. Mathews and MacLeod (1986), however, instructed their subjects to ignore completely material in the unattended channel.

In an earlier study, Mathews and MacLeod (1985) found that anxious as compared to nonanxious subjects evidenced greater interference from threat-related words in a Stroop colour-naming task. Moreover, while all anxious subjects showed interference effects with social threat words, only those with physical worries were equally disrupted by physical threat words. Watts, McKenna, Sharrock and Trezise (1986) also found that spider phobics were selectively disrupted in colour-naming by spider-related words. These results, then, suggest that threat stimuli demand more processing resources in anxious than nonanxious individuals (Mathews and MacLeod, 1987).

In order to determine whether this processing bias is due to conscious attention to threat stimuli or to an attempt by anxious subjects to deny entry of threat words into consciousness (Mathews and MacLeod, 1987), MacLeod, Mathews and Tata (1986) used a probe detection task to test attentional deployment. They found that GAD patients had quicker probe detection when it was preceded by a threat-related word. This indicates that the anxious subjects showed an attentional shift toward threat stimuli. Together these results demonstrate that anxious individuals will automatically and selectively attend to threatening stimuli in their environment. Furthermore, Mathews and MacLeod (1987) point out that this bias will be evident only when there is competition for processing resources.

These studies, then, support the CT view that anxious individuals show a hypervigilance for threat and danger cues within their environment. Moreover, this selectivity in cognitive processing can occur outside of awareness. In addition, numerous empirical studies on self-efficacy have shown that, when confronted with a fear situation, anxious individuals report an increased sense of vulnerability and underestimate their ability to cope with the situation (e.g. Bandura and Adams, 1977; Bandura, Adams and Beyer, 1977).

Cognitive Products

Depression

In a study of 50 clinically depressed patients, Beck (1967) first noted that the primary ideation of these patients involved themes of negative self-evaluation, hopelessness and pessimistic view of the world. Since then, studies using structured questionnaires (e.g. Automatic Thoughts Questionnaire, Cognitions Checklist and Crandell Cognition Inventory) have supported Beck's initial observation (Beck, Brown, Steer, Eidelson and Riskind, 1987; Blackburn, Jones and Lewin, 1986; Crandell and Chambless, 1986; Dobson and Shaw, 1986; Eaves and Rush, 1984; Harrell and Ryon, 1983; Hollon *et al.*, 1986). However, the ideational content of depressed patients has not yet been investigated by means of such recall assessment procedures as "think aloud" or "thoughtsampling" (Clark, in press). "Think aloud" involves the audiotaping and subsequent content analysis of subjects' spontaneous self-verbalizations during performance of a task, while "thought sampling" requires subjects to report their current cognitions when cued by a random sampling device (Kendall and Hollon, 1981, pp. 90–106).

Anxiety

Beck, Laude and Bohnert (1974) and, more recently, Hibbert (1984) found that GAD patients reported thoughts and images of physical or psychological threat to one's personal domain during anxiety attacks. As in depression, this finding was confirmed later with more structured, self-report questionnaires (e.g. Beck *et al.*, 1987; Chambless, Caputo, Bright and Gallagher, 1984; Sutton-Simon and Goldfried, 1979). Moreover, think-aloud and thought-listing procedures have identified threat-related self-verbalizations associated with agoraphobia (Emmelkamp and Felten, 1985; Mavissakalian, Michelson, Greenwald, Kornblith and Greenwald, 1983; Michelson, 1986). Thus, the view that cognitions involving threat and vulnerability are associated with anxiety states has been empirically supported.

THE CONTENT-SPECIFICITY HYPOTHESIS

Given the view that anxiety and depression each exhibit a unique cognitive profile, CT further postulates that differentiation between affective states is possible because of the degree of content specificity in cognitive functioning. In Table 1 we have presented the major cognitive differences between anxiety and depression. Note that it is primarily the content of the faulty information processing system that distinguishes anxiety and depression. This content-specificity hypothesis is at variance with other cognitive-clinical models such as Ellis' rational-emotive therapy in which a few core irrational beliefs are thought to underlie all emotional disorders (Ellis, 1977).

Until recently, few empirical studies directly compared the cognitive functioning of anxious and depressed individuals. At the schema level, Greenberg and Alloy (1987) investigated the content-specificity hypothesis in an analogue study of anxious and depressed students. Using an SRET paradigm, they found that anxious-nondepressed subjects recalled more anxiety-relevant self-referent adjectives, while a mixed depressed-anxious group rated as self-descriptive more negative depression-relevant trait words. Ingram, Kendall, Smith, Donnell and Ronan (1987) employed an SRET to show that depressed-nonanxious subjects had enhanced recall of self-referent trait adjectives with depressive content, while anxious-nondepressed individuals evidenced greater recall of anxiety-relevant words. Greenberg and Beck (1987) found that clinically depressed patients recalled more depression-relevant words than did the anxious subjects. Although there were no significant between-group differences in recall of the anxiety-relevant adjectives, nevertheless the anxious patients did recall more negative than positive anxiety-relevant items. The depressed and control subjects did not show significant differences in their recall of these stimuli. Finally, Beck, Riskind, Brown and Steer (in press) found that patients with a major depressive disorder (MDD) reported significantly more hopelessness about the future than GAD patients. These data, then, support the content-specificity hypothesis by suggesting that different maladaptive schemas are activated during anxiety and depression.

Beck and Emery (1985, p. 103) first noted a number of differences in the way depressed and anxious individuals interpret information. In Table 1 we have listed several of these differences in cognitive processing. Bulter and Mathews (1983) did investigate processing bias using interpretations of ambiguous scenarios as the dependent variable. However, their depressed group evidenced as much anxiety as the anxious sample, thus making interpretation of the results equivocal. Based on the Attributional Style Questionnaire, Ingram *et al.* (1987) found that depressed as compared to test-anxious subjects minimized positive and maximized negative experiences. Brown, Beck, Steer and Riskind (1986) compared MDD and GAD patients on their likelihood estimates for an imagined "worst" and "best" possible outcome to a current life problem using the Fantasied Outcome Test. The depressed patients had significantly higher likelihood estimates for negative events than did the anxious patients. In the MacLeod *et al.* (1986) study, the attentional bias toward threat stimuli was evident with anxious but not depressed patients. Together these results provide empirical support for the content-specificity hypothesis at the cognitive processing level. Differences are evident in the manner in which anxious and depressed individuals process certain types of information.

The content-specificity hypothesis has been more extensively investigated at the cognitive product level. In a number of studies, measures of depressive cognitions showed a higher correlation with depressed mood than with noncorresponding mood states (Clark, 1986; Harrell, Chambless and Calhoun, 1981; Thorpe, Barnes, Hunter and Hines, 1983; Wickless and Kirsch, 1987). Ingram *et al.* (1987) found that "purely" depressed subjects reported significantly more negative automatic thoughts than did nondepressed controls, while the anxious and "normal" subjects failed to differ on this variable. In a clinical study involving well-differentiated samples of anxious and depressed patients, Beck *et al.* (1987) found that the depressed group reported significantly more negative cognitions and the anxious patients more anxiety-relevant thoughts and images, as indicated by scores on the Cognitions Checklist.

When considering anxious cognitions, data from the analogue studies are less consistent. Some studies report higher correlations between threat-related thoughts and anxiety (Clark, 1986; Parkinson and Rachman, 1981; Wickless and Kirsch, 1987), while others fail to support this finding (Harrell *et al.*, 1981; Thorpe *et al.*, 1983). In an earlier study, LaPointe and Harrell (1978) did not find cognitive-affective specificity with either depressed or anxious self-statements.

Taken together, the few studies that have directly compared clinically anxious and depressed patients have provided empirical support for the content-specificity hypothesis. Clearly, more comparative research is needed, particularly at the processing and schema levels.

CONCLUSION

We have briefly outlined a cognitive theory of psychopathology with particular emphasis on anxiety and depression. Two issues of major importance to CT, that of cognitive profiles and the content-specificity hypothesis, were discussed and their empirical status evaluated. As evidenced by the research literature, there is now considerable support for the salience of cognitive factors in anxiety and depression. Data are also encouraging for many of the more specific hypotheses of CT, although inconsistent findings have been reported.

There are a number of reasons why attempts to empirically investigate cognitive factors may be particularly difficult. First, the private, subjective nature of our subject matter necessitates a considerable degree of interference with the dependent variables used to assess cognitive constructs. Consequently, inappropriate or insensitive methods will yield conflicting results. Thus, researchers must ensure that the measures and procedures they employ possess adequate ecological and construct validity.

Secondly, we believe analogue studies often produce inconsistent results because they provide only a weak test of CT. Normal student subjects will not show an information processing system dominated by maladaptive schemas. Instead, any faulty cognitive functioning will be transient, situationally specific, and rather secondary in nature. On the other hand, psychiatric patients are a stronger test of the model, since they are expected to show a faulty information processing system dominated by dysfunctional schemas.

And, finally, researchers must be specific about the cognitive constructs investigated in their studies (Kendall and Ingram, 1987). As mentioned earlier, there are numerous constructs aimed at varying analytic levels. Confusion and inconsistency arise when researchers are not specific about the cognitive constructs tapped by their measures. Future studies should employ a multimethod assessment approach in which a number of cognitive constructs at varying theoretical levels are measured.

References

Bandura, A. (1977) Self-efficacy: toward a unifying theory of behavioral change. *Psychological Review*, **84**, 191–215

Bandura, A. and Adams, N. (1977) Analysis of self-efficacy theory of behavioral change. *Cognitive Therapy and Research*, 1, 289–310

Bandura, A., Adams, N. and Beyer, J. (1977) Cognitive processes mediating behavior change. *Journal of Personality and Social Psychology*, **35**, 125–139

Beck, A.T. (1967) *Depression: Causes and Treatment*. Philadelphia: University of Pennsylvania Press

Beck, A.T. (1976) *Cognitive Therapy of the Emotional Disorders*. New York: New American Library

Beck, A.T. (1987) Cognitive models of depression. *Journal of Cognitive Psychotherapy: An International Quarterly*, **1**, 5–37

Beck, A.T. and Emery, G. (1985) *Anxiety Disorders and Phobias: A Cognitive Perspective*. New York: Basic Books

Beck, A.T. and Rush, A.J. (in press) Cognitive therapy. In *Comprehensive Textbook of Psychiatry IV*, edited by H.J. Kaplan and B.J. Sadock. Williams and Wilkins Press

Beck, A.T. and Weishaar, M.E. (in press) Cognitive therapy. In *Handbook of Cognitive Therapy*, edited by A. Freeman, K.M. Simon, H. Arkowitz and L. Beulter. New York: Plenum Press

Beck, A.T., Laude, R. and Bohnert, M. (1974) Ideational components of anxiety neurosis. *Archives of General Psychiatry*, **31**, 319–325

Beck, A.T., Rush, A.J., Shaw, B.F. and Emery, G. (1979) *Cognitive Therapy of Depression*. New York: Guilford Press

Beck, A.T., Brown, G., Steer, R.A., Eidelson, J.I. and Riskind, J.H. (1987) Differentiating anxiety and depression utilizing the Cognition Checklist. *Journal of Abnormal Psychology*, **96**, 179–186

Beck, A.T., Riskind, J.H., Brown, G. and Steer, R.A. (in press) Levels of hopelessness in DSM-III disorders: a test of the cognitive model of depression. *Cognitive Therapy and Research*

Blackburn, I.M., Jones, S. and Lewin, R.J.P. (1986) Cognitive style in depression. *British Journal of Clinical Psychology*, **25**, 241–251

Bradley, B. and Mathews, A. (1983) Negative self-schemata in clinical depression. *British Journal of Clinical Psychology*, **22**, 173–181

Breslow, R., Kocsis, J. and Belkin, B. (1981) Contribution of the depressive perspective to memory function in depression. *American Journal of Psychiatry*, **138**, 227–229

Brown, G.A., Beck, A.T., Steer, R.A. and Riskind, J.H. (1986) Differentiating anxiety from depression: the cognition checklist, fantasied outcome test, hopelessness scale and self concept test. (Paper presented at the annual meeting of the Society for Psychotherapy Research, Wellesley, MA, USA)

Buchwald, A.M. (1977) Depressive mood and estimates of reinforcement frequency. *Journal of Abnormal Psychology*, **86**, 443–446

Bulter, G. and Mathews, A. (1983) Cognitive processes in anxiety. *Advances in Behaviour Research and Therapy*, **5**, 51–62

Burgess, I.S., Jones, L.M., Robertson, S.A., Radcliffe, W.N. and Emerson, E. (1981) The degree of control exerted by phobic and non-phobic verbal stimuli over the recognition behaviour of phobic and non-phobic subjects. *Behaviour Research and Therapy*, **19**, 233–243

Chambless, D.L., Caputo, G.C., Bright, P. and Gallagher, R. (1984) Assessment of fear in agoraphobics: The Body Sensations Questionnaire and the Agoraphobic Cognitions Questionnaire. *Journal of Consulting and Clinical Psychology*, **52**, 1090–1097

Clark, D.A. (1986) Cognitive-affective interaction: a test of the "specificity" and "generality" hypotheses. *Cognitive Therapy and Research*, **10**, 607–623

Clark, D.A. (in press) the validity of measures of cognition: a review of the literature. *Cognitive Therapy and Research*

Clark, D.A. and Beck, A.T. *Cognitive Therapy and Therapy of Anxiety and Depression*. Manuscript in preparation

Clark, D.M. and Teasdale, J.D. (1982) Diurnal variation in clinical depression and accessibility of memories of positive and negative experiences. *Journal of Abnormal Psychology*, **91**, 87–95

Clark, D.M. and Teasdale, J.D. (1985) Constraints on the effects of mood on memory. *Journal of Personality and Social Psychology*, **48**, 1595–1608

Clark, D.M., Teasdale, J.D., Broadbent; D.E. and Martin, M. (1983) Effect of mood on lexical decisions. *Bulletin of the Psychonomic Society*, **21**, 175–178

Clifford, P.I. and Hemsley, D.R. (1987) The influence of depression on the processing of personal attributes. *British Journal of Psychiatry*, **150**, 98–103

Craighead, W.E., Hickey, K.S. and DeMonbreun, B.G. (1979) Distortion of perception and recall of neutral feedback in depression. *Cognitive Therapy and Research*, **3**, 291–298

Crandell, C.J. and Chambless, D.L. (1986) The validation of an inventory for measuring depressive thoughts: the Crandell Cognitions Inventory. *Behaviour Research and Therapy*, **24**, 403–411

Davis, H. (1979) Self-reference and the encoding of personal information in depression. *Cognitive Therapy and Research*, **3**, 97–110

Deffenbacher, J.L., Zwemer, W.A., Whisman, M.A., Hill, R.A. and Sloan, R.D. (1986) Irrational beliefs and anxiety. *Cognitive Therapy and Research*, **10**, 281–292

DeMonbreun, B.G. and Craighead, W.E. (1977) Distortion of perception and recall of positive and neutral feedback in depression. *Cognitive Therapy and Research*, **1**, 311–329

Derry, P.A. and Kuiper, N.A. (1981) Schematic processing and self-reference in clinical depression. *Journal of Abnormal Psychology*, **90**, 286–297

Dobson, K.S. and Shaw, B.F. (1986) Cognitive assessment with major depressive disorders. *Cognitive Therapy and Research*, **10**, 13–29

Dobson, K.S. and Shaw, B.F. (1987) Specificity and stability of self-referent encoding in clinical depression. *Journal of Abnormal Psychology*, **96**, 34–40

Dunbar, G.C. and Lishman, W.A. (1984) Depression recognition-memory and hedonic tone: a signal detection analysis. *British Journal of Psychiatry*, **144**, 376–382

Eaves, G. and Rush, J.A. (1984) Cognitive patterns in symptomatic and remitted unipolar major depression. *Journal of Abnormal Psychology*, **93**, 31–40

Ellis, A. (1962) *Reason and Emotion in Psychotherapy*. Secaucus, NJ: The Citadel Press

Ellis, A. (1977) The basic clinical theory of rational-emotive therapy. In *Handbook of Rational-Emotive Therapy*, edited by A. Ellis and R. Grieger. New York: Springer.

Emmelkamp, P.M.G. and Felten, M. (1985) The process of exposure *in vivo*: cognitive and physiological changes during treatment of acrophobia. *Behaviour Research and Therapy*, **23**, 219–223

Eysenck, M.W., Mathews, A. and Richards, A. (1987) Anxiety and the interpretation of ambiguity. Unpublished manuscript. Birkbeck College and St George's Hospital Medical School, London, UK

Ferguson, T.J., Rule, B.G. and Carlson, D. (1983) Memory for personally relevant information. *Journal of Personality and Social Psychology*, **44**, 251–261

Finkel, C.B., Glass, C.R. and Merluzzi, T.V. (1982) Differential discrimination of self-referent statements by depressives and nondepressives. *Cognitive Therapy and Research*, **6**, 173–183

Foa, E.B. and McNally, R.J. (1986) Sensitivity to feared stimuli in obsessive-compulsives: a dichotic listening analysis. *Cognitive Therapy and Research*, **10**, 477–485

Fogarty, S.J. and Hemsley, D.R. (1983) Depression and the accessibility of memories: a longitudinal study. *British Journal of Psychiatry*, **142**, 232–237

Greenberg, M.S. and Alloy, L.B. (1987) Depression versus anxiety: schematic processing of self- and other-referent information. Manuscript in preparation. Center for Cognitive Therapy, University of Pennsylvania and Northwestern University, USA

Greenberg, M.S., and Beck, A.T. (in press) Cognitive approaches to psychotherapy: theory and therapy. In *Emotion and Psychotherapy*, edited by R. Plutchik and H. Kellerman.

Greenberg, M.S. and Beck, A.T. (1987) Depression versus anxiety: a test of the content specificity hypothesis. Manuscript submitted for publication. Center for Cognitive Therapy, University of Pennsylvania, USA

Greenberg, M.S., Vazquez, C.V. and Alloy, L.B, (in press) Depression versus anxiety: differences in self and other schemata. In *Cognitive Processes in Depression*, edited by L.B. Alloy. New York: Guilford

Hamilton, E.W. and Abramson, L.Y. (1983) Cognitive patterns and major depressive disorder: a longitudinal study in a hospital setting. *Journal of Abnormal Psychology*, **92**, 173–184

Harrell, T.H. and Ryon, N.B. (1983) Cognitive-behavioral assessment of depression: clinical validation of the Automatic Thoughts Questionnaire. *Journal of Consulting and Clinical Psychology*, **51**, 721–725

Harrell, T.H., Chambless, D.L. and Calhoun, J.F. (1981) Correlational relationship between self-statements and affective states. *Cognitive Therapy and Research*, **5**, 159–173

Hasher, L., Rose, K.C., Zacks, R.T., Sanft, H. and Doren, B. (1985) Mood, recall, and selectivity effects in normal college students. *Journal of Experimental Psychology: General*, **114**, 104–118

Hibbert, G.A. (1984) Ideational components of anxiety: their origin and content. *British Journal of Psychiatry*, **144**, 618–624

Hollon, S.D., Kendall, P.C. and Lumry, A. (1986) Specificity of depressotypic cognitions in clinical depression. *Journal of Abnormal Psychology*, **95**, 52–59

Ingram, R.E. and Kendall, P.C. (1986) Cognitive clinical psychology: implications of an information processing perspective. In *Information Processing Approaches to Clinical Psychology*, edited by R.E.Ingram. Orlando: Academic Press

Ingram, R.E., Kendall, P.C., Smith, T.W., Donnell, C. and Ronan, K. (1987) Cognitive specificity in emotional distress. *Journal of Personality and Social Psychology*, **53**

Jones, R.G. (1969) A factored measure of Ellis' irrational belief system, with personality and maladjustment correlates. *Dissertation Abstracts International*, **29**, 4379B (University Microfilms No. 69-6443)

Kelly, G.A. (1955) *The Psychology of Personal Constructs*. New York: W.W. Norton and Company

Kendall, P.C. and Hollon, S.D. (1981) Assessing self-referent speech: methods in the measurement of self-statements. In *Assessment Strategies for Cognitive-Behavioral Interventions*, edited by P.C. Kendall and S.D. Hollon. Orlando: Academic Press

Kendall, P.C. and Ingram, R.E. (1987) The future for cognitive assessment of anxiety: let's get specific. In *Anxiety and Stress Disorders: Cognitive-Behavioral Assessment and Treatment*, edited by L. Michelson and L.M. Ascher. New York: Guilford Press

Kent, G. (1985) Cognitive processes in dental anxiety. *British Journal of Clinical Psychology*, **24**, 259–264

Kuiper, N.A. and Derry, P.A. (1982) Depressed and nondepressed content self reference in mild depressives. *Journal of Personality*, **50**, 67–79

LaPointe, K.A. and Harrell, T.H. (1978) Thoughts and feelings: correlational relationships and cross-situational consistency. *Cognitive Therapy and Research*, **2**, 311–322

Loeb, A., Beck, A.T. and Diggory, J. (1971) Differential effects of success and failure on depressed and nondepressed patients. *Journal of Nervous and Mental Disease*, **152**, 106–114

MacLeod, C., Mathews, A. and Tata, P. (1986) Attentional bias in emotional disorders. *Journal of Abnormal Psychology*, **95**, 15–20

MacLeod, C., Tata, P. and Mathews, A. (1987) Perception of emotionally valenced information in depression. *British Journal of Clinical Psychology*, **26**, 67–68

Mathews, A. and Bradley, B. (1983) Mood and the self-reference bias in recall. *Behaviour Research and Therapy*, **21**, 233–239

Mathews, A. and MacLeod, C. (1985) Selective processing of threat cues in anxiety states. *Behaviour Research and Therapy*, **23**, 563–569

Mathews, A. and MacLeod, C. (1986) Discrimination of threat cues without awareness in anxiety states. *Journal of Abnormal Psychology*, **95**, 131–138

Mathews, A. and MacLeod, C. (1987) An information-processing approach to anxiety. *Journal of Cognitive Psychotherapy: An International Quarterly*, **1**, 105–115

Mavissakalian, M., Michelson, L., Greenwald, D., Kornblith, S. and Greenwald, M. (1983) Cognitive-behavioral treatment of agoraphobia: paradoxical intention vs self-statement training. *Behaviour Research and Therapy*, **21**, 75–86

Michelson, L. (1986) Treatment consonance and response profiles in agoraphobia: the role of individual differences in cognitive, behavioral and physiological treatments. *Behaviour Research and Therapy*, **24**, 263–275

Mogg, K., Mathews, A. and Weinman, J. (in press) Memory bias in clinical anxiety. *Journal of Abnormal Psychology*

Nelson, R.E. and Craighead, W.E. (1977) Selective recall of positive and negative feedback, self-control behaviors, and depression. *Journal of Abnormal Psychology*, **86**, 379–388

Nunn, J.D., Stevenson, R.J. and Whalan, G. (1984) Selective memory effects in agoraphobic patients. *British Journal of Clinical Psychology*, **23**, 195–201

O'Banion, K. and Arkowitz, H. (1977) Social anxiety and selective memory for affective information about the self. *Social Behavior and Personality*, **5**, 321–328

Parkinson, L. and Rachman, S. (1981) Part III. Intrusive thoughts: the effects of an uncontrived stress. *Advances in Behaviour Research and Therapy*, **3**, 111–118

Peterson, C. and Seligman, M.E.P. (1985) The learned helplessness model of depression: current status of theory and research. In *Handbook of Depression: Treatment, Assessment, and Research*, edited by E.E. Beckham and W.R. Leber. Homewood, Ill.: The Dorsey Press

Pietromonaco, P.R. and Markus, H. (1983) The nature of negative thoughts in depression. *Journal of Personality and Social Psychology*, **48**, 799–807

Powell, N. and Hemsley, D.R. (1984) Depression: a breakdown of perceptual defence? *British Journal of Psychiatry*, **145**, 358–362

Roth, D. and Rehm, L.P. (1980) Relationships among self-monitoring processes, memory, and depression. *Cognitive Therapy and Research*, **4**, 149–157

Silverman, J.S. Silverman, J.A. and Eardley, D.A. (1984) Do maladaptive attitudes cause depression? *Archives of General Psychiatry*, **41**, 28–30

Sutton-Simon, K. and Goldfried, M.R. (1979) Faulty thinking patterns in two types of anxiety. *Cognitive Therapy and Research*, **3**, 193–203

Teasdale, J.D. and Russell, M.L. (1983) Differential effects of induced mood on the recall of positive, negative and neutral words. *British Journal of Clinical Psychology*, **22**, 163–171

Teasdale, J.D. and Taylor, R. (1981) Induced mood and accessibility of memories: an effect of mood state or of induction procedure? *British Journal of Clinical Psychology*, **20**, 39–48

Teasdale, J.D., Taylor, R. and Fogarty, S.J. (1980) Effects of induced elation-depression on the accessibility of memories of happy and unhappy experiences. *Behaviour Research and Therapy*, **18**, 339–346

Thorpe, G.L., Barnes, G.S., Hunter, J.E. and Hines, D. (1983) Thoughts and feelings: correlations in two clinical and two nonclinical samples. *Cognitive Therapy and Research*, **7**, 565–574

Watts, F.N., McKenna, F.P., Sharrock, R. and Trezise, L. (1986) Colour naming of phobic-related words. *British Journal of Psychology*, **77**, 97–108

Weissman, A.N. and Beck, A.T. (1978) *Development and validation of the Dysfunctional Attitudes Scale.* Paper presented at the annual meeting of the Association for Advancement of Behavior Therapy, Chicago

Wickless, C. and Kirsch, I. (1987) Cognitive correlates of anger, anxiety, and sadness. Manuscript submitted for publication, University of Connecticut, USA

Williams, J.M.G. and Broadbent, K. (1986) Distraction by emotional stimuli: use of a Stroop task with suicide attemptors. *British Journal of Clinical Psychology*, **25**, 101–110

Willner, P. and Neiva, J. (1986) Brief exposure to uncontrollable but not to controllable noise biases the retrieval of information from memory. *British Journal of Clinical Psychology*, **25**, 93–100

Zwemer, W.A. and Deffenbacher, J.L. (1984) Irrational beliefs, anger, and anxiety. *Journal of Counseling Psychology*, **31**, 391–393

THE EFFECTS OF SELF-FOCUSED ATTENTION ON PERSPECTIVE-TAKING AND ANXIETY

R. GLEN HASS
Brooklyn College and The Graduate Center, The City University of New York

and

DONNA EISENSTADT
St. Mary's College of Maryland

Evidence is examined that pertains to two of the basic assumptions underlying self-awareness theory: that self-focused attention causes one to adopt an external perspective in which one views oneself like an observer; and that self-focus leads to self-dissatisfaction and negative affect. Experimental evidence is reviewed and found to offer convincing support for the perspective-taking assumption. An experiment that used a disguised measure of mood to test the negative affect assumption is reported. As predicted by self-awareness theory, subjects who saw their reflection in a mirror while completing the disguised mood measure were found to have more negative affect than subjects who did not face the mirror.

KEYWORDS: Self-awareness, self-focus, perspective-taking, direction of attention, mood, affect

Self-awareness theory (Duval & Wicklund, 1972; Wicklund, 1975) examines the psychological consequences of focusing attention on oneself, versus focusing attention elsewhere. According to the theory, external stimuli guide whether one's attention is focused outward toward the external environment, or back toward oneself. Distracting stimuli, engaging activities, and tasks that require conscious or effortful participation draw one's attention outward toward those external events. By contrast, stimuli such as mirrors, cameras, tape recorders, or an audience direct the focus of attention back on oneself. According to the theory, self-directed attention precipitates self-evaluation on currently salient dimensions — a comparison of what one believes one is like with one's ideal. Recognition of these real/ideal discrepancies normally produces self-dissatisfaction, followed by efforts to reduce the negative feelings either by focusing attention elsewhere, or by efforts to reduce the discrepancy.

In this paper we shall examine the evidence regarding two of the assumptions underlying self-awareness theory: the assumption that when self-focused one directs one's attention back toward oneself from an external perspective, and the assumption that self-focused attention generates negative affect.[1]

[1]Terms like "perspective" and "viewpoint" have multiple meanings. They can refer to the mental, or conceptual position of an individual (the evaluative orientation from which an interpretation is made), or they can refer to the physical location from which an observation occurs (as in the visual orientation of a person). Because researchers have used the terms to mean both things, some confusion and misinterpretation has resulted. We will use the term "perspective" to mean *visual* perspective, and "standards," "evaluative perspective," or the like when we mean more than just visual orientation.

Correspondence to: R. Glen Hass, Department of Psychology, Brooklyn College, CUNY, Brooklyn, New York 11210, USA.

SELF-AWARENESS AND PERSPECTIVE-TAKING

Over the years a number of theorists in addition to Duval and Wicklund have taken the position that awareness of the self is associated with a process by which an individual views himself or herself from an external vantage point. Acquiring the ability to take the perspective of another person was conceptualized by Piaget (1966/1924) as playing a central role in the loss of egocentrism by the developing individual. And seeing ourselves as others see us was viewed by the symbolic interactionists Cooley, Mead, and Dewey to play a central role in the development of a sense of self and individuality. For example, Cooley (1902) used the term "looking glass self" to describe the self-image we create by imagining ourselves through the eyes of another. "We perceive in another's mind some thought of our appearance, manners, aims, deeds, character, friends and so on" (Cooley, 1902, p. 184).

According to Mead (1934) and Duval and Wicklund (1972), when self-aware a person experientially leaves himself or herself and takes an external viewpoint as an observer of his or her behavior. Mead often used the phrase "getting outside oneself experientially" to describe the process of self-awareness. Duval and Wicklung (1972) agree, saying "the feeling [Mead] describes of being outside one's self does coincide with our theoretical notion . . . In short, the causal agent self has figuratively come outside itself and focuses upon itself in retrospect" (p. 34). There is now experimental evidence from several sources that supports the existence of this phenomenon.

Visual perspectives

In a series of experiments, Hass (1984a) tested the visual aspect of the bi-directional focus of attention assumption of self-awareness theory. According to the theory, a high level of self-focused attention causes a person to adopt an external, reflexive visual perspective. It is as if one takes the physical perspective of an outside observer looking back at oneself. By contrast, when self-focus is low, attention is directed outward, away from oneself and toward the surroundings. As a result, events that occur on the face in the same plane as the eyes should appear different depending on the perspective from which they are observed.

In each of three experiments (Hass, 1984a), subjects were asked to draw the capital letter *E* on their forehead. The subjects believed they were alone, but the experimenter could covertly observe whether they drew the *E* so that it was oriented correctly for an external observer (appearing "E" to the experimenter), or oriented from a perspective inside the subject's head (appearing "Ǝ" to the experimenter). In two of the experiments the self-awareness manipulation was visual (a video camera placed to the side of the subject in the first study, and behind the subject in the second). In the third experiment the self-focus manipulation was auditory (an audio tape recorder and microphone placed in front of the subject). In all three experiments subjects in the high self-awareness condition were more likely to draw the *E* from the perspective of an external observer than were subjects in the low self-awareness condition. Both visual ("What do I look like?") and auditory ("What do I sound like?") manipulations of self-focused attention produced an external, reflexive *visual* perspective.

In a fourth experiment, Hass (1984b) manipulated self-attention by making subjects aware of an internal process, their heartbeat. Replicating earlier results obtained by Fenigstein and Carver (1978), the heartbeat feedback increased self-attributions made by subjects for responsibility on a series of hypothetical positive or negative events (Duval & Wicklund, 1973). This manipulation of self-focus did not, however, affect the direction subjects drew the *E* on their forehead. Apparently, making people aware of aspects of themselves that are external leads them to take the external perspective of an observer of themself. But awareness of internal processes does not evoke an external perspective, even though awareness of internal events causes some other self-focusing effects, such as heightened self-attribution of responsibility. This distinction between self-awareness manipulations that lead to external perspective-taking and those that do not appears to follow the distinction between public and private self-awareness proposed by Carver and Scheier (1981).

When subjects in these experiments drew an *E* on their forehead, who did they orient it for, themselves or someone else? Several forms of evidence suggest that they oriented the *E* so that it looked correct to themselves. First of all, the subjects believed they were alone and unobservable, especially when self-focus was manipulated via an audio tape recorder. There was neither a person nor equipment that could observe the direction the *E* was drawn, so far as they knew. They were their only observer, and therefore the only person for whom the *E* could have been oriented.[2]

Secondly, if in the high self-focus conditions subjects were imagining some other observer and re-orienting the *E* for him/her, the mental activity required to do so should have added to the time it took subjects to respond. Subjects were instructed to draw the *E* as quickly as they could and then press a button that stopped a timer. No differences in time to draw the *E* were found between high self-focus and low self-focus conditions in any of the experiments. Orienting the *E* from an internal perspective is normal when one is alone and not self-focused. When one's attention is self-focused, orienting the *E* for an external perspective becomes more likely, but with no increased latency of response. So, it does not appear that one way of drawing the *E* is natural while the other is unnatural.

Finally, many subjects expressed surprised amusement when they discovered or the experimenter pointed out during the debriefing that the *E* could have been oriented differently from the way they had drawn it. Apparently subjects just drew the *E* quickly without realizing at that moment that there was an option in how to orient it. Or, put another way, it seems likely that *the E always looked correct to the subject* — its orientation depending on the circumstances and the subject's phenomenological perspective at the moment (Hass, 1984a).

Further evidence that self-focus produces an external, self-directed perspective comes from a study by Stephenson and Wicklund (1984). Subjects gave verbal instructions, directing another person's movements through a finger maze. The other person could not see the maze and had to rely on the subject's directions to proceed. Because the two people were seated face-to-face, they had opposite spatial perspectives of the maze. Therefore, the subject had to give directions appropriate to the external, subject-directed orientation of the other person. The more able the subject was to adopt an external perspective, the fewer errors she should have made in directing the other person through the maze. As hypothe-

[2]If subjects had suspected that they could be covertly observed, that suspicion should have been present equally in both the high and low self-awareness conditions. Any such suspicion could not have produced the differences between the conditions that were found.

sized, a manipulated increase in self-focus facilitated perspective-taking performance (i.e., reduced the number of errors in directions they gave) among subjects who were low in dispositional self-consciousness (Fenigstein, Scheier, & Buss, 1975). Subjects high in self-consciousness were already so attuned to an external perspective that they made few errors regardless of the experimental treatment.

Actor/observer attributional perspectives

Other evidence that self-awareness leads to the adoption of the self-directed perspective of an outside observer of oneself comes from research on the topic of actor/observer differences in causal attributions. Two people in a situation, an actor and an observer, will often differ systematically in the explanations they offer for the causes of the actor's behavior (Jones & Nisbett, 1971). Several explanations for this phenomenon have been offered. The one most relevant here proposes that we tend to explain events in terms of whatever aspect of the situation is the focus of our attention (c.f., Storms, 1973). The actor, whose attention is directed toward events in his or her surroundings, leans toward interpretations based on circumstances in the environment. The passive observer, whose attention is directed toward the actor in the situation, is more likely to view the behavior as caused by characteristics of the actor.

If manipulations of self-awareness cause an individual to adopt an external, like-an-observer perspective toward his or her own behavior, then such manipulations should affect causal explanations in a manner similar to that found in the studies of actor/observer differences. Duval and Wicklund (1973) asked subjects to read a series of hypothetical situations, each of which presented the possibility that the subject or someone else was responsible for the outcome. In two experiments Duval and Wicklund demonstrated that self-awareness manipulations could direct the level of responsibility subjects assigned themselves for the outcomes. In the first study, a manipulation that *reduced* self-focused attention *lowered* the percentage subjects saw themselves as responsible for negative events. In the second study, a manipulative that *increased* self-focused attention *raised* the percentage of responsibility subjects assigned to themselves for events half of which were positive and half of which were negative. Increasing or decreasing self-awareness affected the extent to which subjects focused attention on themselves from the perspective of an observer, and correspondingly affected the extent to which they acted like observers when forming causal attributions.

Perspective-taking and memory

A final category of evidence that self-awareness evokes an external, self-directed perspective comes from the study of memory. Most studies of personal memory have focused on forgetting. Nigro and Neisser (1983), however, conducted four studies in which they investigated subjects' memories for specific instances of a group of events, such as "watching television," and "giving a public presentation." After generating the memories, subjects were asked to indicate the perspective from which the past event was re-experienced: as an onlooker or observer from an external vantage point seeing oneself from the outside, or from within oneself viewing "the field." Although their research was intuitively driven, rather than testing any specific theoretical predictions, Nigro and Neisser found that heightened self-awareness was an important component of memories in which subjects most often reported recalling events from an external observer's perspective.

Summary and a remaining question

The evidence is compelling that self-focused attention provokes one to adopt an external perspective in which one takes the visual orientation of an observer of oneself, as suggested by theorists such as Mead (1934) and Duval and Wicklund (1972; Wicklund, 1975). The evidence comes from several different areas of research. We have seen that heightened self-awareness evokes an external visual perspective like that of an observer of oneself: It causes people to drawn an *E* on their forehead from an external perspective (Hass, 1984a), and it facilitates guiding someone with an observer's perspective through a maze (Stephenson & Wicklund, 1984). Heightened self-awareness causes one to behave more like an observer than an actor when making causal attributions (Duval & Wicklund, 1973). And higher levels of self-awareness are related to remembering events from the external perspective of an observer (Nigro & Neisser, 1983).

There is evidence that self-aware individuals take the external perspective of an observer. But who is that observer, oneself or an imagined other? This question is closely related to the issue of the standards that are used for the real/ideal self-evaluation that is caused by self-awareness (Duval & Wicklund, 1972; Wicklund, 1975). For example, if you play the violin in front of a mirror, by whose standards do you evaluate your performance, your own or your violin instructor's?

On the one hand, the symbolic interactionists clearly state that the process of self-evaluation involves imagining oneself as one would be perceived by another person. For example, Mead (1934) took the position that one becomes self-aware by considering the viewpoint of others toward oneself. And Cooley's (1902) term "the looking glass self" captured his belief that we view ourselves through the eyes of others who can be distinct and particular or vague and general, but are always there.

Duval and Wicklund (1972), on the other hand, assert that one uses one's own evaluative standards when self-aware, though the dimensions and standards used for self-evaluation can be influenced by other people in the same way that dimensions and standards used to evaluate any object can be influenced by others (e.g., your violin instructor may influence your criteria regarding the artistic merit of various ways of interpreting a musical composition).

Even though evaluative audiences should be extremely powerful agents in the arousal of self-focused attention, most researchers have avoided using real or imagined audiences as manipulations of self-awareness. The highly social nature of many audiences makes interpretation of their impact ambiguous. For example, it becomes difficult to determine whose standards are being used for evaluation, one's own or the audience's. Other social influence effects, such as anticipated rewards and punishments from the audience, also cloud the interpretation of results.

In fact, one of the most impressive aspects of the very large body of research that has been generated by self-awareness theory is that self-evaluation effects predicted by the theory can be produced by manipulations (such as mirrors, cameras and tape recorders) that do not have the immediate social impact and consequences of audiences.

It is important to distinguish between the consequences of self-focus generated by audiences and those generated by other manipulations. Mirrors, cameras, and tape recorders arouse self-evaluation in which one's own standards are the basis on which performance is evaluated. Non-evaluative audiences and audiences not capable of appropriate evaluation (e.g., first graders listening to a master violinist) probably also arouse one's own standards of evaluation. But most evaluative audiences, and audiences that generate evaluative concerns, probably arouse an awareness of the standards that we believe them (the audience) to be applying to our behavior, leading us to imagine ourselves through their eyes in much the manner proposed by the symbolic interactionists. The more important the audience is to us, the more likely is this tendency.

The increased adherence to one's own standards caused by a mirror, in contrast to increased standards of others when one is in the presence of an evaluative audience has been shown by Froming, Walker and Lopyan (1982). In their research Froming et al. used two groups of subjects, one who opposed the use of punishment in learning but believed that other people favored it, and another group who favored the use of punishment but believed others opposed it. The subjects served as "teachers" in a situation in which they were to punish incorrect responses by administering electric shock. In comparison to a control group, the presence of a mirror led subjects to deliver shock levels more like their personal standard (decreased shock levels in the former group, and increased levels in the latter). By contrast, the presence of an evaluative pair of observers led to shock levels more similar to the presumed standards that the evaluative audience was applying (increased shock levels in the former group, and decreased shock in the latter).

In their original presentation of self-awareness theory, Duval and Wicklund (1972) take pains to point out distinctions between their position and the symbolic interactionist position of Mead (1934) and Cooley (1902). For example, they make clear their view that self-awareness leads one to view him- or herself from one's own external vantage point, and to apply one's own standards of evaluation to oneself as a self-observer. Our own view corresponds to that originally proposed by Duval and Wicklund (1972), and is empirically supported by the *E*-on-the-forehead studies (Hass, 1984a). High self-aware subjects in those experiments (a) drew the *E* from an external perspective, even though there was no other observer known to them; and (b) drew the *E* from an external perspective as fast as low self-aware subjects drew it from an internal perspective, suggesting that high self-aware subjects drew it oriented correctly for their own external perspective, rather than taking the additional processing time to turn it around for an imagined other person. Furthermore, (c) both high and low self-awareness subjects often expressed surprise and/or amusement upon realizing that the *E* could have been drawn oriented differently from the way they had drawn it, providing further evidence that they drew the *E* from their own perspective at the moment, be it internal or external.

More recently, however, Stephenson and Wicklund (1983, 1984) have proposed a position more similar to that of the symbolic interactionists. They describe self-awareness as increasing one's ability to view and interpret events from, and better understand the perspective of another person.

In the Stephenson and Wicklund (1984) finger maze experiment reviewed earlier, the other person's visual perspective was the same as the subject's own external, like-an-observer visual perspective, so the predictions cannot be separated. In another series of experiments, Stephenson and Wicklund (1983) studied the effects of self-awareness on the ability of subjects to take the perspective of another person in the experimental setting. For example, in one of the experiments subjects were given the task to write a short story based on a set of stimulus materials. They were to write the story from the perspective of another person who had not seen two critical parts of the stimulus materials seen by the subject. In order to successfully accomplish the task, the subject had to disregard the information that had not been seen by the target subject. Stephenson and Wicklund found that high self-aware subjects were better able to perform the task of taking the other person's perspective than were control subjects. Similarly, high self-aware subjects were found to make fewer errors on a task in which they were to assign responsibility for a portion of a group product. Finally, high self-aware subjects made better use of available information when asked to predict the food preferences of another subject.[3]

Stephenson and Wicklund (1983) interpret these results to indicate that self-focused attention leads to a better understanding of another's perspective. An alternative explanation for the results seems possible, however. In each of the three experiments subjects had a task to perform that was assigned to them by the experimenter. In each situation they were directed to imagine themselves from the perspective of a particular other person. Among the most well established findings in research on self-awareness theory is that self-awareness can increase adherence to standards, and can enhance performance on tasks by increasing motivation (cf. Duval & Wicklund, 1972; Liebling & Shaver, 1973; Wicklund, 1975; Wicklund & Duval, 1971). Consequently, it becomes difficult to know the extent to which the results were due to high self-aware subjects' spontaneously taking the perspective of the other person as a consequence of heightened self-focus, or taking their perspective as a motivated effort to perform better at their assigned task (and also to live up to a standard of fairness in Experiment 2).

Whether self-awareness increases one's tendency to observe oneself from one's own external vantage point and apply one's own standards of evaluation, or leads one to see oneself through the eyes, and presumably through the evaluative standards, of another is an unresolved question. It is probably the case that both are true. For example, being observed by others who are evaluating us would lead us to imagine ourselves from the perspective and standards of the audience, whereas manipulations of self-awareness that do not imply an evaluative audience would create an external perspective, with the self as its own observer.

SELF-AWARENESS AND NEGATIVE AFFECT

According to self-awareness theory (Duval & Wicklund, 1972; Wicklund, 1975) self-directed attention provokes self-evaluation on currently salient dimensions. The discrepancy between what one believes one is like and one's ideal normally produces self-criticism, self-dissatisfaction and negative affect, followed by efforts to reduce the negative feelings either by directing one's attention elsewhere, or by efforts to reduce the discrepancy.[4]

[3]In all three experiments (Stephenson & Wicklund, 1983), arousing a personal concern in the mind of the high self-aware subjects (e.g., that an assessment would be made of the subject's neuroticism or food-related health problems) overwhelmed the effect of the self-awareness manipulation. Apparently it made another evaluative dimension salient for the subject, and attention was focused on it rather than the other experimental task.

[4]Success experiences can produce positive discrepancies and self-aggrandizement, but they are "fleeting phenomena" which "may slip into self-criticism as aspirations again rise beyond the level of attainment" (Wicklund, 1975, p. 248).

Self-focused attention has been shown to be related to the experience, as well as the successful treatment of chronic depression (cf. Brockner, Hjelle, & Plant, 1985; Ingram, Lumry, Cruet, & Sieber, 1987; Ingram & Smith, 1984; Pyszczynski & Greenberg, 1986; Schmitt, 1983), and alcoholism (Hull, 1981). Self-awareness has also been found to be related to aversive experiences in everyday life (Csikszentmihalyi & Figurski, 1982). And self-awareness has been shown to intensify the experience of other moods, both positive and negative, e.g., repulsion, sexual attraction, and fear (Carver, Blaney, & Scheier, 1979; Scheier, 1976; Scheier & Carver, 1977).

Our focus here is not on the relationship between self-awareness and chronic emotion, nor is it on the intensifying effects of self-awareness on other powerful mood inducing manipulations. Instead, our focus is on the more limited issue of the self-criticism and self-dissatisfaction that is assumed by the theory to result normally whenever attention is drawn to the self. The negative affect hypothesized to be aroused by self-focused attention is a critical element in the theory, since it energizes all the other predictions of the theory, whether they be efforts to redirect one's attention or to reduce the real/ideal discrepancy.

The negative affect aroused by most self-awareness manipulations (e.g., looking into a mirror, or hearing one's voice on a tape recorder) is probably weak compared to the normal experience of emotion. It should also be difficult to assess using the typical measure of mood: a paper-and-pencil questionnaire. A paper-and-pencil mood measure, such as an adjective check list, suffers from several problems when it comes to studying the effect of self-awareness manipulations on mood. First of all, paper-and-pencil mood measures make subjects aware that mood is being measured. Subjects' expectations and other demand characteristics become possible artifacts as a result. Second, such measures require that subjects are aware of and can accurately articulate their mood. Third, since such measures require that subjects focus on themselves in order to complete the questionnaire, the mood measure itself should heighten self-focus, reducing the impact of manipulated differences in self-awareness between experimental conditions. And finally, the mood questionnaires require concentration and take time to fill out, lessening the impact of any self-awareness manipulation that might have preceded it.

What is needed is a measure of mood that can be administered *during* the self-awareness manipulation, without subjects being aware that mood is being measured. Such a mood measure has been developed by Hass and Katz (1988). The measure is disguised as research on "Subliminal Perception." Subjects view material flashed on a computer screen below threshold. They are told that while their conscious mind cannot read it, their unconscious mind can. (In fact, what is flashed on the screen are not words at all, but world-like strings of letters.) Subjects are then shown a multiple choice list of words and are asked to pick the one that feels to them to be most similar in meaning to the word that was flashed on screen. One of the words is a mood-related word selected from one of several standard mood checklists. The mood words were selected to reflect the dimensions of anxiety and depression, with special emphasis on self-satisfaction/dissatisfaction. The subject receives a positive and a negative mood score based on the number of mood words selected over all the trials.

The rationale for the measure is similar to that of any projective test. The stimuli have nothing to do with mood, so when subjects select mood words that "feel" correct, they are presumed to be indicating something about how they are feeling at that moment. In validation research Hass and Katz used a mood induction procedure to manipulate mood and found that the mood measure successfully discriminated the mood conditions that were created. The measure has also been used successfully in another experiment on the topic of negative affect aroused by ambivalent feelings that White Americans have toward Blacks (Hass & Katz, 1989).

In the present experiment, the assumption of self-awareness theory that self-focused attention evokes negative feelings of self-criticism and self-dissatisfaction was tested by comparing the mood results for subjects who completed the mood measure under a high self-awareness condition, with subjects who responded in a low self-awareness condition.

Method

Subjects. Thirty-three undergraduates participated in order to satisfy a course requirement. Subjects were randomly assigned to either a high self-awareness condition (n = 17) or a low self-awareness condition (n = 16).

Mood measure. Subject's mood was assessed using Hass and Katz' (1988) mood measure. This measure requires subjects to attend to a computer monitor on which a string of letters was flashed during each trial. The letters were flashed faster than they could be read (approximately 1 msec), although it could be seen that something was flashed. Subjects were then instructed to select, from among four choices, the word that felt most similar in meaning to the one that was presented. (Subjects were told that the word that was flashed on the screen was not among the four alternatives.) On each trail one of the four choices represented a mood word. The remaining three words were constructed to have comparable length and physical appearance to the mood item. There were a total of 40 trials: 20 in which the mood word was positive (e.g., satisfied, cheerful, contented), and 20 in which the mood word was negative (e.g. uncertain, tense, unworthy).

Self-awareness manipulation. Self-awareness was manipulated through either the presence (high self-awareness) or absence (low self-awareness) of a mirror. The mirror was situated on a table approximately 120° to the left of the subject when facing the computer monitor. In front of the mirror was a small box with two lights. Subjects were required to report the color of the light (green or red) before responding on each trial. The sequence of colors was randomly determined for the 40 trials. In order to see the lightbox, subjects had to turn their head toward it. In so doing, subjects in the high self-awareness condition could not avoid seeing their faces in the mirror.

Procedure. Subjects were tested individually. They were seated at a table within a cubicle, separated from the experimenter by a partition. The computer monitor and a partial keyboard were on the table. Subjects were told that the purpose of the experiment was to study "subliminal perception." It was explained that they almost certainly would not be able to consciously perceive the words flashed on the screen, and that the research was investigating the effect of the words on the unconscious mind.

Subjects were instructed to look at a spot between two parallel lines in the middle of the screen when they heard a beep tone. The character string was flashed between those lines and then masked by a string of "#"s. Next, the message, "What Color Is The Light?" appeared, and subjects were to look over their left shoulder at the lightbox and report whether the light was red or green. There was a seven-second delay between the presentation of the beep and the onset of the light. This delay had the effect of requiring subjects in the high self-awareness condition to look at their image in the mirror for several seconds prior to reporting the color of the light. After reporting the color of the light, the multiple choice list of four words appeared on the computer screen and subjects selected the word that felt to them to be most similar to the "word" that had flashed on the screen moments before.

Subjects were told ahead of time that the words would be flahed "faster than their conscious mind could read them. Even if their conscious mind would not be able to read the words and they might get frustrated, the words would register in their unconscious." In order to make sure that subjects did not give up or just respond randomly to a seemingly impossible task, subjects were informed prior to beginning the task that they would receive an instant lottery ticket if their score exceeded a predetermined level. It was emphasized that virtually everyone could achieve the requisite score if they paid attention when performing the task. All subjects were given an instant lottery ticket at the conclusion of the 40 trials.

Following completion of the task, subjects were probed for suspicions about the experiment. None of the subjects reported any awareness that the research involved measuring mood, and none reported any suspicion about the presence of the mirror.

Results

Each subject received mood scores based on the number of positive mood words selected (out of 20), the number of negative mood words selected (out of 20), and a composite mood score (positive minus negative mood scores).

As predicted by self-awareness theory, subjects who saw their reflection in a mirror just prior to responding to each of the 40 items of the mood measure had lower composite mood scores than subjects in the no mirror condition ($t = 3.49$, $p < .01$). The theory predicts an increase in self-criticism and self-dissatisfaction, so the fact that the lowered mood scores in the mirror condition were primarily due to an increase in negative mood ($t = 2.26$, $p < .05$), rather than a decrease in positive mood ($t = 1.23$, *ns*) is also in accord with the theory.

Subjects in the high self-awareness condition had to look toward the mirror prior to each trial. As a result, subjects could not avoid looking at the mirror. Nor could they get absorbed in the task and ignore the mirror. The impact of the mirror was reinstated on each trial, providing a strong test of its effect.

In this research subjects' mood was measured without their awareness, reducing the potential of experimental demand and other artifacts that might otherwise cloud the interpretation of the results. Also eliminated was the tendency of paper-and-pencil questionnaire measures of mood to increase self-awareness because of their self-examining nature.

The advantage of the mood measure used in this study is that it is disguised. It is not an especially sensitive measure of mood in general, nor is it able to discriminate subtle differences in types of mood. It is, however, adequate to test for broad differences in positivity of mood between groups, as was the purpose here.

CONCLUSION

In this paper we have examined evidence for two of the most important assumptions that underly self-awareness theory: the assumption that self-focused attention produces an external, reflexive perspective causing one to view oneself as an observer; and the assumption that self-awareness leads to negative affect, presumably because self-focus makes salient discrepancies between what one is like and one's ideal.

Existing experimental evidence supports both assumptions of the theory.

References

Brockner, J., Hjelle, L., & Plant, R.W. (1985). Self-focused attention, self-esteem, and the experience of state depression. *Journal of Personality*, **53**, 425–434.

Carver, C.S., Blaney, P.H., & Scheier, M.F. (1979). Focus of attention, chronic expectancy, and responses to a feared stimulus. *Journal of Personality and Social Psychology*, **37**, 1186–1195.

Carver, C.S., & Scheier, M.F. (1981). *Attention and self-regulation: A control theory approach to human behavior*. New York: Springer-Verlag.

Cooley, C.H. (1902). *Human nature and the social order*. New York: Scribner's.

Csikszentmihalyi, M., & Figurski, T.J. (1982). Self-awareness and aversive experience in everyday life. *Journal of Personality*, **50**, 15–28.

Duval, S., & Wicklund, R.A. (1972). *A theory of objective self-awareness*. New York: Academic Press.

Duval, S., & Wicklund, R. A. (1973). Effects of objective self-awareness on attribution of causality. *Journal of Experimental Social Psychology*, **9**, 17–31.

Fenigstein, A., & Carver, C.S. (1978). Self-focusing effects of false heartbeat feedback. *Journal of Personality and Social Psychology*, **36**, 1241–1250.

Fenigstein, A., Scheier, M.F., & Buss, A.H. (1975). Public and private self-consciousness: Assessment and theory. *Journal of Consulting and Clinical Psychology*, **43**, 522–527.

Froming, W.J., Walker, G.R., & Lopyan, K.J. (1982). Public and private self-awareness: When personal attitudes conflict with societal expectations. *Journal of Experimental Social Psychology*, **18**, 476–487.

Hass, R.G. (1984a). Perspective taking and self-awareness: Drawing an *E* on your forehead. *Journal of Personality and Social Psychology*, **46**, 788–798.

Hass, R.G. (1984b). *Perspective taking and self-awareness: The effect of false heartbeat feedback*. Unpublished manuscript, Brooklyn College CUNY.

Hass, R.G., & Katz, I. (1988). *A disguised measure of mood*. Unpublished manuscript, Brooklyn College and The Graduate Center CUNY.

Hass, R.G., & Katz, I. (1989). *The effect of racial ambivalence on self-dissatisfaction and negative mood*. Unpublished manuscript, Brooklyn College and The Graduate Center CUNY.

Hull, J.G. (1981). A self-awareness model of the causes and effects of alcohol consumption. *Journal of Abnormal Psychology*, **90**, 586–600.

Ingram, R.E., Lumry, A.E., Cruet, D., & Sieber, W. (1987). Attentional processes in depressive disorders. *Cognitive Therapy and Research*, **11**, 351–360.

Ingram, R.E., & Smith, T.W. (1984). Depression and internal versus external focus of attention. *Cognitive Therapy and Research*, **8**, 139–151.

Jones, E.E., & Nisbett, R.E. (1971). The actor and the observer: Divergent perceptions of the causes of behavior. In E.E. Jones et al. (Eds.) *Attribution: Perceiving the causes of behavior*. Morristown, N.J.: General Learning Press.

Liebling, B.A., & Shaver, P. (1973). Evaluation, self-awareness, and task performance. *Journal of Experimental Social Psychology*, **9**, 297–306.

Mead, G.H. (1934). *Mind, self and society*. Chicago: University of Chicago.

Nigro, G., & Neisser, U. (1983). Point of view in personal memories. *Cognitive Psychology*, **15**, 467–482.

Piaget, J. (1966). *Judgment and reasoning in the child*. Totowa, N.J.: Littlefield, Adams. (Original work published 1924).

Pyszczynski, T., & Greenberg, J. (1986). Evidence for a depressive self-focusing style. *Journal of Research in Personality*, **20**, 95–106.

Scheier, M.F. (1976). Self-awareness, self-consciousness, and angry aggression. *Journal of Personality*, **44**, 627–644.

Scheier, M.F. & Carver, C.S. (1977). Self-focused attention and the experience of emotion: Attraction, repulsion, elation and depression. *Journal of Personality and Social Psychology*, **35**, 625–636.

Schmitt, J.P. (1983). Focus of attention in the treatment of depression. *Psychotherapy: Theory, research and practice*, **20**, 457–463.

Stephenson, B., & Wicklund, R.A. (1983). Self-directed attention and taking the other's perspective. *Journal of Experimental Social Psychology*, **19**, 58–77.
Stephenson, B., & Wicklund, R.A. (1984). The contagion of self-focus within a dyad. *Journal of Personality and Social Psychology*, **46**, 163–168.
Storms, M.D. (1973). Videotape and the attribution process: Reversing actors' and observers' points of view. *Journal of Personality and Social Psychology*, **27**, 165–175.
Wicklund, R.A. (1975). Objective self-awareness. In L. Berkowitz (Ed.). *Advances in experimental social psychology* (Vol. 8, pp. 233–275). New York: Academic Press.
Wicklund, R.A. & Duval, S. (1971). Opinion change and performance facilitation as a result of objective self awareness. *Journal of Experimental Social Psychology*, **7**, 319–342.

A TERROR MANAGEMENT ANALYSIS OF SELF-AWARENESS AND ANXIETY: THE HIERARCHY OF TERROR

TOM PYSZCZYNSKI

University of Colorado at Colorado Springs

JEFF GREENBERG

University of Arizona

SHELDON SOLOMON

Skidmore College

JAMES HAMILTON

University of Colorado at Colorado Springs

In this article, we apply terror management theory to the operation of self-awareness processes. According to the theory, self-esteem consists of accepting a cultural conception of reality and believing that one is living up to the standards of value inherent in that conception. The function of self-esteem is to buffer the anxiety that results from the awareness of human vulnerability and mortality that results from our capacity for self-awareness. We argue that self-awareness leads to comparisons with standards, and to behavior aimed at reducing any discrepancies that are detected, because of the potential for existential terror that self-awareness creates. Existential terror is seen as the emotional manifestation of the instinct for self-preservation. Management of this terror is conceptualized as the superordinate goal in a hierarchy of standards through which behavior is regulated. A hierarchical terror management model is proposed. This structure provides a unique analysis of the self-system and its relationship to other attitudes, values, and beliefs. The theory posits several dynamic principles that specify how self-awareness and disruptions determine the movement of conscious attention through various levels of the hierarchy. The implications of this analysis for unresolved theoretical questions about self-awareness processes, unconscius sources of motivation, and clinical problems are discussed.

KEYWORDS: Self-awareness, self-regulation, anxiety, self-focused attention, terror management

Since its initial publication, the theory of objective self-awareness (Duval & Wicklund, 1972) has inspired a great deal of research, considerable controversy, and several revisions and reformulations. In recent years, the theory has also been used as a point of departure for analyses of a variety of clinical problems, such as depression, anxiety, and alcoholism (for a review, see Pyszczynski, Hamilton, Greenberg, & Becker, in press). Despite this high level of activity, a number of very basic questions about self-awareness processes remain unanswered. More importantly, the very basic question of *why* self-awareness produces some of its most important effects has not been addressed. In this article, we apply the recently formulated *terror management* theory

Correspondence should be directed to the first author at: Department of Psychology, University of Colorado, Colorado Srings, CO 80933–7150, USA.

(Greenberg, Pyszczynski, & Solomon, 1986; Solomon, Greenberg, & Pyszczynski, 1989, in press) in an attempt to shed light on self-awareness processes. This analysis assigns anxiety a very central role in the operation of self-awareness processes. We start with an overview of concepts and issues central to self-awareness theory, then present a brief overview of the terror management perspective, and, finally, present a hierarchical model of the self-system and explore its implications concerning critical issues concerning self-awareness, anxiety, terror management, and unconscious sources of motivation.

SELF-AWARENESS PROCESSES

Objective Self-Awareness Theory

Duval and Wicklund's (1972) theory of objective self-awareness started with the assumption that conscious attention can be directed either outward, togward the environment, or inward, toward the self. When attention is focused externally, the individual is in a state of subjective self-awareness. Environmental input is experienced directly, without conscious consideration of its implications for self. When attention is focused on the self, however, the individual is in a state of objective self-awareness — the self becomes the object of attention. The individual not only experiences environmental input, but experiences the fact that he or she is experiencing that input. Most importantly, the state of objective self-awareness is posited to be an inherently self-evaluative state.

According to the theory, focusing attention on the self instigates a self-evaluative process in which one's current state, on whatever dimension is currently most salient, is compared with whatever standard for that dimension is salient. Falling short of the standard produces negative affect, which leads to attempts to either escape the self-focused state or reduce the discrepancy between current state and standard. Duval and Wicklund initially posited that, because people's standards are usually at least slightly beyond reach, self-awareness would inevitably be an aversive state. This position was later revised to take into account the possibility that people might sometimes exceed their standards (Wicklund, 1975). Exceeding the standard was assumed to produce positive affect and a tendency to maintain the self-focused state. Wicklund argued, however, that, because people tend to raise their aspirations after successes, this positive state would tend to be short-lived.

Objective self-awareness theory is clearly a motivational, drive-reduction analysis. Self-focused attention affects behavior by virtue of the affect produced by confrontation with discrepancies between self and standards.

A Cybernetic Model of Self-Regulation

Carver and Scheier's (1981; Carver, 1979; Scheier & Carver, 1988) Cybernetic model of self-regulation is essentially an integration of Duval and Wicklund's self-awareness theory with the general control systems approach to self-regulation, developed by Powers (1973, 1978) and others (e.g., Ashby, 1952). The central feature of such control systems analyses is the negative feedback loop, in which a comparator assesses discrepancies between perceptual input of some kind and a reference value. Detection of discrepancies then sets in motion processes aimed at closing the gap between the perceptual input and the reference value. This, of course, provides an alternative means of conceptualizing the comparison between self and standard posited by Duval and Wicklund to be an inherent consequence of self-focused attention.

Carver and Scheier adopted most, but not all, of the central propositions of self-awareness theory. From their perspective, self-focus is conceptualized as part of a self-regulatory negative feedback loop that functions to keep one "on-track" in one's pursuit of various goals. Consistent with Duval and Wicklund, they posit that self-focus leads to a comparison of current state with standards, and that detection of a negative discrepancy instigates behavior aimed at reducing that discrepancy. They add that disruptions of discrepancy-reducing behavior lead to an assessment of the likelihood that the discrepancy will be reduced. If the probability of successful discrepancy reduction is high, one continues to attempt to reduce the discrepancy. However, if the probability of successful discrepancy reduction is low, one experiences negative affect, withdraws from the feedback loop, disengages from the goal, and diverts attention from the self.

Perhaps the most important point of divergence between the objective self-awareness and cybernetic theories is centered on the mechanism through which self-focused attention leads to discrepancy reducing behavior. Duval and Wicklund clearly view such behavior as resulting from negative affect that is produced by the detection of a discrepancy between self and standard. Carver and Scheier, on the other hand, do not view such goal-directed behavior as driven by negative affect. Rather, they view dispassionate discrepancy reduction in response to detection of discrepancies as an inherent feature of all self-regulating systems. From their perspective, affect is viewed as a consequence of the assessment of the likelihood of successful discrepancy reduction that occurs when ongoing attempts at discrepancy reduction are disrupted. More recently, they also suggested that affect may be generated by a meta-monitoring system that assesses the rate of progress of the first level self-regulatory system in reducing discrepancies (Carver & Scheier, in press). From their perspective, affect may play a role in disengagement from goals, but does not play a role in motivating goal-directed behavior itself.

A Schema Activation Model

Whereas Carver and Scheier's cybernetic model maintained the assumption that self-focused attention leads to a comparison with standards, Hull and Levy's (1979) schema activation model did not. Rather, they argued that the only invariant consequence of directing attention toward the self is an increase in the accessibility of schematically organized self-referent information. Although they conceded that self-focus may sometimes instigate self-evaluation, they did not see comparison of current state with standard as a normal consequence of self-awareness. Self-awareness was seen as functioning to facilitate the processing of self-relevent information.

The idea that self-focus activates the self-schema was also adopted by Carver and Scheier (1981). Thus, self-focus was posited to lead to a comparison with standards only if a behavioral standard is currently salient. If no such standard is salient, self-focus simply activates the self-schema and increases the accessibility of self-referent information.

Summary

Although the three major theories of self-awareness processes agree on many points, there are several points of contention between them. Indeed, they provide very different perspectives on the very nature of the self-aware state. Although there are many other differences, it seems to us that the most important points of contention center around three questions:

1. *Why does self-awareness instigate self-evaluative processes?* Although the notion that self-awareness instigates self-evaluative processes is central to both the Duval and Wicklund and Carver and Scheier approaches to self-awareness processes, neither theory broaches the question of why this might be so. Rather, this link between self-awareness and self-evaluation is taken as an unexplained postulate by both theories. Because Hull and Levy's analysis did not give self-evaluation a prominent role, they, of course, did not consider this question either. For the most part, this omission has not presented serious problems for researchers working with the theories. The assumption that self-awareness leads to self-evaluation has been extremely useful for generating testable hypotheses, even in the absence of an explanation of why this occurs. We suggest, however, that this issue must be addressed if one wishes to provide a complete analysis of self-awareness processes. Furthermore, we suggest that because of the centrality of this question, its answer is likely to have implications for other aspects of our understanding of how self-awareness affects thoughts, feelings, and behavior.

2. *What role does affect play in discrepancy reduction?* According to the original objective self-awareness formulation, self-focused attention affects behavior by virtue of the affect that it generates. Detection of negative discrepancies between self and standards creates negative affect; the person then engages in discrepancy-reducing behavior in order to reduce this negative affect. Carver and Scheier, on the other hand, explicitly state that negative affect is not a cause of discrepancy-reducing behavior. They argue that discrepancy reduction in response to discrepancy-detection is simply an inherent feature of all self-regulating systems, whether living or not. From their perspective, a discrepancy is simply a bit of information that is used by the system as a basis for deciding how to behave. Although they see affect as playing a role in decisions regarding whether to disengage from goals, they maintain that it does not play a role in discrepancy reduction.

3. *Does self-awareness always lead to self-evaluation*? From the perspective of Duval and Wicklund's original theory, self-awareness is an inherently self-evaluative state. Whenever people become self-aware, they are assumed to compare themselves with standards. Hull and Levy, on the other hand, downplayed the importance of self-evaluation. Although they acknowledged that self-awareness may sometimes lead to self-evaluation, they argued that an increase in the accessibility of self-referent information is the only invariant effect of self-directed attention. Unfortunately, they did not specify the conditions under which self-awareness is especially likely to lead to comparison with standards. Finally, although Carver and Scheier place a great deal of emphasis on the self-evaluative properties of self-awareness, they acknowledge that such evaluations take place only when a behavioral standard is currently salient. From their perspective, self-awareness does not instigate self-evaluation if no standard is salient at the time.

In this paper we use terror management theory (Greenberg et al., 1986; Solomon, et al., 1989, in press) to address these issues. In the following section, we present a brief overview of the theory. We then use the theory as a point of departure for addressing the question of why self-awareness leads to discrepancy reduction. This analysis, in turn, provides insights into the other two questions posed above, and also has implications for a variety of other problems.

TERROR MANAGEMENT THEORY

Terror management theory (Greenberg et al., 1986; Solomon et al., 1989, in press) addresses the questions of why people need self-esteem, how self-esteem is related to other aspects of people's conceptions of reality, and how the need for self-esteem affects behavior. The theory is based largely on Ernest Becker's (1971, 1973, 1975) attempts to synthesize the various social science disciplines to provide what he referred to as a "general science of man." In the following paragraphs we present the aspects of the theory that are most relevant to understanding the operation of self-awareness processes. For a more thorough exposition of the theory, see Solomon et al. (1989).

The Curse of Self-Awareness

According to Becker, the success and adaptability of the human species resulted from the evolution of a set of highly sophisticated intellectual abilities that sets us apart from all other living creatures. The abilities to think in terms of cause and effect, to project ourselves in time and imagine things that have yet to occur, and, most importantly, to reflect on ourselves as objects of attention all provide incredible flexibility and adaptability to our behavior. These abilities free us from the necessity of relying on "hard wired", instinctual, fixed response patterns, and enable us to adapt our behavior to a constantly changing environment. Interestingly, these very same abilities play prominent roles in contemporary theories of motivation, under the labels of attribution (e.g., Abramson, Seligman, & Teasdale, 1978; Weiner, 1986), expectancy (e.g., Atkinson, 1981; Carver & Scheier, 1981, Rotter, 1954), and self-focused attention e.g., Carver & Scheier, 1981; Duval & Wicklund, 1972).

Unfortunately, these uniquely human abilities also give rise to some uniquely human problems. As a result of our highly sophisticated intellectual abilities, we inevitably become aware of the tenuous nature of existence, of the ever-present potential for pain and injury, and, most importantly, of the inevitability and unavoidability of death. This awareness of our vulnerability and mortality gives rise to the potential for paralyzing terror. Awareness that the only real certainty in life is that one will eventually die is simply too much to bear for any animal with an instinct for self-preservation. Without some means of managing this terror, life would bog down because of the overwhelming terror created by self-awareness. Interestingly, the same abilities that gave rise to the potential for terror also gave rise to the species' solution to this dilemma. As Rank (1932/1950) put it:

> Consciousness mediated man's knowledge, if not his recognition of sexual processes and death, and yet it had become a kind of insurance against death . . . thus there appears finally the paradox that man feels immortal just because of his fleeting consciousness, which death extinguishes . . . Death, which was recognized by consciousness, was denied by individual self-consciousness (p. 191).

Humans developed means to deny their vulnerability and mortality symbolically by creating cultural worldviews, which provide a basis for self-value.

The Cultural Anxiety-Buffer

From the perspective of terror management theory, a culture is a shared symbolic conception of reality. Cultures function to minimize the anxiety that results from awareness of human vulnerability and mortality by imbuing the world with meaning, order, stability, and permanence, and by providing the individual with some hope of averting aversive experience, and, ultimately, of transcending death. Although there is great diversity in the specific forms that cultural worldviews take, all cultures provide a description of how the world was created, a prescription for what people should do to lead meaningful and valuable lives, and the promise of safety and immortality to those who live up to the standards of the culture (via just world beliefs, immortality symbols, and religious beliefs). The cultural worldview thus consists of a set of beliefs about reality and a set of standards of value that are derived from those beliefs. When one lives up to those standards, one acquires self-esteem and the protection promised by the culture.

The cultural worldview enables the individual to manage terror by providing a context within which he or she can conceive of him or herself as valuable and significant. This sense of value, which we refer to as self-esteem, provides a buffer against the anxiety that can be caused by self-awareness. From this perspective, self-esteem is acquired by internalizing a conception of reality and the standards of value that are part of that conception[1], and then living up to those standards. To paraphrase Becker, having self-esteem requires that one conceive of oneself as a person of primary value in a world of meaning. People are motivated to maintain high levels of self-esteem because self-esteem provides a buffer against the anxiety that results from their awareness of their vulnerability and mortality.

Consistent with this analysis, a large body of research has shown that self-esteem deficits are associated with a wide range of anxiety-related problems (e.g., for a review, see Solomon et al., in press). It has also recently been shown that exposing subjects to death-related stimuli increases their tendency to claim that they possess positive characteristics and that they do not possess negative characteristics (Paulhus & Levitt, 1987). Presumably these reminders of mortality increase subjects' need for self-esteem. In studies designed to provide a direct test of the self-esteem as anxiety-buffer hypothesis, it has been shown that increasing subjects' self-esteem makes them less prone to anxiety in response to both threat of electric shock and gorey scenes from a film about death (Greenberg, Solomon, Lyon, & Pyszczynski, in preparation). These studies consistently support the terror management notion that self-esteem functions to buffer anxiety.

Research has also supported the proposition that cultural worldviews serve an anxiety-buffering function. In a series of nine experiments, Rosenblatt, Greenberg, Solomon, Pyszczynski, and Lyon (1989) and Greenberg, Pyszczynski, Solomon, Rosenblatt, Veeder, Kirkland, and Lyon (in press) have shown that inducing subjects to think about their mortality increases their tendency to respond negatively to those who threaten the cultural worldview and positively to those who uphold it. Given that the cultural worldview is a cultural creation that depends on consensual validation from others for its maintenance, it follows that people should react positively to those who support it and negatively to those who challenge it. To the extent that the cultural worldview functions to buffer individuals against anxiety, it follows that reminders of what they are frightened of should increase their need to keep the anxiety-buffer strong, and thus intensify their reactions to those who impinge on it. In support of this reasoning, Rosenblatt et al. demonstrated that mortality salience led to particularly

[1] We use the term "cultural worldview" to emphasize the fact that the individual's conception of reality is derived from the broader cultures to which he or she is exposed. We do not wish to imply, however, that all members of a culture share the same beliefs and values. Each individual constructs his/her own individualized cultural worldview out of the diverse array of sources to which he/she is exposed throughout the process of socialization. Thus although the broader culture to which one belongs exerts a strong influence on the content of one's individualized cultural worldview, and certain aspects of that conception will be shared by most members of a given culture, there will also be considerable variability in the specifics of the cultural worldviews held by any set of individuals.

negative reactions to a cultural deviant and particularly positive reactions to a hero. Greenberg et al. (in press) showed that mortality salience led to particularly positive reactions to an ingroup member and an individual who praised the culture and to particularly negative reactions to an outgroup member, an individual with dissimilar attitudes, and an individual who criticized the culture. For a more thorough review of these and other studies supporting terror management theory hypotheses, see Solomon et al. (1989).

To summarize, because of the human capacity for self-awareness, people inevitably must face the fact that they will someday die. Because of our instinct for self-preservation, this awareness creates the potential for paralyzing terror. Humankind dealt with this problem by the creation of shared symbolic conceptions of reality (cultures) that imbue the individual with value and provide hope of avoiding aversive experience and ultimately transcending death. Individuals are thus protected from the anxiety that results from awareness of their vulnerability and mortality by a cultural anxiety-buffer consisting of two components: (a) maintaining faith in a cultural worldview, and (b) believing that one is meeting the standards of value associated with that worldview.

A Terror Management Analysis of Self-Awareness Processes

Given the foregoing analysis of the function of self-esteem, our answer to the question of why self-awareness leads to self-evaluation is fairly straightforward. According to the theory, self-awareness is a prerequisite for the experience of existential terror. Becker saw self-awareness as particularly important in the genesis of terror. It is when we are self-aware that our individual creatureliness and isolation is especially salient. This potential for anxiety is counteracted by self-esteem, which is achieved by meeting cultural standards of value.

To the extent that self-awareness creates the potential for terror, and to the extent that this terror is assuaged by meeting cultural standards of value, it follows that one would compare oneself with such standards when one becomes self-aware. Only by assessing the extent to which we are currently meeting these standards can we be assured of our value and thus that we are relatively safe from the things that frighten us. If this comparison reveals that we are indeed meeting our standards of value, the anxiety-buffer is strengthened. If, on the other hand, the comparison reveals that we are falling short of our valued goals, this releases anxiety that signals the need for behavior to bolster the threatened anxiety-buffer. By engaging in a self-evaluative process and then attempting to bring ourselves in closer line with our standards, we short-circuit the potential for terror that self-awareness would otherwise create.

This analysis implies that, because of the potential for terror that self-awareness creates, reactions to the self-aware state are generally focused on bolstering the cultural anxiety-buffer. In other words, when people become self-aware, they should be more attuned to the implications for self of their own behavior and the events that happen around them, they should behave in ways that maximize their sense of value, and they should be especially prone to employ defensive strategies when their self-esteem is threatened. Consistent with this reasoning, research has shown that self-awareness does indeed appear to increase the tendency to encode information in terms of its self-relevance. For example, Hull and Levy (1979) have shown that private self-consciousness is associated with better recall of words previously rated for self-descriptiveness but not for words evaluated in other ways. Research conducted by Turner (1980) and Geller and Shaver (1976) is also generally consistent with this proposition. Furthermore, a large number of studies have documented the wide variety of ways in which self-awareness leads to behavior more in tune with both personal and social standards of value (for reviews, see Carver & Scheier, 1981; Scheier & Carver, 1988; or Wicklund, 1975). Finally, it also appears that self-awareness encourages the use of self-esteem maintenance strategies such as the self-serving attributional bias and self-handicapping (e.g., Federoff & Harvey, 1976; Kernis, Zuckerman, Cohen, & Spadofora, 1982).

A terror management analysis also suggests that self-awareness should encourage defense of the cultural worldview. Thus, when self-aware, people should be especially sensitive to information that supports or threatens their attitudes, beliefs, and values. The fact that self-awareness increases attitude-behavior consistency (e.g. Carver, 1975) suggests, at least in a general way, that self-awareness increases people's concern for their standards. The theory would also make the more direct prediction that self-awareness should lead to greater sensitivity to information relevant to the cultural worldview, increased resistance to persuasion in response to counter-attitudinal messages, and more extreme reactions toward those who support and attack the cultural worldview. Unfortunately, we know of no studies that have directly tested these hypotheses.

THE HIERARCHICAL STRUCTURE OF MOTIVATION

The foregoing analysis suggests that the motivating force behind the self-evaluative and discrepancy-reducing behaviors that self-awareness sets in motion is the leakage of existential terror that self-awareness causes. To avoid confrontation with this terror, the individual attempts to ensure that he or she is meeting the standards of value that provide self-esteem and, consequently, freedom from anxiety. One might ask, however, how this could possibly be true. Although people may sometimes contemplate their mortality and worry about the various tragedies that could befall them, these are certainly not topics that most people spend a great deal of time considering. Furthermore, it seems unlikely that conscious consideration of one's mortality is a particularly frequent consequence of entering the self-aware state. Although there is some evidence that self-awareness leads to a comparison with standards, there is as of yet no evidence that self-awareness increases one's tendency to think about death.

We suggest that it is precisely *because* self-awareness leads to self-evaluative thinking that confrontation with the existential dilemma is averted. To fully explain how this process works, we must first consider how the standards through which self-esteem is acquired are structured and how the various sources of anxiety that trouble people are related to each other. Carver & Scheier's (1981) concept of a *hierarchy of standards* provides a useful tool for considering these relations.

Borrowing from Power's (1978) earlier application of cybernetic modelling to human self-regulation, Carver & Scheier (1981) proposed that goals and standards are hierarchically organized, from simple and concrete, to complex and abstract. As one moves up to increasingly abstract levels of the hierarchy, the standard at any given level becomes a criterion behavior through which the next highest level standard can be met. Thus for an academic psychologist, the goal of getting an article published in a respected journal becomes a criterion behavior through which he or she can achieve the next highest level standard of getting recognition for his or her research. Being recognized for his/her research becomes a criterion behavior through which he/she can meet the next highest standard of becoming a respected member of the academic community, and so on up the hierarchy. Similarly, moving down the hierarchy, writing an interesting and compelling paper becomes the criterion behavior through which the goal of publishing one's work is accomplished. Conducting a methodologically sound and conceptually interesting study becomes the criterion behavior through which the goal of writing an interesting paper is accomplished, and so on.

Toward the bottom of the hierarchy, are standards that regulate physical action, muscle tensions, and other micro-level constituents of the more abstract and meaningful behavior toward which people's conscious attention is usually focused. At this level, the standards dictate position of one's body, speed at which one moves, differences in muscle tension, and other criteria for accomplishing coordinated action. These low-level standards are rarely the focus of conscious attention; indeed, there is evidence that consciously attending to low-level standards often disrupts performance of higher level acts (e.g., Bryan & Harter, 1899; Langer & Imber, 1979). Nonetheless, meeting these low level standards is essential if we are to meet the more abstract goals to which we aspire. Interestingly, this analysis is consistent with a long tradition in cognitive psychology of conceptualizing perceptual and conceptual schemata as hierarchically organized (e.g., Bartlett, 1932; Bransford, 1979).

As one moves down the hierarchy, there are an increasing number of alternative pathways through which each superordinate goal can be met. Our analysis views success at a given level of the hierarchy as a requirement for satisfaction of the next highest level goal in a fashion crudely analogous to graded post-synaptic transmission potentials in the neural transmission process. A neuron at rest will remain at rest until a threshold is reached, at which point the nerve impulse is engendered. Stimulation from a number of neurons, none of which in isolation would be sufficient to fire the neuron, can be summed to reach the threshold. Similarly, in our model, meeting a standard at one level will result in meeting the next highest level standard if that success is sufficiently significant to reach threshold by itself, or if that success is in close temporal proximity to other successes on the same level of the hierarchy. Thus, satisfaction of superordinate goals is sometimes accomplished by meeting a single subordinate standard and sometimes requires meeting several such standards of lower value. For example, a professor who desires recognition for his/her work may be able to accomplish this by having one article accepted by a highly prestigious journal; alternatively, the superordinate goal could be reached by being complimented by a student for one's lecture, being interviewed by a local newspaper about his/her research, and having a paper accepted for presentation at a regional convention, all on the same day. Although none of these latter events in isolation would be sufficient to satisfy the superordinate goal, in combination they may do so.

Carver & Scheier have suggested that near the very top of this hierarchy is the superordinate goal of maintaining a positive self-image. As one moves up the hierarchy, there is an increasingly greater number of pathways through which each goal can be met. For example, meeting the very global goal of maintaining a positive self-image can be achieved by meeting standards in a wide variety of domains, such as intellectual pursuits, athletics, romance, and morality. Subordinate to the goal of maximizing self-esteem are the many specific sources of identity to which one is committed (cf., Wicklund & Gollwitzer, 1982). These various sources of identity enable one to achieve and maintain self-esteem.

Our analysis suggests, however, that there are levels in the hierarchy superordinate to the goal of maintaining self-esteem. At the very top of the hierarchy is the goal of survival and continued existence. Following theorists such as Darwin & Freud, we assume that the single most important goal of all individual living organisms is that of maintaining one's own life. At a species level, the self-preservation instinct maximizes the likelihood that one's genes will be passed on and that the species will continue to exist.[2] The fear of death, that we posit to be the basic motivating force behind the need for self-esteem, is simply the emotional manifestation of the self-preservation instinct. Reacting with fear to any threat to one's continued existence is adaptive because it signals the need for behavior to reduce the threat.

Thus, we suggest that all goals, in one way or another, serve the superordinate goal of life preservation. The fear of death is the emotional manifestation of this superordinate goal that energizes and directs behavior. This is not to say that everything people do always facilitates the preservation of their lives. Unfortunately, because of the way some individuals' hierarchies are structured, meeting goals subordinate to this overarching goal may sometimes actually reduce their chances of continued existence. For example, in order to increase self-esteem by winning the approval of one's peers, an adolescent may consume large quantities of alcohol, drive at breakneck speeds, or get involved in violent confrontations with others.

In specifying what goals are immediately subordinate to the overarching need for self-preservation, we find it useful to distinguish between direct and symbolic means of assuring one's continued existence. Direct means of life preservation generally involve tending to one's biological needs: procuring food, water, and shelter; tending to pains, illnesses, and injuries; maintaining warmth, circulation, and other things of this nature. Although of obvious importance for sustaining life, regulation of these needs is beyond the scope of this paper. Our focus, is on the symbolic means through which one copes with the emotional manifestation of the self-preservation instinct. A graphic depiction of this hierarchy is presented in Figure 1.

Terror management theory posits that the cultural anxiety-buffer is the major means through which humans cope with the fear of death (which results from the instinct for self-preservation). Thus, the superordinate symbolic goal that people pursue is that of maintaining the integrity of the cultural anxiety-buffer, which consists of two interrelated components, the cultural worldview and self-esteem. Maintaining the cultural worldview gives the individual a sense of meaning. Maintaining self-esteem gives the individual a sense of value. As we have argued throughout this paper, people acquire equanimity by conceiving of themselves as objects of primary value in a world of meaning.

Within this framework, the cultural worldview serves the function of managing terror in two basic ways. First, it provides a benevolent structure or framework for perceiving the world. The cultural worldview helps us organize and simplify the vast array of sensory information that we take in on a daily basis, and imbues existence with meaning, order, stability, and permanence. As many theorists have suggested, people are highly motivated to maintain a consistent, coherent conception of reality (e.g., Becker, 1971; Festinger, 1957; Heider, 1958; Kruglanski, 1980; for a more thorough discussion of the terror management perspective on this need, see Solomon et al., 1989). Second, the cultural worldview provides the standards through which individuals evaluate themselves and acquire self-esteem. Without a view of the world that specifies what is valuable, there is no basis for perceiving oneself as having value. Thus, a meaningful worldview is a prerequisite for self-esteem.

From this perspective, self-esteem is achieved by conceiving of oneself as meeting the standards of value inherent in the worldview to which one subscribes. Identity commitments can thus be conceptualized as the constellation of attributes, roles, and

[2] It has recently been argued that preservation of one's genes rather than oneself is the primary motive underlying behavior (e.g., Dawkins, 1976; Wilson, 1978). With rare exceptions, however, preserving one's own life is the optimal means of enhancing the likelihood that one's genes will be passed on. Thus whether self-preservation is focused on the self or one's genes does not alter our reasoning.

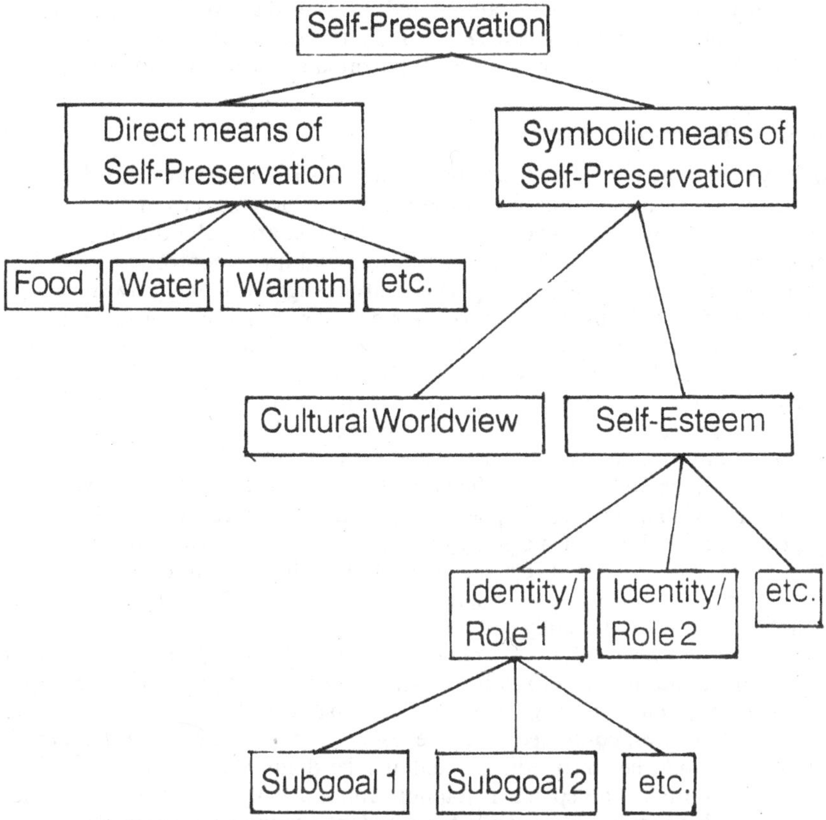

Figure 1 Direct and symbolic means of self-preservation: A Hierarchy.
Note. A more thorough depiction of the structure of the direct means to self-preservation or the cultural worldview would be beyond the scope of this paper.

traits that follow from the standards of value inherent in one's worldview. The requirements for these attributes are then met by achieving various identity-relevant goals, and these goals are achieved by pursuing various courses of action or strategies, and so on, down to the lowest levels of the hierarchy at which these subgoals are transformed into concrete action. From the level of self-esteem downwards, our analysis of the structure of the hierarchy is quite similar to that initially proposed by Carver & Scheier (1981). Our perspective diverges from theirs, however, in the motivational basis for self-regulation and in many specific aspects of the manner in which the hierarchy operates.

To summarize, we suggest that the superordinate goal of all behavior is the preservation of one's continued existence, and that the emotional manifestation of this need is the fear of death. This goal is served by both direct, concrete behavior aimed at maintaining one's health and well-being, and by the maintenance of a symbolic dual component cultural anxiety-buffer, consisting of a cultural worldview and self-esteem. Self-esteem is achieved by living up to the standards of value prescribed by the cultural worldview. This sense of self-worth can be attained by pursuing a variety of life goals that imply that one is a valued contributor to one's culture. These goals are achieved by pursuing increasing less abstract strategies and subgoals that eventually translate into concrete action. The entire system is driven by the potential for existential terror engendered by awareness of the everpresent potential for death and tragedy.

Dynamic Properties of the Hierarchy

As we have previously suggested, self-awareness gives rise to self-evaluative and self-esteem-maintaining behavior because this protects the individual from the terror that self-awareness would otherwise create. By meeting standards subordinate to the goal of terror management, the individual is able to avoid direct confrontation with the terrifying prospect of inevitable death. This analysis suggests that self-awareness may influence the level of the hierarchy at which one thinks about one's current pursuits.

As Carver & Scheier have suggested, the vast majority of one's conscious attention is focused on the intermediate levels of the hierarchy at which one's specific life goals are represented. Most people probably rarely think about death or their ultimate individual value. Rather, they think about their goals and aspirations relevant to their careers, relationships, hobbies, and the means through which these goals are achieved. Nonetheless, people sometimes shift their attention, both upward and downward in the hierarchy. Both Vallacher & Wegner (1987) and Carver & Scheier (1981) have suggested that difficulties in achieving a goal leads to a shifting of attention toward the lower level means by which the original goal can be achieved. For example, having a manuscript rejected by a journal might lead a researcher to reconsider his or her approach to writing up the study in question.

We suggest, however, that if attempts to meet the standard continue to be unsuccessful, attention begins to shift toward other directions in the hierarchy. Thus, although failure in pursuit of a goal initially leads to a focus toward lower level means of achieving that goal, continued failure leads attention to move toward alternative means of achieving the superordinate goal at a level equivalent to the one initially pursued. To continue the spatial metaphor, continued failure leads one to move laterally in the hierarchy. For example, for a student pursuing a pre-medical program, continued failure in the courses required to complete that degree is likely to lead to thoughts of alternative means of achieving the superordinate goal of obtaining a college degree. Wicklund & Gollwitzer's (1982) analysis of responses to shortcomings in pursuit of particular identity commitments is highly consistent with this proposition. They proposed and provided evidence that an inability to achieve symbols of one's preferred self-definition motivates the pursuit of alternative symbols of the threatened identity.

In some cases, an individual may be unable to meet any of the possible subgoals at a given level of the hierarchy. For example, our frustrated pre-med student may find that he or she is unable to meet the requirements for any degree program. If this happens, attention is likely to move upwards in the hierarchy. Thus the person may begin to question his/her general intelligence, and, if other goals relevant to a positive self-image are also not being achieved, the person eventually may come to question his/her ultimate value as a person. Continued questioning of one's value as a person may ultimately lead one either to question the underlying cultural worldview or to a direct consideration of death and the experience of existential terror. Stripped of self-esteem, the individual may be left with only his or her temporary creaturely existence to ponder. We are suggesting, then, that persistent failure eventually pushes conscious attention up the hierarchy toward the more basic, and largely unconscious, goals that motivate us.

To summarize, we suggest that disruptions increase one's level of self-focus (cf.

Greenberg & Pyszczynski, 1986), and, initially, push attention downwards in the hierarchy, toward lower level means by which the current discrepancy can be reduced. If this is ineffective, attention then shifts laterally, toward alternative means of achieving the goal superordinate to the one currently being pursued. If none of these standards can be met, attention shifts up to the next highest level of the hierarchy, and then, given continued failure, laterally again, and then upwards toward the top of the hierarchy. It should be noted that one need not actually attempt concrete behavior to meet each of these goals. Rather, it is probably the individual's assessment of the likelihood that the various goals can be met that determines movement through the hierarchy.

Of course, in most cases, disruptions usually do not reverberate very far up the hierarchy. Usually there are alternative means through which one's middle level goals can be successfully achieved. Our analysis also implies that, if one does move to a higher level in the hierarchy, successful discrepancy reduction at this higher level will reduce the negative affect that was created by the initial discrepancy. Research demonstrating compensatory increases in the favorability of one's global self-concept after failure on a specific task is generally consistent with this proposition (Greenberg & Pyszczynski, 1985). Furthermore, if alternative means are not likely to be successful, people usually disengage from their goals and avert attention from the self through distractions or alcohol (cf. Gibbons & Wicklund, 1976; Hull, 1981), and thus, at least temporarily, avoid confrontation with high-level discrepancies.

However, in some instances, people may be unable or unwilling to escape the self-focused state when faced with such generalized inability to reduce discrepancies. Pyszczynski & Greenberg (1987) have suggested that such an inability to exit a self-regulatory cycle after the loss of a central source of self-worth is the proximal cause of reactive depression. The dynamic principles of movement in the hierarchy suggest that such an inability to disengage when faced with general pessimism about reaching one's goals is likely to shake the very foundations of one's system of equanimity. In such instances, people are likely to become conscious of doubts about their general value as human beings, and, eventually, of deep existential concerns about the meaning of existence.

The present analysis suggests that in such cases, continued self-focus is likely to eventually lead to a vertical shift upward toward focus on the cultural worldview itself. Thus, people are likely to begin to question the values from which self-esteem is derived and the conception of reality from which those values are derived. Again, dealing with the problem at this very high level is likely to effectively reduce the need to attempt discrepancy reduction at a lower level. Steele (1988) has recently shown that inducing subjects to think about their higher-level values reduces their need to employ other means to reduce cognitive dissonance that was aroused by specific counter-attitudinal behavior. Anecdotal reports of people coping with specific difficulties by emphasizing their religious beliefs also demonstrate the effectiveness of such high-level coping strategies.

Unfortunately, individuals who are unable to maintain a sense of individual value may often have a difficult time finding solace in the cultural worldview. The system of meaning adopted by these individuals has essentially failed them. Thus, unless they are able to find a new and more benevolent set of beliefs and values, they will be likely to experience existential terror in a conscious and direct way. Clinical observations that depressed people often perceive life as meaningless and futile and experience thoughts and images of death are generally consistent with these propositions (APA, DSM-III-R, 1987).

In general, then, we are suggesting that, although the potential for experiencing the deeper sources of anxiety is present whenever one becomes self-aware, it is usually short-circuited by meeting standards relatively low in the hierarchy. However, failures at a subordinate level can reverberate up the hierarchy. Reverberation up the hierarchy is determined largely by the level of complexity and differentiation present in the hierarchy (cf. Linville, 1985). The more alternative means of meeting standards at each level of the hierarchy, the less continued failure to meet any one standard will reverberate up the hierarchy. Various means of meeting goals can be viewed metaphorically as pillars upon which self-esteem is built. The more pillars that are available to support the structure, the less damage to any one pillar will threaten the structure as a whole.

IMPLICATIONS OF A HIERARCHICAL TERROR MANAGEMENT PERSPECTIVE

Self-Awareness Processes

Let us now return to the questions about self-awareness processes with which we began our analysis. A terror management perspective suggests that self-awareness leads to comparisons with standards and attempts to bring behavior into line with standards because of the potential for existential terror that self-awareness would otherwise create. By meeting cultural standards of value, the individual attains self-esteem and is buffered against the anxiety that can be produced by awareness of vulnerability and mortality. Thus, self-awareness would be expected to instigate behavior to bolster either the self-esteem or cultural worldview components of the anxiety-buffer.

From this perspective, negative affect plays a central role in the process of self-regulation. Awareness of discrepancies between self and standard allow a leakage of existential terror. This leakage of terror, which is subjectively experienced and labelled as anxiety, embarassment, shame, or guilt, then motivates behavior aimed at reducing the discrepancy. The higher in the hierarchy at which the focal discrepancy exists, the greater and more pervasive the negative affect that is experineced. This is because as one moves up the hierarchy there are fewer layers available to buffer one against the ultimate source of anxiety. Conversely, the lower in the hierarchy toward which one is focused, the less affect that is released.

This analysis implies that although affect may play a major role in discrepancy reduction when one's attention is focused at a high level of abstraction, it may play little or no role when one is focused at more concrete levels. As Carver & Scheier (1981) have suggested, it seems unlikely that the conscious experience of affect is involved in the sorts of discrepancy reduction involved in moving one's arm to a desired location or in the changes in muscle tension necessary to accomplish such movements. Based on observations of this sort, they argued that affect does not play a role in discrepancy reduction at any level. We suggest that although the conscious experience of affect does not directly drive reduction of low-level discrepancies, the potential for affect inherent in the higher-level standards to which these low-level standards are subservient does play a critical role. The closer one's attention gets to the higher levels of the hierarchy, the more affect is released and the greater a role this affect plays in discrepancy reduction. Stated differently, the more cognizant one becomes of the implications of a discrepancy for one's system of value and meaning, the greater the role that affect plays in self-regulation.

Our terror management analysis also implies that there may indeed be other responses to self-awareness besides comparison with standards and discrepancy reduction. If the purpose of such comparison is the avoidance of existential terror, then other means of accomplishing this goal should also be possible. As Hull (1981) and colleagues have suggested, because of its self-awareness reducing properties, alcohol is often ingested by highly self-aware individuals who are faced with irreducible discrepancies. Similarly, self-awareness may sometimes lead to a preoccupation with internal bodily sensations and symptoms (cf. Pennebaker, 1982) because such a focus may also distract one from higher level concerns. If self-awareness-produced comparisons with standards are conceptualized as serving a specific function, then other means of achieving this same end should also be likely to emerge when in the self-focused state.

The present formulation also has implications for Duval & Wicklund's (1972) original contention that self-awareness is inevitably an aversive state. The terror management perspective suggests that self-awareness always has the *potential* to be an aversive state because of the role that self-awareness plays in the genesis of terror. However, because people usually attempt to regulate towards a positive self-image when they become self-focused, self-awareness need not lead to the conscious experience of anxiety. As Wicklund (1975) suggested, self-focus can lead to positive or negative affect, depending on the outcome of the comparison with standards.

Unconscious Sources of Motivation

Terror management theory posits that, although the fear of death plays a central role in motivating behavior, people are rarely aware of this fear. Maintenance of the cultural anxiety-buffer enables us to repress awareness of this terror and dread. The foregoing hierarchical analysis suggests a simple mechanism through which such unconscious sources of motivation can affect behavior. To the extent that people are able to focus their attention on only a single level of the hierarchy at a time, it follows that they will be generally unaware of the influence of higher level needs. To the extent that we spend most of our time focused on our specific occupational and social goals and the means through which these goals are achieved, it follows that we will rarely be consciously aware of how these goals affect our self-esteem, and even more rarely will be aware of the existential terror that lies behind the need for self-esteem.

To illustrate this model of unconscious motivation, consider the case of achievement-oriented behavior. Most psychologists would probably agree that the need for self-esteem has important effects on such behavior. Yet people rarely think about their general value as a person when they are pursuing their achievement-oriented goals. Rather, they think about the goals themselves and the means through which these goals can be achieved. Although they may sometimes think about the identity-relevant traits that such goals serve, such as intelligence or creativity, it is probably relatively rare for a person to consciously think that their achievements demonstrate their value as individuals. When one is regulating towards one's goals at low levels of the hierarchy, such awareness is even less likely. We simply suggest that the penultimate goal of terror management is even less likely to find its way into consciousness.

Indeed, because of the emotional upset that awareness of one's mortality would create, we suggest that such awareness is actively kept out of consciousness. The whole purpose of maintaining the cultural anxiety-buffer is to facilitate this repression. Thus, to the extent that one is successfully immersed in the cultural drama, conscious confrontation with the ultimate source of anxiety is unlikely to occur.

Clinical Implications

Our analysis has implications for a wide range of psychological disturbances and clinical problems (for a review of theory and research on the role of self-awareness in such disorders, see Pyszczynski et al., in press). For example, the hierarchical model provides a potentially useful way of integrating two phenomenologically distinct conditions that have both been referred to as "anxiety" problems. On the one hand, the term "anxiety" is used to refer to circumscribed fears, such as phobias. On the other hand, psychoanalytic and existential writers have used the term "anxiety" to refer to global and pervasive feelings of dread, uncertainty, and so forth. The hierarchical model suggests that anxieties about specific day-to-day life concerns derive from deeper concerns about vulnerability and death. Whereas circumscribed sources of anxiety reflect actual or imagined discrepancies at relatively low levels in the hierarchy, deeper sources of anxiety reflect difficulties at the higher levels. Specific, conscious goals at a relatively low level of abstraction are thus believed to serve needs that lie outside of the person's awareness. The hierarchy model provides a single framework for understanding both types of anxiety.

In addition to positing that higher-level unconscious needs motivate lower level goal-seeking, this analysis also implies that failures at the lower levels can eventually threaten higher level strivings. For example, specific social rejections can lead one to question one's general self-worth, and such questions can subsequently lead to conscious struggles with the underlying existential concerns that motivate one's strivings for self-esteem.

One interesting implication of this model is that individuals who report "freefloating" or existential anxiety may be doing so because of continual difficulties in achieving low-level goals, which ultimately led to reverberation up the hierarchy. For such an individual, a therapeutic solution might be to become more successful in attaining these low-level goals, thus shoring up the lower level pillars upon which self-esteem is based. In this way, the individual can imbed him-herself back within the security of the cultural anxiety-buffer and end the confrontation with the higher level problems.

In his book on existential psychotherapy, Yalom (1980) proposed that the reverse strategy may also sometimes be useful; individuals consciously attending to lower level concerns may need to bring their deeper concerns into awareness. By doing so, they may come to understand that there are many more lower level means by which they can achieve their higher level goals than they previously realized. In conjunction with guidance from a psychotherapist, this realization may encourage the individual to develop more fruitful strategies for meeting their needs.

In addition to its general implications for psychotherapy, the hierarchical terror management model also suggests answers to questions concerning basic symptoms of specific disorders. For example, it has often been noted that depressed individuals experience a great deal of anxiety (e.g., Gotlib, 1984; Hollon & Kendall, 1980). Self-regulatory perseveration theory (Pyszczynski & Greenberg, 1987) posits that depression is instigated when one is both unable to reduce a central discrepancy and unwilling to withdraw from self-regulatory pursuits. The current model suggests that this perseverated focus on an irreducible negative discrepancy will eventually shift awareness upward in the hierarchy. Depressed individuals are therefore likely to experience anxiety not just about their self-worth, but also about the validity of the cultural worldview and the inevitability of death. Indeed, despairing and morbid thoughts are very common characteristics of depressive thought (APA, DSM-III-R, 1987).

The hierarchical model may also be useful for explaining a variety of specific anxiety-related phenomena, such as hypochondriasis, somatization disorder, and obsessive-compulsive neurosis. All of these disorders may be characterized as involving an urgent focus on low-level goal-directed behavior in order to circumvent awareness of higher-level problems. Such behavior may have the added advantage of giving the individual the sense that he/she is effectively meeting his/her goals. Becker (1975) offered a similar analysis in more general terms:

> Man immunizes himself against terror by controlling his fascination, by localizing it and developing working responses toward the sources of it. The result is that he becomes a reflex of small terrors and small fascinations in place of overwhelming ones (p. 148).

This attentional diversion strategy is not likely to be effective in the long run; it is a stop-gap measure that will not protect the individual from anxiety when serious stressors occur because it is not a real solution to the basic problem. Such terror focalization strategies are only likely to be attempted by individuals who cannot maintain faith in their self-worth or the validity of their worldview in more conventional ways.

Likewise, disorders characterized by overly general negative self-referent thought, such as depression (cf. Beck, 1967), may reflect a tendency to respond to specific setbacks at lower levels by focusing attention on the higher order goals that the lower ones serve. Such a tendency may be related to the extent of differentiation in the individual's goal hierarchy (cf. Linville, 1985; Pyszczynski & Greenberg, 1987). Clearly, a better understanding of the development and dynamics of the goal hierarchy would enhance the utility of self-regulatory theories for understanding such clinical phenomena.

CONCLUSION

We hope that conceptualizing self-awareness within a broader model of human motivation will result in fruitful new avenues of self-awareness research. Although Carver & Scheier (1981) did include self-awareness within a general model of self-regulation, their model took insufficient account of the fact that human beings are more than simple self-regulating systems. At the most basic level, human beings are animals. Terror management theory recognizes that like other animals, humans are driven by needs and the emotions that result from the potential and actual satisfaction and thwarting of those needs. At the same time, the theory builds on the notion that, unlike other animals, humans are faced with the knowledge of their own vulnerability and inevitable mortality. Self-awareness is viewed as both an important cause of this existential dilemma and as a mediator of the self-evaluation process that enables the individual to achieve value and either literally or symbolically transcend death.

In presenting this model, we offered answers to three important questions about self-awareness: why self-awareness instigates self-evaluative processes, what role affect plays in discrepancy reduction, and whether self-awareness always leads to self-evaluation. Only future research can determine the validity of these answers. We ourselves are not sure what the final verdict from this research will be, but we believe that, at the very least, it will explore some fascinating aspects of the human capacity for self-reflection and its role in the tragedy of the human condition.

References

Abramson, L. Y., Seligman, M. E. P., & Teasdale, J. D. (1978). Learned helplessness in humans: Critique and reformulation. *Journal of Abnormal Psychology*, **87**, 49–74.

American Psychological Association (1987). *Diagnostic and statistical manual of mental disorders* (3rd ed., revised) (DSM-III-R). Washington, DC.

Ashby, W. R. (1952). *Design for a brain.* New York: Wiley.

Atkinson, J. W. (1981). Studying the personality in the context of an advanced motivational psychology. *American Psychologist*, **36**, 117–128.

Bartlett, F. C. (1932). *Remembering: A study in experimental and social psychology.* Cambridge, England: Cambridge University Press.

Beck, A. T. (1967). *Depression: Clinical, experimental, and theoretical aspects.* New York: Hoeber.

Becker, E. (1971). *The birth and death of meaning.* New York: Free Press.

Becker, E. (1973). *The denial of death.* New York: Free Press.

Becker, E. (1975). *Escape form evil.* New York: Free Press.

Bransford, J. D. (1979). *Human cognition: Learning, understanding, and remembering.* Belmont, CA: Wadsworth.

Bryan, W. L., & Harter, L. (1899). Studies on the telegraphic language: The acquisition of a hierarchy of habits. *Psychological Review*, **6**, 345–378.

Carver, C. S. (1975). Physical aggression as a function of objective self-awareness and attitude toward punishment. *Journal of Experimental Social Psychology*, **11**, 510–519.

Carver, C. S. (1979). A cybernetic model of self-attention processes. *Journal of Personality and Social Psychology*, **37**, 1251–1281.

Carver, C. S., & Scheier, M. (1981). *Attention and self-regulation.* New York: Springer-Verlag.

Carver, C. S., & Scheier, M. F. (in press). Origins and functions of positive and negative affect: A control-process view. *Psychological Review.*

Dawkins, R. (1976). *The selfish gene.* London: Oxford University Press.

Duval, S., & Wicklund, R. A. (1972). *A theory of objective self-awareness.* New York: Academic Press.

Federoff, N. A., & Harvey, J. H. (1976). Focus of attention, self-esteem, and attribution of causality. *Journal of Research in Personality*, **10**, 336–345.

Festinger, L. (1957) *A theory of cognitive dissonance.* Evanston, Ill: Roy, Peterson.

Geller, V., & Shaver, P. (1976). Cognitive consequences of self-awareness. is.Journal of Experimental Social Psychology, **12**, 99–108.

Gibbons, F. X., & Wicklund, R. A. (1976). Selective exposure to self. *Journal of Research in Personality*, **10**, 98–106.

Gotlib, I. H. (1984). Depression and general psychopathology in university students. *Journal of Abnormal Psychology*, **93**, 19–30.

Greenberg, J., & Pyszczynski, T. (1985). Compensatory self-inflation: A response to the threat to self-regard of public failute. *Journal of Personality and Social Psychology*, **49**, 273–280.

Greenberg, J., & Pyszczynski, T. (1986). Persistent high self-focus after failure and low self-focus after success: The depressive self-focusing style. *Journal of Personality and Social Psychology*, **50**, 1039–1044.

Greenberg, J. Pyszczynski, T., & Solomon, S. (1986) The causes and consequences of the need for self-esteem: A terror management theory. In R. F. Baumeister (Ed.), *Public self and private self* (pp. 189–212). New York: Springer-Verlag.

Greenberg, J., Solomon, S., Lyon, D., & Pyszczynski, T. (in preparation). *Evidence for terror management theory III: The anxiety-buffering function of self-esteem.* University of Arizona, Tucson, AZ.

Greenberg, J., Pyszczynski, T., Solomon, S., Rosenblatt, A., Veeder, M., Kirkland, S., & Lyon, D. (in press). Evidence for terror management theory II: The effects of mortality salience on reactions to those who implicitly or explicitly threaten or support the cultural world view. *Journal of Personality and Social Psychology.*

Heider, F. (1958). *The psychology of interpersonal relations.* New York: Wiley.

Hollon, S. D., & Kendall, P. C. (1980). Cognitive self-statements in depression: Development of an automatic thoughts questionnaire. *Cognitive Therapy and Research*, **4**, 383–395.

Hull, J. G. (1981). A self-awareness model of the causes and effects of alcohol consumption. *Journal of Abnormal Psychology*, **90**, 586–600.

Hull, J. G., & Levy, A. S. (1979). The organizational functioning of the self: An alternative to the Duval and Wicklund model of self-awareness. *Journal of Personality and Social Psychology*, **37**, 756–768.

Kernis, M. H., Zuckerman, M., Cohen, A., & Spadofora, S. (1982). Persistence following failure: The interactive role of self-awareness and attributional bias for negative expectancies. *Journal of Personality and Social Psychology*, **43**, 1184–1191.

Kruglanski, A. W. (1980) Lay epistemology process and contents. *Psychological Review*, **87**, 70–87.

Langer, E. J., & Imber, L. G. (1979). When practice makes imperfect: Debilitating effects of overlearning. *Journal of Personality and Social Psychology*, **37**, 2014–2024.

Linville, P. W. (1985). Self-complexity and affective extremity - don't put all your eggs in one cognitive basket. *Social Cognition*, **3**, 94–120.

Paulhus, D. L., & Levitt, K. (1987). Desirable responding triggered by affect-automatic egotism. *Journal of Personality and Social Psychology*, **52**, 245–259.

Pennebaker, J. W. (1982). *The psychology of physical symptoms.* New York: Springer-Verlag.

Powers, W. T. (1973). *Behavior: The control of perception.* Chicago: Aldine.

Powers, W. T. (1978). Quantitative analysis of purposive systems- some spadework at foundations of scientific psychology. *Psychological Review*, **85**, 417–435.

Pyszczynski, T., & Greenberg, J. (1987). Self-regulatory perseveration and the depressive self-focusing style: A self-awareness theory of reactive depression. *Psychological Bulletin*, **102**, 1–17.

Pyszczynski, T., Hamilton, J., Greenberg, J., & Becker, S. (in press). Self-awareness and psychological dysfunction. In C. R. Snyder & D. Forsyth (Eds.), *Handbook of social and clinical psychology: The health perspective.*

Rank, O. (1932/1950). *Psychology and the soul.* (Translated by W. D. Turner). Philadelphia: University of Pennsylvania Press.

Rosenblatt, A., Greenberg, J., Solomon, S., Pyszczynski, T., & Lyon, D. (1989). Evidence for terror management theory I: the effects of mortality salience on reaction to those who vilate and uphold cultural values. *Journal of Personality and Social Psychology*, **57**, 681–690.

Rotter, J. B. (1954). *Social learning and clinical psychology.* New York: Prentice-Hall.

Scheier, C. S., & Carver, M. F. (1988). A model of behavioral self-regulation: Translating intention into action. In L. Berkowitz (Ed.), *Advances in experimental social psychology*, Vol. 21 (pp. 303–346). New York: Academic Press.

Solomon, S., Greenberg, J., Pyszcynski, T. (1989). *A terror management theory of the role of self esteem in social behavior.* Manuscript submitted for publication. Skidmore College, Sarasota Springs, New York.

Solomon, S., Greenberg, J., Pyszczynski, T. (in press). The critical role of self-esteem in adjustment: A terror management analysis. In C. R. Snyder & D. Forsyth (Eds.), *Handbook of social and clinical psychology: The health perspective.*

Steele, C. (1988). Self-affirmation. In L. Berkowitz (Ed.), *Advances in experimental social psychology*, Vol. 21 (pp. 261–301). New York: Academic Press.

Turner, R. G. (1980). Self-consciousness and memory of trait terms. *Personality and Social Psychology Bulletin*, **6**, 273–277.

Vallacher, R. R., & Wegner, D. M. (1987). What do people think they're doing? Action identification and human behavior. *Psychological Review*, **94**, 3–15.

Weiner, B. (1986). *An attributional theory of motivation and emotion.* New York: Springer-Verlag.

Wicklund, R. A. (1975). Objective self-awareness. In L. Berkowitz (Ed.), *Advances in experimental social psychology* (Vol. 8, pp. 233–275). New York: Academic Press.

Wicklund, R. A., & Gollwitzer, P. M. (1982). *Symbolic self-completion.* Hillsdale, NJ: Erlbaum.

Wilson, E. O. (1976). *The selfish gene.* Cambridge, MA: Harvard University Press.

Yalom, I. D. (1980). *Existential psychotherapy.* New York: Basic Books.

Part 2: TASK-IRRELEVANT COGNITIONS, EXPECTANCIES, AND PERFORMANCE

SELF-EFFICACY CONCEPTION OF ANXIETY

ALBERT BANDURA*

Stanford University, California, USA

In social cognitive theory, perceived self-efficacy to exercise control over potential threats plays a central role in anxiety arousal. Threat is a relational property reflecting the match between perceived coping capabilities and potentially hurtful aspects of the environment. People who believe they can exercise control over potential threats do not engage in apprehensive thinking and are not perturbed by them. But those who believe they cannot manage threatening events that might occur experience high levels of anxiety arousal. Experimental analyses of the microrelation between perceived self-efficacy and anxiety arousal reveal that perceived coping inefficacy is accompanied by high levels of subjective distress, autonomic arousal and catecholamine secretion. Environmental events are not always completely under personal control and most human activities contain some potential risks. The exercise of control over anxiety arousal, therefore, requires not only development of behavioral coping efficacy but also efficacy in controlling dysfunctional apprehensive cognitions. It is not frightful cognitions *per se* but the perceived self-inefficacy to turn them off that is the major source of anxiety arousal. Analyses of the causal structure of self-protective behavior show that anxiety arousal and avoidant behavior are mainly co-effects of perceived coping inefficacy.

KEY WORDS: Self-efficacy, anxiety arousal, avoidant behavior, coping

Analysis of the determinants and mechanisms of anxiety requires specification of the phenomenon. For purposes of the present discussion, anxiety is defined as a state of anticipatory apprehension over possible deleterious happenings. Some conceptions of anxiety, however, endow it with its presumed causes and effects as if they constituted defining properties of the construct itself. Thus, for example, in the tripartite conception (Lang, 1977), anxiety is characterized as a set of loosely coupled components embodying apprehensive cognitions, physiological arousal, and avoidant behavior.

The conceptual and empirical problems associated with tripartite conceptions of anxiety have been addressed elsewhere and will not be reviewed here (Bandura, 1986). It deserves noting, however, that to make cognition, affect, and action all constituents of anxiety essentially precludes meaningful theoretical analysis of its origins and functions. If anxiety is defined as avoidant behavior, then the theoretical issue of whether anxiety causes avoidant behavior is reduced to the empty question of whether avoidant behavior causes itself. The assumption that anxiety arousal controls avoidant behavior will be analyzed later in some detail. Similar conceptual problems arise in regarding cognitions as anxiety. Apprehensive cognitions may cause anxiety arousal but they are not, in themselves, anxiety. If anxiety is characterized as apprehensive cognitions, this renders untestable the proposition that cognitions generate anxiety because both are defined as part of the same thing.

Although in definition, anxiety has often been invested with multifaceted properties, in theorizing about it and testing for its origins and effects, the confounding cognitive

*Address correspondence to: Albert Bandura, Department of Psychology, Jordan Hall, Building 420, Stanford University, Stanford, California, 94305, U.S.A.

This research was supported by Public Health Research Grant MH–5162–25 from the National Institute of Mental Health.

and behavioral properties are promptly jettisoned. Anxiety is then properly conceptualized as an emotion of fright indexed by physiological arousal or subjective feelings of agitation. Theories about whether or not anxiety controls self-protective behavior and whether apprehensive thoughts generate anxiety then become testable.

Anxiety involves anticipatory affective arousal that is cognitively labeled as a state of fright. Different types of experienced emotions are characterized by extensive similarities in autonomic arousal and hormonal secretions (Frankenhaeuser, 1975; Levi, 1972; Patkai, 1971). The physiological undifferentiation overshadows any small differences that may appear (Bandura, 1986). Moreover, the differences do not always replicate across different studies or different ways of inducing emotion. Discrepant findings suggest that uncontrolled factors covarying with emotion induction, such as variations in the intensity of the emotion instigators, may be responsible for the differences. Even if the nuances were reliably established, it is doubtful that they would be sufficiently distinguishable in an otherwise common elevated pattern of physiological arousal to serve as the cues specifying the experienced emotion.

The process of labeling one's state of affective arousal as anxiety or some other emotion is heavily influenced by the cognitive and situational context in which the arousal occurs. Situational instigators give emotional specificity to physiological commonality. Thus, affective arousal in the presence of perceived threats is experienced as anxiety or fear, arousal occurring in thwarting and insulting situations as anger, and arousal produced by irretrievable loss of what is highly valued as sorrow (Hunt, Cole and Reis, 1958).

Cognition plays a broader role in human emotion than simply labeling physiological states. Physiological arousal, itself, is often generated cognitively by arousing trains of thought (Beck, 1976; Schwartz, 1971). People frighten themselves by scary thoughts, they work themselves into a state of anger by ruminating about social slights and mistreatments, they become sexually aroused by conjuring up erotic fantasies, and they become depressed by dwelling on gloomy cognitive scenarios. The trains of thoughts that occupy one's consciousness thus create physiological arousal as well as help to define what one is feeling.

Perceived Coping Self-Efficacy and Anxiety Arousal

In social cognitive theory (Bandura, 1986), perceived self-efficacy to exercise control over potentially threatening events plays a central role in anxiety arousal. Threat is not a fixed property of situational events. Nor does appraisal of the likelihood of aversive happenings rely solely on reading external signs of danger or safety. Rather, threat is a relational property concerning the match between perceived coping capabilities and potentially hurtful aspects of the environment. Therefore, to understand people's appraisals of external threats and their affective reactions to them it is necessary to analyze their judgments of their coping capabilities which, in large part, determine the subjective perilousness of environmental events.

People who believe they can exercise control over potential threats do not conjure up apprehensive cognitions and, hence, are not perturbed by them. But those who believe they cannot manage potential threats experience high levels of anxiety arousal. They tend to dwell on their coping deficiencies and view many aspects of their environment as fraught with danger. Through such inefficacious thought they distress themselves and constrain and impair their level of functioning (Beck, Emery and Greenberg, 1985; Lazarus and Folkman, 1984; Meichenbaum, 1977; Sarason, 1975).

There is a good deal of research documenting the influential role of perceived control in anxiety and stress reactions (Averill, 1973; Miller, 1980). A sense of personal control can be achieved either behaviorally or cognitively. In behavioral control, individuals do things that forestall or attenuate aversive events. In cognitive control, individuals operate under the belief that they are capable of managing threatening situations should they arise. Although actual and perceived control are clearly distinguishable at the operational level, there is often substantial variance between perception and actuality, and perceived self-efficacy operates anticipatorily in regulating anxiety arousal in both forms of control.

Being able to exercise control over potential threats can diminish anxiety because the capability is used to reduce or to prevent painful experiences. But stress reduction by behavioral control involves much more than simply curtailing painful events. The experiences accompanying the exercise of behavioral control produce substantial cognitive changes in perceived self-efficacy that continue to affect autonomic arousal after the behavioral episodes have ceased (Bandura, Cioffi, Taylor and Brouillard, 1988). In some studies of behavioral control, threatening events occur undiminished but they are promptly transformed to nonaversive ones when their occurrence is personally controlled (Gunnar-vonGnechten, 1978). Hence it is simply the exercise of initiatory control, not the curtailment of the events themselves, that reduces anxiety. The anxiety-reduction effects stem from the sense of control rather than from increased predictability of aversive events (Gunnar, 1980). That a sense of control diminishes anxiety, even across markedly different domains of functioning, is strikingly demonstrated by Mineka, Gunnar, and Champoux (1986) in a developmental study. Monkeys who had been reared under conditions in which they exercised control over food months later showed little fear or avoidance of novel threats, whereas the same threats were highly frightening to monkeys who could not develop a sense of control because food had been given to them independently of their actions. In situations in which the opportunity to wield behavioral control exists but is unexercised, it is the self-knowledge that one can exercise control should one choose to do so rather than its application that reduces anxiety reactions (Glass, Reim and Singer, 1971).

The converging lines of evidence indicate that much of the anxiety reductive effects of behavioral control stem anticipatorily from perceived capability to wield control over aversive events rather than simply from attenuating them when they occur. Thus, perceived control even without the actuality reduces anxiety. People who are led to believe they can exercise some control over painful stimuli display lower autonomic arousal and less performance impairment than do those who believe they lack personal control, even though they are equally subjected to the painful stimuli (Geer, Davison and Gatchel, 1970; Glass, Singer, Leonard, Krantz and Cummings, 1973). Repeated failures arouse anxiety when ascribed to personal incapability, but the same painful experiences leave people unperturbed if ascribed to situational factors (Wortman, Panciera, Shusterman and Hibscher, 1976).

Microrelation Between Perceived Self-Efficacy and Anxiety Arousal

That perceived coping efficacy operates as a cognitive mediator of anxiety has been stringently tested by creating different levels of perceived self-efficacy and relating them at a microlevel to different manifestations of anxiety. In these studies, phobics' self-percepts of efficacy are raised to differential levels by different modes of efficacy induction, whereupon their level of anxiety arousal is measured in anticipation and during encounters with phobic threats (Bandura, Reese and Adams, 1982). In addition to instating different levels of efficacy to remove ambiguities about the direction of causality, validation of self-efficacy theory regarding anxiety arousal and avoidant behavior involves verification of microrelations across different domains of functioning. The self-efficacy appraisal is in the cognitive domain, whereas the predicted effects are in the domain of avoidant behavior, autonomic arousal, or plasma catecholamine secretion.

Subjective Distress

Let us consider first the effects of perceived coping inefficacy on intensity of subjective distress. People experience high anticipatory and performance distress on coping tasks on which they perceive themselves to be inefficacious, but as the strength of their perceived self-efficacy increases their anxiety arousal declines. At high strengths of perceived self-efficacy, threatening tasks are performed with virtually no apprehensiveness. The inefficacy-anxiety relationship is replicated regardless of whether perceived self-efficacy is altered by enactive, vicarious, emotive, or cognitive means (Bandura, 1982).

The intensity of subjective distress in anticipation and performance even of the same coping task varies as a function of levels of perceived self-efficacy (Bandura, Reese and Adams, 1982). The perceived self-efficacy of different groups of phobics was raised to differential levels either by modeling or guided mastery experiences, whereupon their anxiety reactions to the same coping task were measured. Subjects in the low and medium levels of perceived efficacy then received additional efficacy-enhancing treatment until they achieved the next level of perceived self-efficacy and their anxiety arousal was again assessed. As shown in Figure 1, the greater the perceived self-inefficacy, the higher is the subjective distress regardless of whether self-percepts of efficacy are instated enactively or vicariously or whether the analysis involves anticipatory or performance anxiety based on intergroup or intrasubject variations in level of perceived self-efficacy. Perceived coping inefficacy similarly predicts level of subjective distress in other domains of functioning involving academic and athletic stressors (Krampen, 1988; Leland, 1983).

Autonomic Arousal

The generality of the relationship between perceived self-inefficacy and anxiety is further replicated using physiological indices of anxiety arousal. Elevation in blood pressure and cardiac acceleration were measured in phobics during anticipation and performance of intimidating tasks corresponding to strong, medium, and weak strength of perceived self-efficacy. The scope of perceived self-efficacy was expanded by modeling coping strategies until a full range of efficacy strengths was instated for each person. The coping tasks for the test of autonomic arousal were individually selected to correspond to the three strengths of perceived self-efficacy according to each person's particular scope of efficacy. What may be a coping task of low perceived efficacy for one individual might fall in the category of strong perceived efficacy for another. Thus, physiological arousal was examined as a function of differential strength of self-efficacy regardless of what the particular task might be. Following the assessment, subjects received guided mastery treatment with repeated efficacy probes until they all perceived themselves to be maximally self-efficacious on all coping tasks. Then their autonomic reactions were again measured.

Figure 2 shows the mean change from the baseline level in heart rate and blood pressure as a function of differential strength of perceived self-efficacy. Subjects were viscerally unperturbed by coping tasks they regarded with utmost self-efficacy. However, on tasks about which they had moderate doubts about their coping efficacy,

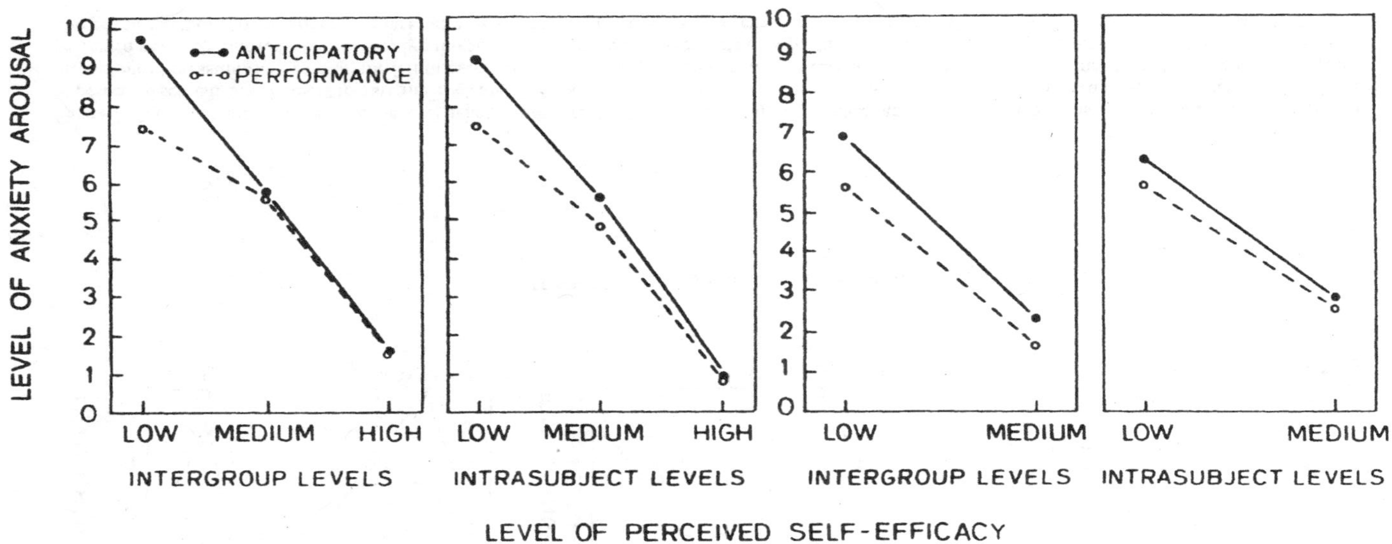

Figure 1. Mean intensity of anticipatory and performance anxiety experienced by different groups of subjects at different levels of perceived self-efficacy (intergroup) and by the same subjects at successively higher levels of perceived self-efficacy (intrasubject). The two left panels present the relationship for perceived self-efficacy raised by mastery experiences; the two right panels present the relationship for perceived self-efficacy raised by vicarious experiences (Bandura, Reese and Adams, 1982).

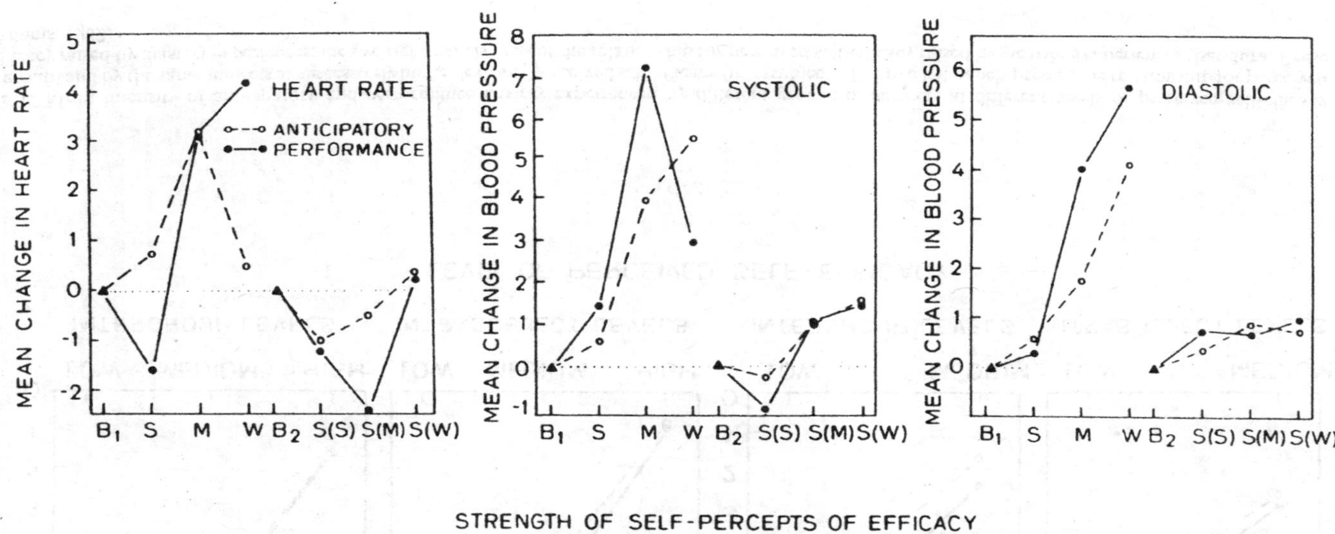

Figure 2. Mean change from the baseline level in heart rate and blood pressure during anticipatory and performance periods as a function of differential strength of perceived self-efficacy. *B* refers to baseline level, and *S*, *M*, and *W* signify strong, medium, and weak strengths of perceived self-efficacy, respectively. For each physiological measure the figure on the left in each panel shows the autonomic reactions related to self-percepts of differing strengths (performance arousal at perceived weak self-efficacy is based on only a few subjects who were able to execute only partial performances). The figure on the right of the same panel shows the autonomic reactions to the same set of tasks after self-percepts of efficacy were strengthened to the maximal level (Bandura, Reese and Adams, 1982).

their heart rate accelerated and their blood pressure rose during anticipation and performance of the activities. After self-percepts of efficacy were fully strengthened, these same coping task demands were managed unperturbedly.

When presented with tasks in the weak self-efficacy range, most subjects promptly rejected them as too far beyond their coping capabilities to even attempt. Indeed, only a few subjects were able to do any of them. Although too few instances precluded a meaningful analysis of performance arousal, data from the anticipatory phase shed light on how visceral reactions change when people withdraw from transactions with threats they judge will overwhelm their coping capabilities. Cardiac reactivity promptly declined but blood pressure continued to climb. After perceived self-efficacy was strengthened to the maximal level, everyone performed these previously intimidating tasks without any visceral agitation.

Heart rate is affected more quickly than blood pressure by personal restructuring of intimidating task demands, which may explain the different pattern of autonomic reactivity at the extreme level of perceived self-inefficacy. Catecholamines, which govern autonomic activity, are released in different temporal patterns during encounters with external stressors (Mefford *et al.*, 1981). Heart rate is especially sensitive to momentary changes in catecholamine patterns, with epinephrine, which is rapidly released, having a more pronounced effect on cardiac activity than on arterial pressure.

Research into the impact of perceived coping inefficacy on endogenous opioid activation further documents the influential role of perceived self-efficacy in autonomic arousal (Bandura, Cioffi, Taylor and Brouillard, 1988). Experiences involving efficacious and inefficacious efforts to cope with cognitive stressors produce cognitive changes in beliefs about personal coping efficacy that have substantial physiological effects in the absence of the stressor. In this study, subjects' heart rate was continuously monitored during a baseline period, while they coped with problem-solving stressors under conditions designed to create high and low perceived controlling efficacy, and when they later appraised their perceived cognitive efficacy. In Figure 3 the changes in heart rate are plotted as a function of strength of perceived self-efficacy. Perceived coping inefficacy was not only accompanied by higher autonomic arousal during the problem solving, but left subjects with a sense of inefficacy that affected autonomic arousal beyond the task. Thereafter, mere self-appraisal of coping efficacy lowered autonomic arousal in those whose perceived self-efficacy had been enhanced but heightened autonomic arousal in those whose sense of coping efficacy was diminished. The weaker the perceived self-efficacy and the greater its decline, the more elevated were the changes in heart rate.

Catecholamine Secretion

Understanding of the physiological mechanisms through which self-percepts of efficacy affect anxiety arousal was carried one step further by linking strength of perceived self-efficacy to release of catecholamines (Bandura, Taylor, Williams, Mefford and Barchas, 1985). As in the previous research, after the range of perceived self-efficacy in phobics was expanded by modeling, phobics were then presented in a randomized order with coping tasks they judged to be in their low, medium, and high self-efficacy range. Throughout this period, continuous blood samples were obtained through a catheter.

Figure 4 presents graphically the microrelation between self-percepts of efficacy and plasma catecholamine secretion. Epinephrine, norepinephrine, and dopac levels were

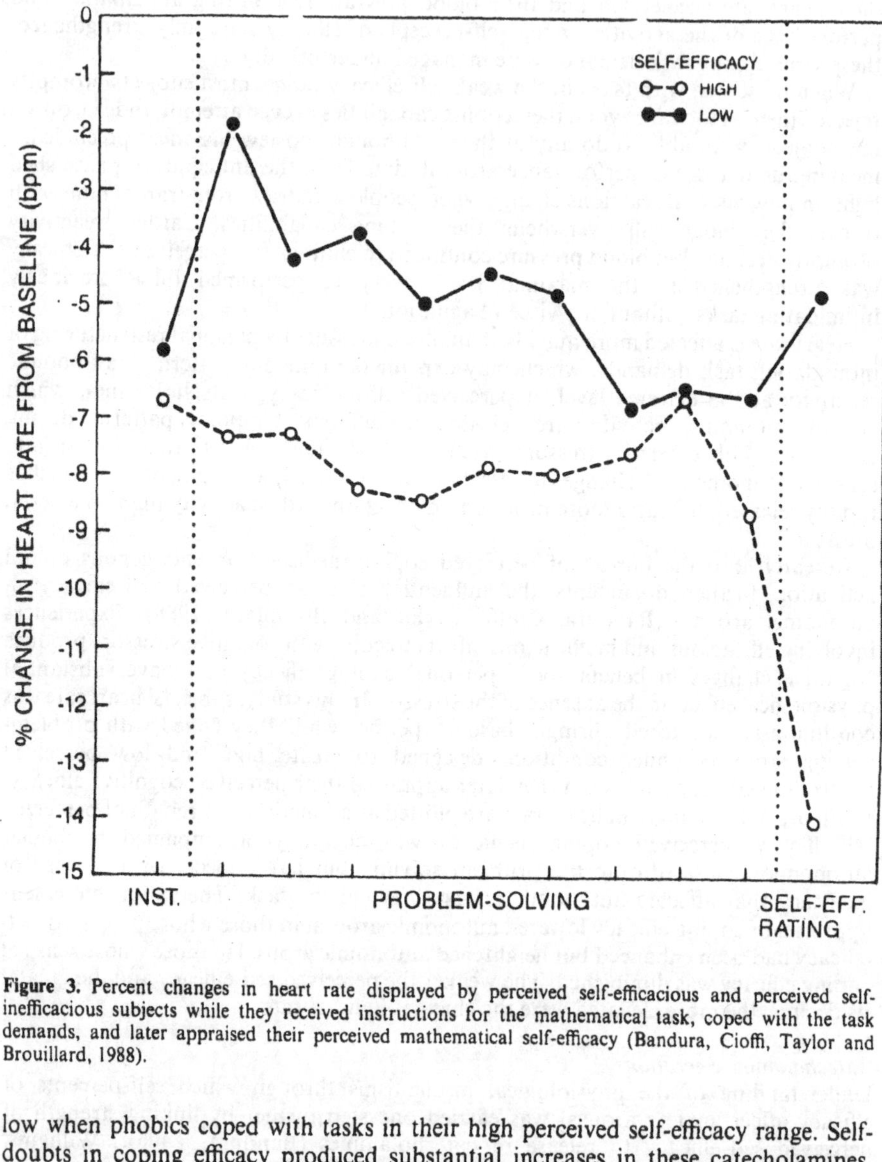

Figure 3. Percent changes in heart rate displayed by perceived self-efficacious and perceived self-inefficacious subjects while they received instructions for the mathematical task, coped with the task demands, and later appraised their perceived mathematical self-efficacy (Bandura, Cioffi, Taylor and Brouillard, 1988).

low when phobics coped with tasks in their high perceived self-efficacy range. Self-doubts in coping efficacy produced substantial increases in these catecholamines. When presented with tasks that exceeded their perceived coping capabilities the phobics instantly rejected them. Catecholamines dropped sharply. The dopac response differs markedly from the other catecholamines. Whereas epinephrine and norepinephrine dropped upon rejection of the threatening task, dopac rose to its highest level, even though the phobics had no intention of coping with the task. Dopac seems to be triggered by the mere apperception that environmental demands overwhelm one's perceived coping capabilities. After perceived coping efficacy was strengthened to the maximal level by guided mastery experiences, coping with the

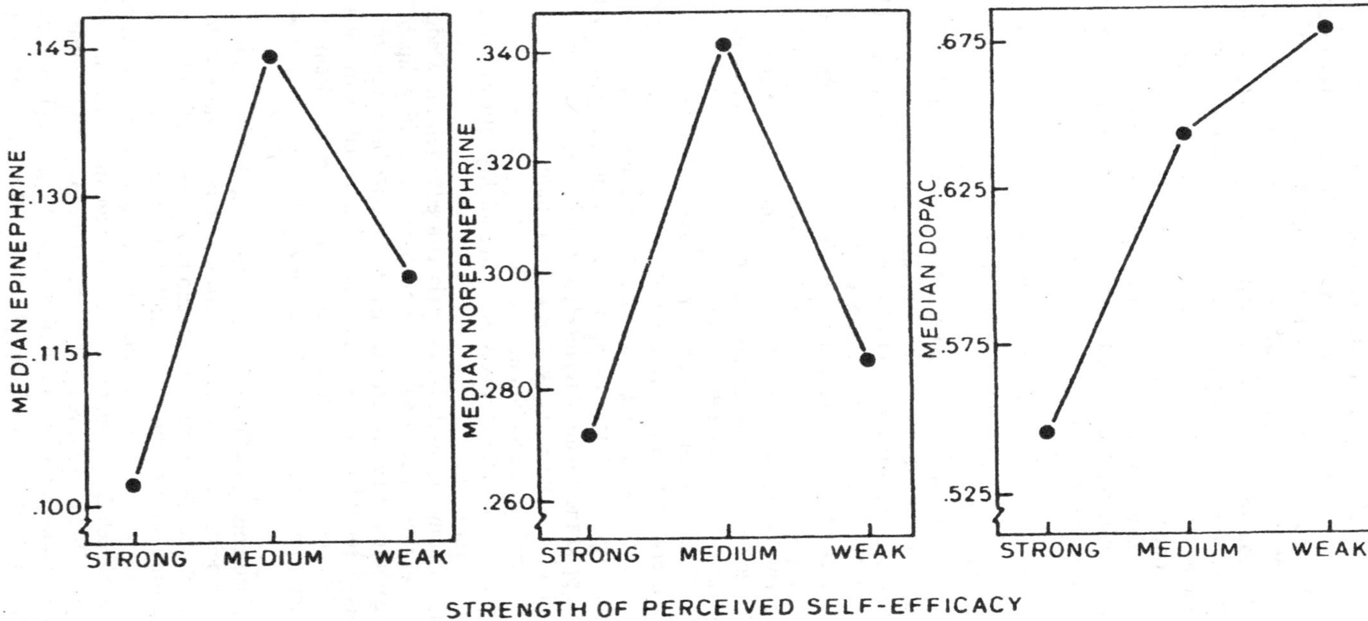

Figure 4. Median level of catecholamine secretion as a function of perceived coping self-efficacy (Bandura, Taylor, Williams, Mefford and Barchas, 1985).

previously intimidating tasks no longer elicited differential catecholamine reactivity. The latter findings indicate that the elevated catecholamine secretions observed in the initial test resulted from a perceived mismatch between perceived coping capabilities and task demands, rather than from properties inherent in the tasks themselves. The coping tasks *per se*, are not the source of variation in anxiety reactions.

The combined results from the different manifestations of anxiety are consistent in showing that anxiety reactions to coping tasks differ when perceived self-efficacy differs, but anxiety reactions to the identical tasks are the same when perceived self-efficacy is raised to the same maximal level. Perceived coping efficacy determines the perceived dangerousness of interactions with threats. People regard contact with phobic threats as potentially dangerous when they believe they cannot control them, but they regard such encounters as nondangerous when they believe they can exercise control over them.

The influential role of personal control in physiological activation is further revealed in microanalysis of changes in catecholamine secretion as phobics gain mastery over phobic threats through guided mastery treatment. Guided mastery is a powerful vehicle for instilling a resilient sense of coping efficacy in people whose psychosocial functioning is seriously impaired by phobic thinking. It provides persuasive confirmatory tests that one can exercise control over potential threats (Bandura, Blanchard and Ritter, 1969; Bandura, Jeffery and Wright, 1974). As functioning is restored, varied self-directed mastery experiences are arranged to strengthen and generalize the sense of coping efficacy (Bandura, Jeffery and Gajdos, 1975). Guided mastery uniformly achieves widespread psychological changes in a relatively short time. It eliminates phobic behavior and anxiety reactions, creates positive attitudes, and eradicates phobic ruminations and nightmares.

Figure 5 summarizes the changes in plasma catecholamine levels at five demarcated stages in the guided mastery treatment. During initial phases, when phobics lacked a sense of coping efficacy, even the mere sight or minimal contact with phobic objects activated catecholamine responses. After participants gained controlling efficacy, their catecholamine level dropped and remained relatively low during the most intimidating interactions with phobic objects. When they were asked to relinquish all control, which left them completely vulnerable, catecholamine reactivity promptly rose. This pattern of results is in accord with a mechanism involving controllability rather than simple extinction or adaptation over time.

We saw earlier that autonomic arousal to stressors is reduced by self-knowledge that one can wield control over them at any time even though that controlling capability is unexercised. Choosing not to exercise control at a particular time, but being able to do so whenever one wants to, should be distinguished from relinquished control in which one is deprived of all means of control while subjected to stressors. Relinquished control leaves one completely vulnerable, whereas freely usable control leaves one in full command.

The effects of perceived coping inefficacy on psychobiological stress reactions can have other important repercussions. There is a growing body of evidence that the ability to exercise control over potential stressors can have significant impact on the immune system. Exposure to stressors with controlling efficacy has no adverse physiological effects. However, exposure to the same stressors without controlling efficacy impairs various cellular components of the immune system (Maier, Laudenslager and Ryan, 1985). Perceived self-inefficacy in exercising control over stressors also activates endogenous opioid systems (Bandura, Cioffi, Taylor and Brouillard, 1988). There is evidence that some of the immunosuppressive effects of

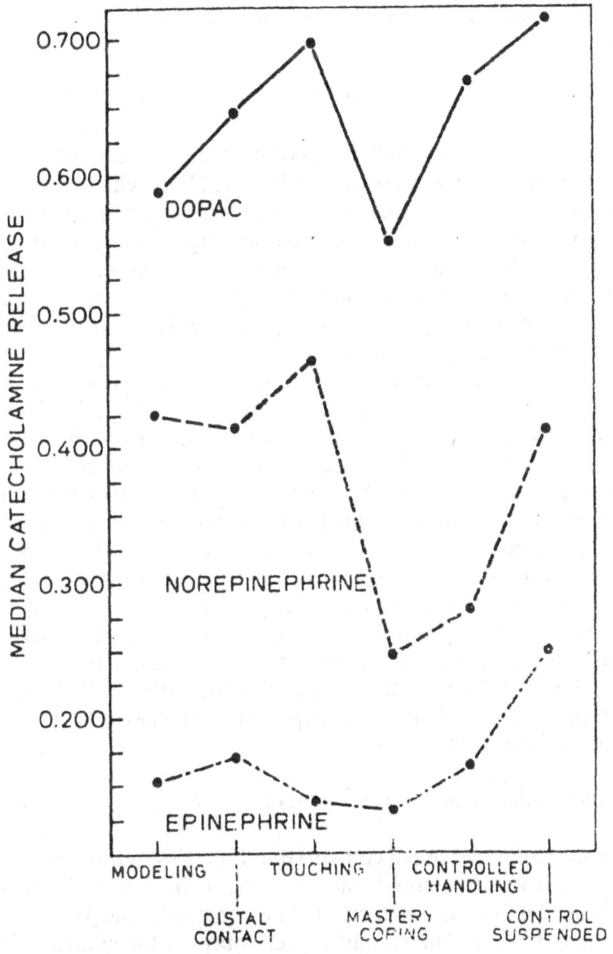

Figure 5. Changes in median level of catecholamine secretion as phobics master coping techniques through guided mastery experiences (Bandura, Taylor, Williams, Mefford and Barchas, 1985).

inefficacy in controlling stressors are mediated by release of endogenous opioids (Shavit and Martin, 1987). When opioid mechanisms are blocked by naloxone, the stress of coping inefficacy loses its immunosuppressive capabilities. Because physiological systems are highly interdependent, the types of physiological reactions that have been shown to accompany perceived coping inefficacy are involved in the regulation of immune systems.

It would be evolutionarily disadvantageous if the stress of coping inefficacy invariably impaired immune function because of the high prevalence of human stressors in everyday life. The findings of some of our current research indicate that acute moderate levels of stress may be immunoenhancing but that a severe sense of coping inefficacy activates high levels of stress that impair cellular components of the immune system.

Self-Efficacy Determinants of Apprehensive Thinking

As alluded to earlier, people's beliefs concerning their efficacy affect the type of cognitive scenarios they generate in coping situations. Those who have a strong sense of efficacy envision success scenarios that foster a problem-solving approach to difficulties they may encounter. In contrast, those who are beset by self-doubts tend to dwell on their personal deficiencies and envision failure scenarios that beget adverse consequences. Such intrusive thinking undermines effective use of capabilities by diverting attention from how best to master problems to concerns over personal deficiencies and possible calamities (Sarason, 1975).

The effect of perceived self-inefficacy on apprehensive thinking has been studied in terms of outcome expectancies. Most outcomes either flow naturally from actions or are linked to them by socially structured contingencies. Therefore, the types of outcomes people anticipate depend largely on their judgments of how well they will be able to perform in given situations. Those who judge themselves highly efficacious expect favorable outcomes, whereas those who expect deficient performances of themselves conjure up negative outcomes. In activities in which competency level determines the ensuing outcomes, self-judged efficacy accounts for most of the variance in expected outcomes (Barling and Abel, 1983; Barling and Beattie, 1983; Godding and Glasgow, 1986). In phobic dysfunctions, the lower the perceived coping efficacy, the more negative are the anticipated consequences in encounters with potential threats (Lee, 1984a,b; Williams and Watson, 1985). When variations in perceived self-efficacy are partialed out, expected outcomes do not account for additional variance in phobic behavior.

Environmental Controllability and Anxiety Arousal

There are two aspects to the exercise of control (Bandura, 1986; Gurin and Brim, 1984). The first concerns the level of personal efficacy to effect changes by productive use of capabilities and enlistment of sustained effort. This constitutes the personal side of the transactional control process. The second aspect concerns the controllability of the environment. This facet represents the level of environmental constraints and the degree to which the incidence of particular environmental events is influenceable by the exercise of personal efficacy.

Neither self-efficacy nor social environments are fixed entities. Operative efficacy is a generative capability in which multiple subskills must be continuously improvised to manage ever-changing circumstances often containing unpredictable and stressful elements. Individuals with the same subskills may, therefore, perform poorly, adequately, or extraordinarily, depending on their self-beliefs of efficacy, which affect how well they use the capabilities they possess. For the most part, the social environment constitutes a potentiality that is actualized by appropriate action. What parts of the potential environment come into play as the actual environment and the forms they take thus depend on how people behave. Human action is, of course, governed largely by perceptions of personal efficacy and social environments rather than simply by their objective properties. Thus, individuals who believe themselves to be inefficacious are likely to effect limited change even in environments that provide many potential opportunities (Bandura and Wood, 1988; Litt, 1988; Wood and Bandura, 1988). Conversely, those who have a firm belief in their efficacy, through ingenuity and perseverance, figure out ways of exercising some measure of control in environments containing more limited opportunities and many constraints.

Many deleterious events are not completely under personal control. Although perceived coping efficacy is a major contributor to anticipatory anxiety and stress reactions, it is not the sole determinant. For example, the more efficacious people judge themselves as drivers, the less anxious they will be on busy thoroughfares. However, even highly self-efficacious drivers will experience some apprehension because they cannot always spot and forestall reckless drivers from ramming them, sideswiping them, or broadswiping them through disregard of traffic signals. In situations where margins for error are narrow, mistakes produce serious consequences, and some limits exist on how much personal control can be wielded over potential threats, the exercise of high perceived self-efficacy will be accompanied by some apprehension. The more predictable and personally controllable potentially deleterious events are, the smaller will be the contribution of extraneous factors to anxiety arousal. However, people who judge themselves to be highly efficacious are especially prone to take on risky activities. To continue with the driving example, individuals who judge themselves highly efficacious venture into congested freeway and urban traffic and thereby create for themselves more taxing and risky environments than do self-inefficacious individuals who confine their driving to relatively safe situations.

Although perceived self-efficacy emboldens venturesomeness, it does not incite wrecklessness. After inefficacious individuals develop a strong sense of coping efficacy, they replace stereotyped self-protective avoidance by flexibly adaptive behavior that is cognitively controlled by judgments of probable affects of prospective actions. They engage in activities of interest to them when it is relatively safe to do so, but they refrain from those that carry high risk.

Thought Control Efficacy and Anxiety Arousal

Human activities are rarely devoid of risks. It is, therefore, natural to give some thought to potential risks in any undertaking and to have some uneasiness about them. But where the risks are extremely low, it is dysfunctional to conjure up magnified subjective dangers or to ruminate apprehensively about highly improbable risks to the point where it creates self-inflicted misery and impairs psychosocial functioning. The exercise of control over anxiety arousal in activities involving some risks may require not only development of coping efficacy, but also efficacy in controlling irrational apprehensive cognitions. The process of efficacious cognitive control is summed up well in the Chinese proverb: "You cannot prevent the birds of worry and care from flying over your head. But you can stop them from building a nest in your head." Self-generated distress is likely to be kept at a relatively low level when both cognitive control and action-based control are fully exercised.

The influential role played by thought control efficacy in anxiety arousal is corroborated in an interesting line of research examining the different properties of perturbing cognitions and their correlates. The results show that it is not the extent of frightful cognitions *per se* that accounts for anxiety arousal but rather the strength of perceived self-efficacy to control them (Kent, 1987; Kent and Gibbons, 1987). Thus, the incidence of frightful conditions is unrelated to anxiety level when variations in perceived thought control efficacy are controlled for, whereas perceived thought control efficacy is strongly related to anxiety level when extent of frightful cognitions is controlled. It appears that people who have a high sense of efficacy that they can exercise control over their thought processes are relatively unperturbed by apprehensive cognitions because they can abort their escalation or perseveration. Analysis of the aversiveness of obsessional ruminations provides further support for efficacious thought control as a key factor in the regulation of cognitively-generated arousal (Salkovskis and Harrison, 1984). It is not the sheer frequency of intrusive cognitions but rather the inefficacy to turn them off that is the major source of distress.

As in efficacious action, ability to control perturbing cognitions requires not only development of skills of thought control, but also a resilient self-belief of efficacy to apply them consistently and persistently (Bandura, 1988b). Thoughts of high intensity are not that easily dismissable (Clark and de Silva, 1985; Salkovskis and Harrison, 1984). Self-doubts of coping capabilities can set in fast. If people are not fully convinced of their personal efficacy they rapidly abandon the strategies they have been taught when they fail to get quick results or suffer setbacks. The findings of research into the regulation of one's own consciousness through the exercise of thought-control efficacy broaden understanding of the process of cognitive self-arousal.

Interactive But Asymmetric Relation

Self-percepts of efficacy are modifiable by four main sources of influence. They include performance mastery experiences; vicarious experiences of observing the attainments of others; verbal persuasion and allied types of social influences that one possesses certain capabilities; and physiological states from which people partly judge their adroitness, strength, and vulnerability to dysfunction. Information that is relevant for judging personal capabilities–whether conveyed enactively, vicariously, persuasively, or physiologically–is not inherently enlightening. Rather, it influences self-efficacy judgment through a process of cognitive appraisal in which multidimensional efficacy information must be selected, weighted, and integrated. A host of factors affect how efficacy-relevant experiences are cognitively processed (Bandura, 1986).

Social cognitive theory posits an interactive, thought asymmetric, relation between perceived self-efficacy and anxiety arousal, with coping efficacy exercising the much greater sway. That is, perceived self-inefficacy in coping with potential threats leads people to approach such situations anxiously, and experience of disruptive arousal may further lower their sense of efficacy that they will perform skillfully. However, people are much more likely to act on their self-percepts of efficacy inferred from various dependable sources of information rather than rely primarily on visceral cues. This is not surprising because self-knowledge based on information about one's coping skills, past accomplishments, and social comparison is considerably more indicative of capability than are the indefinite stirrings of the viscera. Seasoned performers interpret their anticipatory apprehension as a normative situational reaction, rather than as an indicant of personal incapability. They know what they can do once they get started, however much their viscera may be agitating anticipatorily.

The impact of perceived coping inefficacy on anxiety arousal is well established. But the influence of anxiety arousal on self-percepts of efficacy is equivocal. Actual level of physiological arousal has little or no effect on judgments of self-efficacy but perceived autonomic arousal can affect such judgments (Feltz and Mungo, 1983). In prospective studies, perceived self-efficacy predicts subsequent level of anxiety but anxiety level does not predict subsequent perceptions of personal efficacy (Krampen, 1988). Considering the indistinct diagnosticity of visceral information regarding personal capabilities, it is perhaps not surprising that evidence for arousal effects on self-percepts of efficacy is ambiguous and inconsistent.

Anxiety Arousal and Avoidant Behavior as Co-effects of Perceived Coping Inefficacy

Avoidant behavior has traditionally been explained in terms of a dual-process theory (Dollard and Miller, 1950; Mowrer, 1950). According to this view, avoidant behavior is motivated by an anxiety drive, and the reduction of anxiety through escape from threats reinforces the self-protective behavior. To eliminate avoidant behavior, it was considered necessary to eradicate the underlying anxiety. Many therapeutic procedures, therefore, have been keyed to extinguishing anxiety arousal.

The notion that anticipatory anxiety controls avoidant behavior has been investigated extensively using diverse procedures and found seriously wanting (Bandura, 1986; Bolles, 1975; Herrnstein, 1969; Schwartz, 1978). In some studies, feedback of autonomic arousal, which is the principal index of the anxiety drive, is eliminated surgically or blocked pharmacologically. The results show that the sensory experience of autonomic arousal is neither required to learn avoidant behavior, nor does it affect the rate with which such behavior is eliminated (Rescorla and Solomon, 1967; Wynne and Solomon, 1955). In other studies, the occurrence of avoidance behavior is measured after anxiety arousal to threats has been thoroughly eliminated. Avoidance behavior is often performed without autonomic arousal and can persist long after autonomic reactions to threats have been completely eradicated (Black, 1965; Rescorla and Solomon, 1967).

The differential latencies of autonomic and behavioral response systems also pose serious problems for the postulated causal sequence. Since avoidant actions occur faster than it takes to activate autonomic reactions, the former cannot be caused by the latter. Psychological principles need not be reduced to physiological ones, but a postulated psychological mechanism concerning the relationship between autonomic arousal and avoidant behavior cannot violate what is known about the physiological systems that subserve them. Research not only confirms that anticipatory arousal is not the controller of avoidant behavior but it casts doubt on the notion that anxiety reduction reinforces it (Bolles, 1975).

In still other studies, changes in anxiety arousal are related to changes in avoidance behavior during and after treatment. Such studies reveal no consistent relationships between changes in anxiety arousal and phobic behavior (Barlow, Leitenberg, Agras and Wincze, 1969). Elimination of phobic behavior can be preceded by increases in autonomic arousal, by reductions in autonomic arousal, or by no change in autonomic arousal. Neither the pattern nor magnitude of change in autonomic arousal accompanying treatment correlates significantly with the degree of behavioral change (O'Brien and Borkovec, 1977; Orenstein and Carr, 1975; Schroeder and Rich, 1976). The combined evidence from these diverse lines of research is highly consistent in showing that avoidance behavior is not controlled by anxiety arousal. More recently, the anxiety-extinction notion is being couched in terms of habituation. However, habituation is usually invoked presumptively rather than measured independently of behavior change and tested as a predictor of coping behavior.

As has already been shown, perceived self-inefficacy in coping with potential threats gives rise to fearful expectations and avoidance behavior. People avoid situations and activities not because they are beset with anxiety but because they believe they will be unable to manage safely situations they regard as risky. Those who judge themselves as efficacious in managing potential threats, neither fear nor shun them. In contrast, those

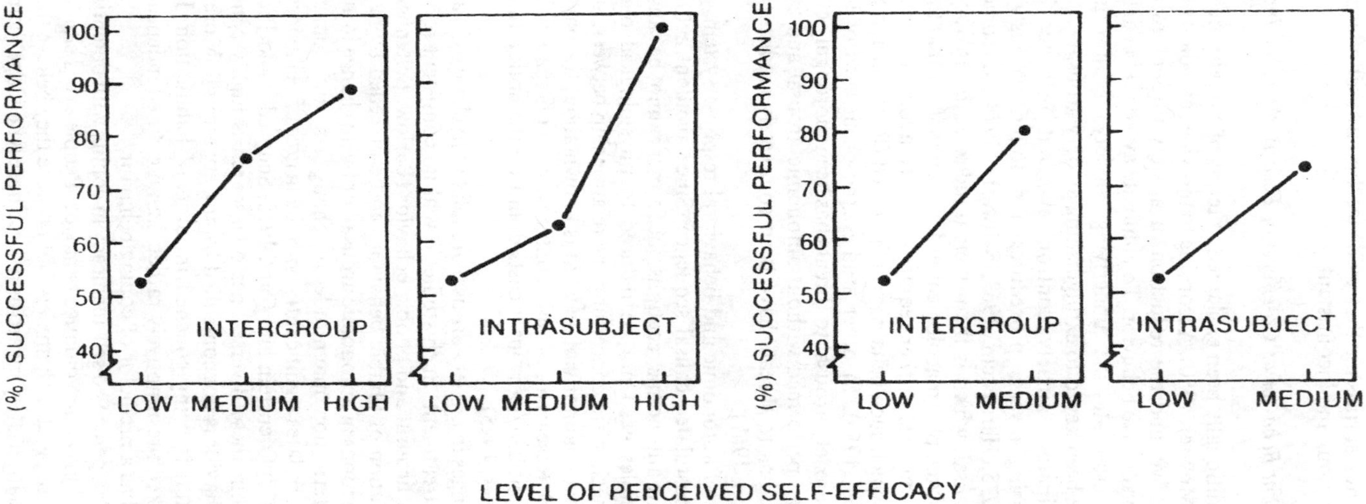

Figure 6. Mean coping attainments as a function of differential levels of perceived self-efficacy. The two left panels present the relationship for perceived self-efficacy raised by mastery experiences, the two right panels present the relationship for perceived self-efficacy raised by vicarious experiences solely by observing coping strategies modeled. The intergroup panels show the coping attainments of groups of subjects whose self-percepts of efficacy were raised to differential levels; the intrasubject panels show the coping attainments for the same subjects after their self-percepts of efficacy were successfully raised to different levels (Bandura, Reese and Adams, 1982).

who judge themselves as inefficacious in exercising control over potential threats envisage their inept coping as producing scary outcomes and are unwilling to have any commerce with situations they believe exceed their coping capabilities (Bandura, 1983).

The causal contribution of self-percepts of efficacy to coping behavior has been investigated by different paradigms, each of which tests the postulated causal links between efficacy instating conditions, the self-efficacy mediator, and behavior (Bandura, 1988b). In one such approach, perceived self-efficacy was raised in phobics from virtually non-existent levels to preselected low, moderate, or high levels by providing them with mastery experiences, or simply by modeling coping strategies for them (Bandura, Reese and Adams, 1982). Their coping behavior was measured after self-percepts of efficacy were developed to the designated levels.

As may be seen in Figure 6, higher levels of perceived self-efficacy are accompanied by higher coping attainments. The efficacy-action relationship is replicated across different phobic dysfunctions and in both intergroup and intrasubject comparisons, regardless of whether perceived self-efficacy was raised by mastery experiences or by vicarious influence. Microanalysis of efficacy-action congruences reveal a close fit between performance and perceived self-efficacy on individual tasks.

The role of perceived self-efficacy and anxiety arousal in the causal structure of avoidant behavior has also been examined in a number of studies. The results show that people base their actions on self-percepts of efficacy in situations they regard as risky. Williams and his colleagues (Williams, Dooseman and Kleifield, 1984; Williams, Turner and Peer, 1985) have analyzed by partial correlation numerous data sets from studies in which perceived self-efficacy, anticipated anxiety, and phobic behavior were measured. Perceived self-efficacy accounts for a substantial amount of variance in phobic behavior when anticipated anxiety is partialed out, whereas the relationship between anticipated anxiety and phobic behavior essentially disappears when perceived self-efficacy is partialed out (Table 1). Williams and Watson (1985) similarly demonstrate the predictive superiority of perceived self-efficacy over perceived dangerous consequences and level of fear arousal associated with performance of threatening activities. The variance contribution of perceived self-efficacy to phobic behavior may be reduced in pretreatment phases where preselection of severe cases markedly curtails the range of self-efficacy scores. Studies of other threatening activities lend further support to the proposed causal model (Hackett and Betz, 1984; McAuley, 1985). Perceived self-efficacy predicts performance whereas anxiety does not. The data taken as a whole indicate that anxiety arousal and avoidant behavior are largely coeffects of perceived coping inefficacy rather than causally linked.

It is interesting to speculate on why the belief that anticipatory anxiety arousal controls avoidant behavior remains firmly entrenched in psychological thinking despite substantial evidence to the contrary. A possible answer may lie in the force of confirmatory biases in judgments of causality (Nisbett and Ross, 1980). Confirming instances in which anxiety and avoidance occur jointly are likely to remain highly salient, whereas nonconfirming instances in which anxiety and approach behavior occur together, or avoidance occurs without anxiety command less attention. It is not that the nonconfirming instances are any less prevalent. Quite the contrary. People commonly perform activities at lower strengths of perceived self-efficacy despite high anxiety arousal. Thus, for example, actors strut on stage, athletes engage in competitive athletic activities, and students take intimidating examinations although beset by aversive anticipatory arousal. Similarly, people regularly take self-protective

Table 1 Relationship between perceived self-efficacy and anticipated anxiety to coping behavior when the other factor is partialled out

	COPING BEHAVIOR	
	ANTICIPATED ANXIETY with Self-Efficacy Controlled	PERCEIVED SELF-EFFICACY with Anticipated Anxiety Controlled
Williams & Rappoport (1983)		
Pretreatment 1	−0.12	0.40*
Pretreatment 2	−0.28	0.59**
Posttreatment	0.13	0.45*
Follow – up	0.06	0.45*
Williams *et al.* (1984)		
Pretreatment	−0.36*	0.22
Posttreatment	−0.21	0.59***
Williams *et al* (1985)		
Pretreatment	−0.35*	0.28*
Posttreatment	0.05	0.72***
Follow – up	−0.12	0.66***
Telch *et al.* (1985)		
Pretreatment	−0.56***	−0.28
Posttreatment	0.15	0.48**
Follow – up	−0.05	0.42*
Kirsch *et al.* (1983)		
Pretreatment	−0.34*	0.54***
Posttreatment	−0.48**	0.48**
Arnow *et al.* (1985)		
Pretreatment	0.17	0.77***
Posttreatment	−0.08	0.43*
Follow-up	−0.06	0.88***

*p<.05 **p<.01 ***p<.001

action without having to wait for anxiety to impel them to action. They strap on seat belts to prevent injury, disinfect things to protect against disease producing organisms, and disconnect electrical appliances before repairing them without having to conjure up an anxious state before they can take action. These different types of disconfirming occurrences tend to be ignored in judging the relation between anxiety and avoidance.

Empowerment Versus Anxiety Extinction or Habituation

Theories concerning the determinants and mechanisms of avoidant behavior shape the form of therapeutic practices. The anxiety control theory sponsors treatments emphasizing nonreinforced exposure to aversive situations until anxiety is extinguished. All therapists need do, according to this view, is get clients to expose themselves to threats without untoward consequences. If such exposure is repeated often enough they will eventually lose their anxiety and cease their avoidant behavior.

Findings of studies varying exposure and efficacy-enhancing factors lend little support to the exposure-extinction/habituation notion of change (Bandura, 1988a; Williams, 1987). Different modes of treatment with equivalent exposure produce different levels of perceived self-efficacy, which predict the level of coping behavior (Bandura, Adams and Beyer, 1977; Bandura, Jeffery and Wright, 1974; Williams, Dooseman and Kleifield, 1984). The amount of nonreinforced elicitation of anxiety arousal during the exposure, which presumably governs habituation and fear extinction, has no consistent effect on the rate and level of change of avoidant behavior (Emmelkamp and Mersch, 1982; Hafner and Marks, 1976; Mathews, Gelder and Johnston, 1981). According to the fear extinction/habituation notion, withdrawal from threats under high anxiety only reinforces avoidant behavior. Contrary to this view, agoraphobics told to cope with threats but to exercise personal control by withdrawing temporarily when highly anxious and trying again, increase their perceived self-efficacy and coping behavior comparably to those told to cope with threats until their anxiety abates (Rachman, Craske, Tallman and Solyom, 1986). Brief avoidance under high anxiety with renewed effort was construed as exercise of personal control rather than as escape. In treatments relying on unassisted exposure, brief distributed encounters with threats that limit opportunities to gain coping efficacy produce little change, whereas prolonged coping ensuring confirmatory mastery experiences achieve positive results. Therapeutic changes are more enduring if treatment by unassisted coping fosters positive self-appraisal of efficacy (Marshall, 1985). As these various studies illustrate, people preside as cognizing agents over their own change rather than exposure to threats automatically habituating or extinguishing their reactivity.

In enactive modes of treatment it is not mere exposure to threats, but mastery experience gained through exercise of personal agency that is the vehicle of change (Bandura, 1986; Williams, Dooseman and Kleifield, 1984). In vicarious modes of treatment it is not mere exposure, but the modeling of effective coping strategies and socially comparative indicants of capability that constitute the critical influences. Thus, phobics who have been exposed to a successful model raise their perceived self-efficacy and coping behavior when the model is alleged to be similar to them, whereas they do not benefit from the same exposure if the model is alleged to be different from them (Prince, 1984). In persuasory modes of influence, it is not mere exposure to verbal representations of threats, but the social power and credibility of the persuader that convinces participants that they have the capability to cope more effectively.

The greatest benefits that psychological treatments can bestow are not specific remedies or affective extinctions, but the tools with which to cope effectively with whatever future situations might arise. To the extent that treatment equips people to exercise control over events in their lives they are less vulnerable to distress and debility. The exercise of control involves a generative capability in which multiple subskills must be continuously improvised to manage ever changing circumstances. Therefore, in any activity, skills and self-beliefs of efficacy that ensure their effective use are required for successful functioning. Variations in self-beliefs of efficacy produce variable utilization of skills. When people are assured of their capabilities they get the most out of their talents whereas, when they are beset by self-doubts, they tend to behave ineffectually despite well-developed skills (Bandura and Wood, 1988; Wood and Bandura, 1988).

Guided mastery treatment provides the most effective vehicle for empowering people with the cognitive and behavioral tools needed to exercise personal control (Bandura, 1988b). Guided mastery experiences are not only ideally suited for cultivating generative coping skills, but they provide highly persuasive confirmatory tests of personal capability to exercise control over potential threats. Changes result from cognitive processing of performance information rather than being implanted directly by the performances *per se*. Self-efficacy theory provides guides for how to structure mastery experiences to maximize their efficacy-enhancing impact.

The empowerment model applies to adoption of beneficial self-protective behavior as well as to elimination of dysfunctional apprehensiveness and self-protectiveness. People are helped to adopt preventive health practices not by trying to scare them into healthy ways but by empowering them with the self-regulatory skills and self-beliefs of efficacy for exercising personal control over their own motivation and health habits (Beck and Lund, 1981; Maddux and Rogers, 1983). Each of the modes of efficacy influence can be put to the service of developing the resilient sense of perceived self-efficacy needed to override difficult circumstances that inevitably arise in the transactions of everyday life.

References

Averill, J.R. (1973). Personal control over aversive stimuli and its relationship to stress. *Psychological Bulletin*, **80**, 286–303.

Bandura, A. (1982). Self-efficacy mechanism in human agency. *American Psychologist*, **37**, 122–147.

Bandura, A. (1983). Self-efficacy determinants of anticipated fears and calamities. *Journal of Personality and Social Psychology*, **45**, 464–469.

Bandura, A. (1986). *Social foundations of thought and action: A social cognitive theory*. Englewood Cliffs, NJ: Prentice-Hall.

Bandura, A. (1988a, in press). Self-regulation of motivation and action through goal systems. In V. Hamilton, G.H. Bower & N.H. Frijda (Eds.), *Cognitive perspectives on emotion and motivation*. Dordrecht: Martinus Nijhoff.

Bandura, A. (1988b). Perceived self-efficacy: Exercise of control through self-belief. In J.P. Dauwalder, M. Perrez & V. Hobi (Eds.), *Annual series of European research in behavior therapy* (Vol. 2, pp. 27–59). Lisse (NL): Swets & Zeitlinger.

Bandura, A., Adams, N.E. & Beyer, J. (1977). Cognitive processes mediating behavioral change. *Journal of Personality and Social Psychology*, **35**, 125–139.

Bandura, A., Blanchard, E.B. & Ritter, B. (1969). Relative efficacy of desensitization and modeling approaches for inducing behavioral, affective, and attitudinal changes. *Journal of Personality and Social Psychology*, **13**, 173–199.

Bandura, A., Cioffi, D., Taylor, C.B. & Brouillard, M.E. (1988, in press). Perceived self-efficacy in coping with cognitive stressors and opioid activation. *Journal of Personality and Social Psychology*.

Bandura, A., Jeffery, R.W. & Gajdos, E. (1975). Generalizing change through participant modeling with self-directed mastery. *Behaviour Research and Therapy*, **13**, 141–152.

Bandura, A., Jeffery, R.W. & Wright, C.L. (1974). Efficacy of participant modeling as a function of response induction aids. *Journal of Abnormal Psychology*, **83**, 56–64.

Bandura, A., Reese, L. & Adams, N.E. (1982). Microanalysis of action and fear arousal as a function of differential levels of perceived self-efficacy. *Journal of Personality and Social Psychology*, **43**, 5–21.

Bandura, A., Taylor, C.B., Williams, S.L., Mefford, I.N., Barchas, J.D. (1985). Catecholamine secretion as a function of perceived coping self-efficacy. *Journal of Consulting and Clinical Psychology*, **53**, 406–414.

Bandura, A. & Wood, R.E. (1988). Effect of perceived controllability and performance standards on self-regulation of complex decision making. Submitted for publication.

Barling, J. & Abel, M. (1983). Self-efficacy beliefs and performance. *Cognitive Therapy and Research*, **7**, 265–272.

Barling, J. & Beattie, R. (1983). Self-efficacy beliefs and sales performance. *Journal of Organizational Behavior Management*, **5**, 41–51.

Barlow, D.H., Leitenberg, H., Agras, W.S. & Wincze, J.P. (1969). The transfer gap in systematic desensitization: An analogue study. *Behaviour Research and Therapy*, **7**, 191–196.

Beck, A.T. (1976). *Cognitive therapy and the emotional disorders*. New York: International Universities Press.

Beck, A.T., Emery, G. and Greenberg, R.L. (1985). *Anxiety disorders and phobias*. New York: Basic Books.

Beck, K.H. & Lund, A.K. (1981). The effects of health threat seriousness and personal efficacy upon intentions and behavior. *Journal of Applied Social Psychology*, **11**, 401–415.

Black, A.H. (1965). Cardiac conditioning in curarized dogs: The relationship between heart rate and skeletal behaviour. In W.F. Prokasy (Ed.), *Classical conditioning: A symposium* (pp. 20–47). New York: Appleton-Century-Crofts.
Bolles, R.C. (1975). *Learning theory*. New York: Holt, Rinehart & Winston.
Clark, D.A. & de Silva, P. (1985). The nature of depressive and anxious, intrusive thoughts: Distinct or uniform phenomena? *Behaviour Research and Therapy*, **23**, 383–393.
Dollard, J. & Miller, N.E. (1950). *Personality and psychotherapy*. New York: McGraw-Hill.
Emmelkamp, P.M.G. & Mersch, P.P. (1982). Cognition and exposure *in vivo* in the treatment of agoraphobia: Short-term and delayed effects. *Cognitive Therapy and Research*, **6**, 77–90.
Feltz, D.L. & Mugno, D.A. (1983). A replication of the path analysis of the causal elements in Bandura's theory of self-efficacy and the influence of autonomic perception. *Journal of Sport Psychology*, **5**, 263–277.
Frankenhaeuser, M. (1975). Experimental approaches to the study of catecholamines and emotion. In L. Levi (Ed.), *Emotions: Their parameters and measurement* (pp. 209–234). New York: Raven.
Geer, J.H., Davidson, G.C. & Gatchel, R.I. (1970). Reduction of stress in humans through nonveridical perceived control of aversive stimulation. *Journal of Personality and Social Psychology*, **16**, 731–738.
Glass, D.C., Reim, B. & Singer, J. (1971). Behavioral consequences of adaptation to controllable and uncontrollable noise. *Journal of Experimental Social Psychology*, **7**, 244–257.
Glass, D.C., Singer, J.E., Leonard, H.S., Krantz, D. & Cummings, H. (1973). Perceived control of aversive stimulation and the reduction of stress responses. *Journal of Personality*, **41**, 577–595.
Godding, P.R. & Glasgow, R.E. (1985). Self-efficacy and outcome expectancy as predictors of controlled smoking status. *Cognitive Therapy and Research*, **9**, 583–590.
Gunnar, M.R. (1980). Control, warning signals, and distress in infancy. *Developmental Psychology*, **16**, 281–289.
Gunnar-vonGnechten, M.R. (1978). Changing a frightening toy into a pleasant toy by allowing the infant to control its actions. *Development Psychology*, **14**, 147–152.
Gurin, P. & Brim, O.G., Jr. (1984). Change in self in adulthood: The example of sense of control. In P.B. Baltes & O.G. Brim, Jr. (Eds.), *Life-span development and behavior* (Vol. 6, pp. 281–334). New York: Academic Press.
Hackett, G. & Betz, N.E. (1984). *Mathematics performance, mathematics self-efficacy, and the prediction of science-based college majors*. Unpublished manuscript, University of California, Santa Barbara.
Hafner, R.J. & Marks, I.M. (1976). Exposure *in vivo* of agoraphobics: Contributions of diazepam, group exposure, and anxiety evocation. *Psychological Medicine*, **6**, 71–88.
Herrnstein, R.J. (1969). Method and theory in the study of avoidance. *Psychological Review*, **76**, 49–69.
Hunt, J. McV., Cole, M.W. & Reis, E.E.S. (1958). Situational cues distinguishing anger, fear, and sorrow. *American Journal of Psychology*, **71**, 136–151.
Kent, G. (1987). Self-efficacious control over reported physiological, cognitive and behavioural symptoms of dental anxiety. *Behaviour Research and Therapy*, **25**, 341–347.
Kent, G. & Gibbons, R. (1987). Self-efficacy and the control of anxious cognitions. *Journal of Behavior Therapy and Experimental Psychiatry*, **18**, 33–40.
Krampen, G. (1988). *Competence and control orientations as predictors of test anxiety in students: Longitudinal results*. Unpublished manuscript, University of Trier.
Lang, P.J. (1977). Physiological assessment of anxiety and fear. In J.D. Cone & R.P. Hawkins (Eds.), *Behavioral assessment: New directions in clinical psychology* (pp. 178–195). New York: Brunner/Mazel.
Lazarus, R.S. & Folkman, S. (1984). *Stress, appraisal, and coping*. New York: Springer.
Lee, C. (1984a). Accuracy of efficacy and outcome expectations in predicting performance in a simulated assertiveness task. *Cognitive Therapy and Research*, **8**, 37–48.
Lee, C. (1984b). Efficacy expectations and outcome expectations as predictors of performance in a snake-handling task. *Cognitive Therapy and Research*, **8**, 509–516.
Leland, E.I. (1983). Self-efficacy and other variables as they relate to precompetitive anxiety among male interscholastic basketball players. (Doctoral dissertation, Stanford University, 1983). *Dissertation Abstracts International*, **44**, *1376A*.
Levi, L. (Ed.) (1972). Stress and distress in response to psychosocial stimuli. *Acta Medica Scandinavica*, **191**, Supplement No. 528.
Litt, M.D. (1988). Self-efficacy and perceived control: Cognitive mediators of pain tolerance. *Journal of Personality and Social Psychology*, **54**, 149–160.
Maddux, J.E. & Rogers, R.W. (1983). Protection motivation and self-efficacy: A revised theory of fear appeals and attitude change. *Journal of Experimental Social Psychology*, **19**, 469–479.
Maier, S.F., Laudenslager, M.L. & Ryan, S.M. (1985). Stressor controllability, immune function, and endogenous opiates. In F.R. Brush & J.B. Overmier (Eds.), *Affect, conditioning, and cognition: Essays on the determinants of behavior* (pp. 183–201). Hillsdale, NJ: Lawrence Erlbaum.

Marshall, W.L. (1985). The effects of variable exposure in flooding therapy. *Behavior Therapy*, **16**, 117–135.
Mathews, A.M., Gelder, M. & Johnston, D. (1981). *Agoraphobia: Nature and treatment*. New York: Guilford Press.
McAuley, E. (1985). Modeling and self-efficacy: A test of Bandura's model. *Journal of Sport Psychology*, 7, 283–295.
Mefford, I.N., Ward, M.M., Miles, L., Taylor, B., Chesney, M.A., Keegan, D.L. & Barchas, J.D. (1981). Determination of plasma catecholamines and free 3,4-dihydroxyphenylacetic acid in continuously collected human plasma by high performance liquid chromatography with electrochemical detection. *Life Sciences*, **28**, 447–483.
Meichenbaum, D.H. (1977). *Cognitive behavior modification: An integrative approach*. New York: Plenum.
Miller, (1980). Why having control reduces stress: If I can stop the rollercoaster I don't want to get off. In J. Garber & M.E.P. Seligman (Eds.), *Human helplessness: Theory and research* (pp. 71–95). New York: Academic Press.
Mineka, S., Gunnar, M. & Champoux, M. (1986). Control and early socioemotional development: Infant rhesus monkeys reared in controllable versus uncontrollable environments. *Child Development*, **57**, 1241–1256.
Mowrer, O.H. (1950). *Learning theory and personality dynamics*. New York: Ronald Press.
Nisbett, R. & Ross, L. (1980). *Human inference: Strategies and shortcomings of social judgment*. Englewood Cliffs, NJ: Prentice-Hall.
O'Brien, G.T. & Borkovec, T.D. (1977). The role of relaxation in systematic desensitization: Revisiting an unresolved issue. *Journal of Behavior Therapy and Experimental Psychiatry*, **8**, 359–364.
Orenstein, H. & Carr, J. (1975). Implosion therapy by tape-recording. *Behaviour Research and Therapy*, **13**, 177–182.
Patkai, P. (1971). Catecholamine excretion in pleasant and unpleasant situations. *Acta Psychologica*, **35**, 352–363.
Prince, J.S. (1984). *The effects of the manipulation of perceived self-efficacy on fear-avoidant behavior*. Unpublished doctoral dissertation, Northern Illinois University, De Kalb, Illinois.
Rachman, S., Craske, M., Tallman, K. & Solyom, C. (1986). Does escape behavior strengthen agoraphobic avoidance? *Behavior Therapy*, **17**, 366–384.
Rescorla, R.A. & Solomon, R.L. (1967). Two-process learning theory: Relationships between Pavlovian conditioning and instrumental learning. *Psychological Review*, **74**, 141–182.
Salkovskis, P.M. & Harrison, J. (1984). Abnormal and normal obsessions–a replication. *Behaviour Research and Therapy*, **22**, 549–552.
Sarason, I.G. (1975). Anxiety and self-preoccupation. In I.G. Sarason & D.C. Spielberger (Eds.), *Stress and Anxiety* (Vol. 2, pp. 27–44). Washington, DC: Hemisphere.
Schroeder, H.E. & Rich, A.R. (1976). The process of fear reduction through systematic desensitization. *Journal of Consulting and Clinical Psychology*, **44**, 191–199.
Schwartz, B. (1978). *Psychology of learning and behavior*. New York: Norton.
Schwartz, G.E. (1971). Cardiac responses to self-induced thoughts. *Psychophysiology*, **8**, 462–467.
Shavit, Y. & Martin, F.C. (1987). Opiates, stress, and immunity: Animal studies. *Annals of Behavioral Medicine*, **9**, 11–20.
Williams, S.L. (1987). On anxiety and phobia. *Journal of Anxiety Disorders*, **1**, 161–180.
Williams, S.L., Dooseman, G. & Kleifield, E. (1984). Comparative power of guided mastery and exposure treatments for intractable phobias. *Journal of Consulting and Clinical Psychology*, **52**, 505–518.
Williams, S.L., Turner, S.M. & Peer, D.F. (1985). Guided mastery and performance desensitization treatments for severe acrophobia. *Journal of Consulting and Clinical Psychology*, **53**, 237–247.
Williams, S.L. & Watson, N. (1985). Perceived danger and perceived self-efficacy as cognitive mediators of acrophobic behavior. *Behavior Therapy*, **16**, 136–146.
Wood, R.E. & Bandura, A. (1988). Impact of conceptions of ability on self-regulatory mechanisms and complex decision-making. Submitted for publication.
Wortman, C.B., Panciera, L., Shusterman, L. & Hibscher, J. (1976). Attributions of causality and reactions to uncontrollable outcomes. *Journal of Experimental Social Psychology*, **12**, 301–316.
Wynne, L.C. & Solomon, R.L. (1955). Traumatic avoidance learning: Acquisition and extinction in dogs deprived of normal peripheral autonomic function. *Genetic Psychology Monographs*, **52**, 241–284.

COMPETENCE AND CONTROL ORIENTATIONS AS PREDICTORS OF TEST ANXIETY IN STUDENTS: LONGITUDINAL RESULTS*

GÜNTER KRAMPEN

University of Trier, Federal Republic of Germany

(*Received 11 March, 1988; in final form 19 April, 1988*)

The hypothesis that domain-specific self-related cognitions (self-concept of own competence and control orientations) are predictors of text anxiety in students is tested by longitudinal data. At the beginning and at the end of a school year the following variables were measured twice in a sample of 346 secondary school students (grades six to ten): (1) self-concept of own competence in mathematics, (2) three aspects of locus of control for problem-solving behavior (internality, powerful others control, and chance control), (3) generalized locus of control of reinforcement, (4) test anxiety as well as manifest anxiety. The cross-sequential developmental gradients point toward symmetries in the development of self-related cognitions and test anxiety. The results of cross-lagged correlation analyses show that the null hypothesis (no causal relations exist between the self-related cognitions and test anxiety) can be rejected for the domain-specific aspects of (a low) self-concept of own competence and locus of control (low internality and high chance control), which are confirmed as preceding test anxiety. However, longitudinal results also show that findings of cross-sectional studies tend to overestimate the relations between self-related cognitions and test anxiety in a developmental perspective.

KEY WORDS: Self-related cognitions, test anxiety, longitudinal data.

Among the copious results of studies concerned with the correlates and determinants of test anxiety in students (covering a relatively broad spectrum of variables like features of educational style in family and school, school climate, type of school, reference group, etc.) recently such have increased, in which various constructs of self-related cognitions are analyzed as relevant determinants of anxiety (see, e.g., Schwarzer, 1986; Van der Ploeg, Schwarzer & Spielberger, 1984). This is founded in social cognitive approaches to personality, which differentiate between more or less complex self-related cognitions and relate them to emotional, motivational and behavioral qualities.

Despite their differences, a central assumption of such cognitive approaches (e.g., Bandura, 1986a; Lazarus & Launier, 1978; Peterson & Seligman, 1984) to emotional qualities and coping in general as well as to anxiety in particular is the hypothesis that special types or expressions of self-related cognitions accompany or precede anxiety. More accurately, it must be added, that the view of Lazarus and Launier (1978) is somewhat difficult to interpret because on the one hand they advocate cognitive primacy, on the other they advocate a transactional model of causation between cognitions and emotions. Bandura (1986a) posits a bidirectional but asymmetrical relation between perceived self-efficacy and anxiety, pointing toward the primacy of (low) self-efficacy, but processing in a dynamic cycle of anxiety arousal and decreasing self-efficacy. However, regardless of such indication of a dynamic interaction between self-related cognitions and anxiety, it is similarly assumed in different theoretical conceptions that (test) anxiety results, if a person believes (1) that

*Extended version of a paper read at the conference on Educational Psychology in Tübingen, September 1987. Address correspondence to: Günter Krampen, University of Trier, Department of Psychology, Postfach 3825, D-5500 Trier, Federal Republic of Germany.

an achievement situation/performance test will hinder the attainment of subjectively highly valued objectives or events (e.g., a good grade and its consequences), and (2) that there are no (or at least only few/weak) alternative action possibilities (low self-efficacy in the terminology of Bandura, 1986a) and (3) no (or at least only weak) possibilities of controlling the occurrence of the objective or event (outcome expectancy in the terminology of Bandura, 1986a).

It is not difficult to identify the theoretical expectancy-value basis of this hypothesis (in terms of valences, situation-action or competence expectancies, and action-outcome expectancies; see, e.g., Pekrun, 1984), which—of course—remains highly situation- and action-specific. It makes sense to extend this approach to more general self-related cognitions because the construct of test anxiety implies a more or less generalized tendency of a person to show anxiety reactions before and in achievement situations. Furthermore, achievement situations in school are more or less new and ambiguous action situations, for which at least the anxious student a priori has no adequate cognitive representations.

The social learning theory of Rotter (1982) and its extension to an action-theoretical model of personality (Krampen, 1987a, 1988) postulate that the predictive value of situation- and action-specific person variables is low and that of domain-specific or generalized personality variables is high in such subjectively ill-defined situations. Dealing with domain-specific anxiety (like test anxiety in school) therefore requires the operationalization of self-related cognitions at a medium level in a hierachical model of personality, i.e., domain-specific measurements. Moreover, the action-theoretical model of personality, which stems from the social learning theory and a differentiated expectancy-value model (Krampen, 1987a, 1988), is an integrative frame of reference for situation- and action-specific person variables (e.g., different aspects of valences and expectancies) and personality variables (e.g., self-concept, control and value orientations, etc.). Such variables have up till now been studied mainly separately or additively at best. With reference to the above mentioned recent cognitive research program on test anxiety, domain-specific measurements of self-concepts of own competence and control orientations will be of special relevance.

Research results on the interdependency of test anxiety and domain-specific self-related cognitions can mostly be integrated into this theoretical frame of reference: test anxiety is correlated with low self-concepts of own competence and external control orientations (see, e.g., Hodapp, 1979; Jerusalem, 1984; Nicholls, 1979; Schwarzer, 1986; Van der Ploeg *et al.*, 1984). However, most studies use cross-sectional designs, which make it difficult to test directional causal hypotheses. Only Jerusalem (1984) and Hodapp (1979) analyzed longitudinally the causal relations between self-related cognitions and test anxiety in samples of German students. Jerusalem (1984) restricted himself to empirically testing the undirectional hypothesis that self-concept determines test anxiety; his data confirm this hypothesis for time intervals between 5 and 14 months. Hodapp (1979), who — however — observed only a time span of six weeks, tested the causal hypothesis bidirectionally with the help of cross-lagged correlation analyses and came to the same result. However some results and theoretical considerations allow the reverse causal relationship to be propagated, namely, test anxiety is the determinant of low self-concept and external control orientation (e.g., Jacobs and Strittmatter, 1979; see also the recent discussion between Bandura, 1986b; Kirsch, 1985, 1986; Wilkins, 1986). In addition there exists a third interpretation of the documented relations between (test) anxiety (or more generally: emotions) and self-related cognitions. This interpretation refers to the argument of a priori, conceptual interdependencies between emotions and cognitions (see, e.g., Brandtstädter, 1983; Smedslund, 1978) and, thus, their a priori confounding in conceptualization and measurement. Following this interpretation one can hardly differentiate between causes and effects: test anxiety and self-related cognitions are assumed to be related in a complex, language-transmitted way, which does not allow undirectional interpretations. The question of the adequacy of these three competing interpretations of the interdependency between test anxiety and self-related cognitions is of theoretical relevance as well as of practical relevance (see, e.g., Bandura, 1986b; Kirsch, 1985, 1986; Wilkins, 1986).

The present study focuses on:

(1) Descriptive analyses of the development of domain-specific anxiety and self-related cognitions in secondary school students of grades six to ten (questions regarding the stability/plasticity and the developmental gradients of these variables).

(2) The null hypothesis that there are no causal relationships between test anxiety and domain-specific self-related cognitions (aspects of competence and control orientations) is tested quasi-experimentally; in case that the alternative hypothesis (there is indication of a causal relationship) must be accepted, we will test the causal relationship bidirectionally over the course of time.

(3) Measures of generalized anxiety and locus of control are additionally included in the study, to test the hypothesis of relevance of domain-specific measurements in analyses of test anxiety.

METHOD

Sample

The analyses reported below are based on questionnaire data obtained from 346 secondary school students (grades six to ten) at two times of measurement (interval of ten months). The sample consists of 170 girls and 176 boys with a mean age of M = 13.4 years (SD = 1.36). In spite of a relatively high dropout rate at the second time of measurement (10.1 precent), which can be attributed to the fact that most students who had finished school could not be reached again, no significant dropout effects were observed on any of the variables considered with reference to the data of the first measurement, $t(344) \leq 1.44$.

Variables

The students answered the following questionnaires two times:

(1) *Anxiety Questionnaire for Students* (AFS; Wieczerkowski *et al.*, 1975) measuring test anxiety (PA), manifest anxiety (MA), negative attitude to school (SU) and social desirability (SE).

(2) The *domain-specific IPC Scales* (Krampen, 1984), a 24-item questionnaire constructed in accordance with Levenson's (1974) distinction between internality (I), powerful others control (P) and chance control (C) measuring these three aspects of locus of control orientations for problem-solving behavior in academic settings.

(3) A short, 3-item questionnaire for the measurement of the *self-concept of own mathematical competence* (SKM) measuring self-ratings of own competence by social, intraindividual and criterion-oriented comparisons of own mathematical achievements. The SKM includes self-ratings from bipolar 6-point scales for the

following items: (a) In comparison to other students my math achievements are high above *versus* below average; (b) In comparison to my former math achievements and grades, I have recently improved a lot *versus* I have gotten worse; (c) I understand the subject matter of math lessons very good *versus* very badly.

(4) *LOC-K Scale* (Rinke & Schneewind, 1978), a German version of the "Children Nowicki-Strickland I-E Scale" (Nowicki and Strickland, 1973) measuring highly generalized control orientations on the bipolar dimension of external versus internal locus of control.

Checks of split-half reliability and internal consistency confirm the usefulness of all questionnaires in the present sample for group analyses. The coefficients of internal consistency of all scales at the first and second time of measurement are listed in Table 1. All data were gathered anonymously; questionnaires were assigned to persons by using a stable code.

RESULTS

Different methods of analysis of variance and correlation analysis are used in the following. Given the number of statistical tests applied to the data, we controlled for chance findings within each family of analysis by using either overall tests with a posteriori comparisons or binomial tables to determine the number of significant findings likely to arise by chance given the number of statistical tests/coefficients tested (see Feild & Armenakis, 1974). For all analyses presented below the *number* of significant results obtained *within* each analysis can only be attributed to chance with a probability of $p < .001$. The significance level for each analysis was fixed at a minimum of $p < .05$.

Cross-sequential findings

In the following cross-sequential findings for test anxiety and the self-related cognitions are described, which were analyzed by nonorthogonal analyses of variance (ANOVA) involving the factors Grade Level (G) and Time of Measurement (T) with repeated measurement on the second factor. While no interaction effect of these factors reaches statistical significance, $F(4, 341) \leq 2.31$, almost all main effects turn out to be significant beyond alpha = .05. Effect sizes (in terms of the percentage of variance explained by a main effect) reach medium to large values. Of special interest is the high consistence of cross-sectional (factor G) and longitudinal (factor T) findings. Figures 1 to 5 illustrate these cross-sequential results. The scores of the dependent variables have been transformed to *T-scores* to assure the visual comparison of the presented developmental gradients.

For test anxiety (see figure 1) the main effects for Grade Level, $F(4,341) = 2.99$, $p < .01$ (explained variance: 18.1%), and Time of Measurement, $F(1,341) = 3.90$, $p < .05$ (explained variance: 8.7%), consistently confirm the cross-sectional findings of Schwarzer (1975) of a decrease with grade level/age in German secondary school students. Longitudinally there is—similar to the findings of Jerusalem (1984)—a weak increase in the test anxiety in grade six, but which could not be assured in a posteriori tests. A similar (weak) increase in test anxiety is observed longitudinally as well as cross-sectionally for grade nine, which reaches significance in the Duncan Test ($p < .05$). Thus, before starting the last school year there seems to be a weak increase in

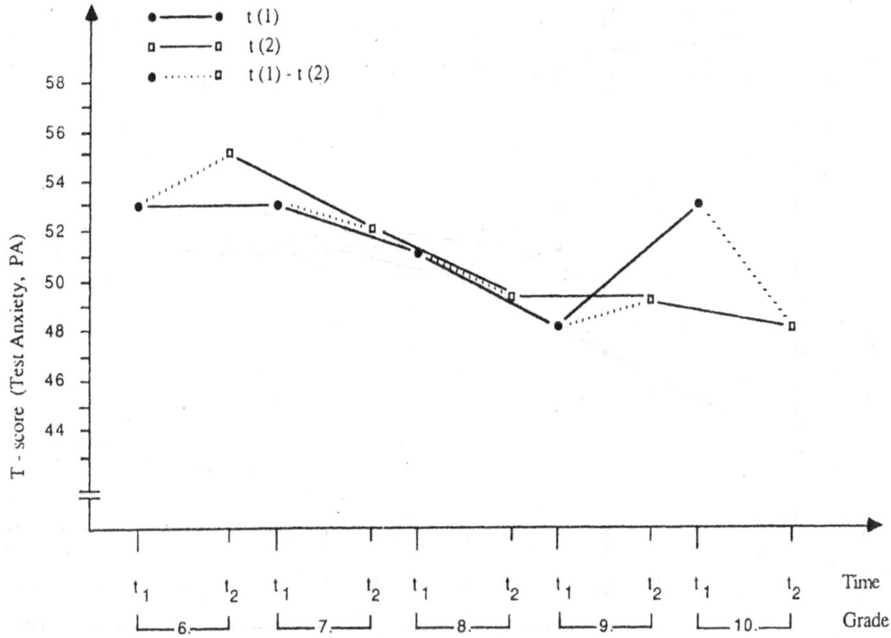

Figure 1 Cross-sequential Findings for Test Anxiety.

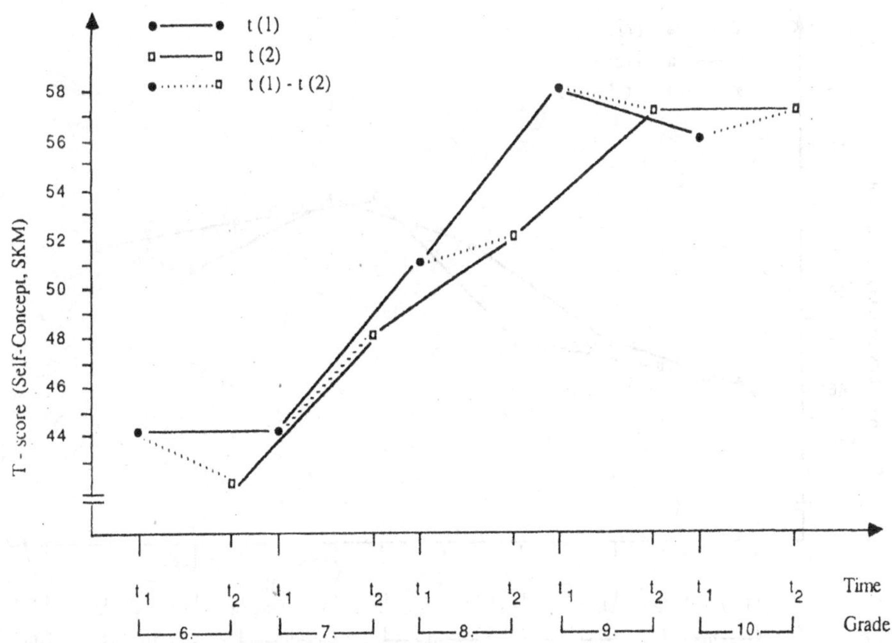

Figure 2 Cross-sequential Findings for the Self-Concept of own Mathematical Competence.

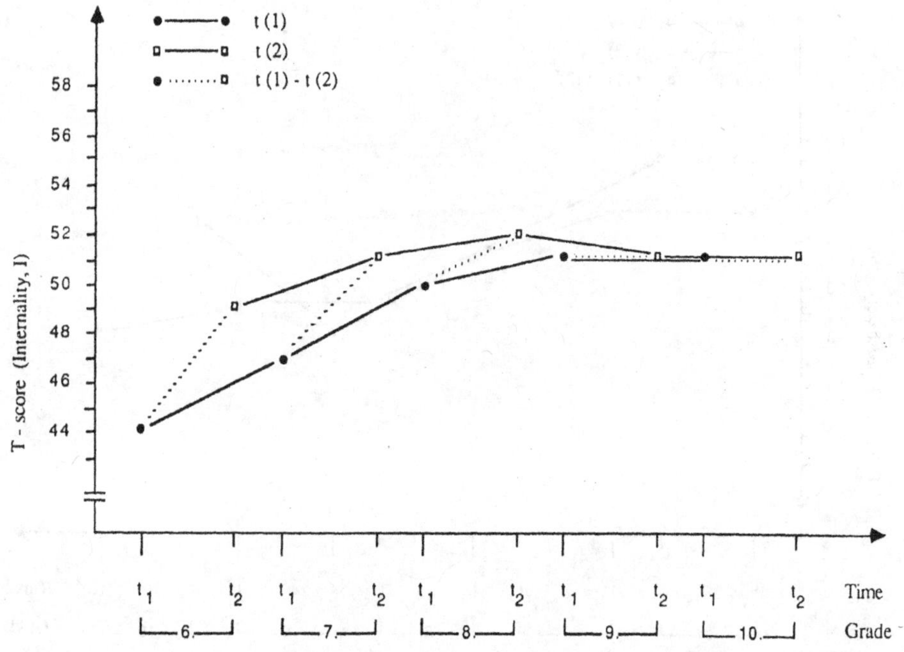

Figure 3 Cross-sequential Findings for Internality in Locus of Control for Problem-solving.

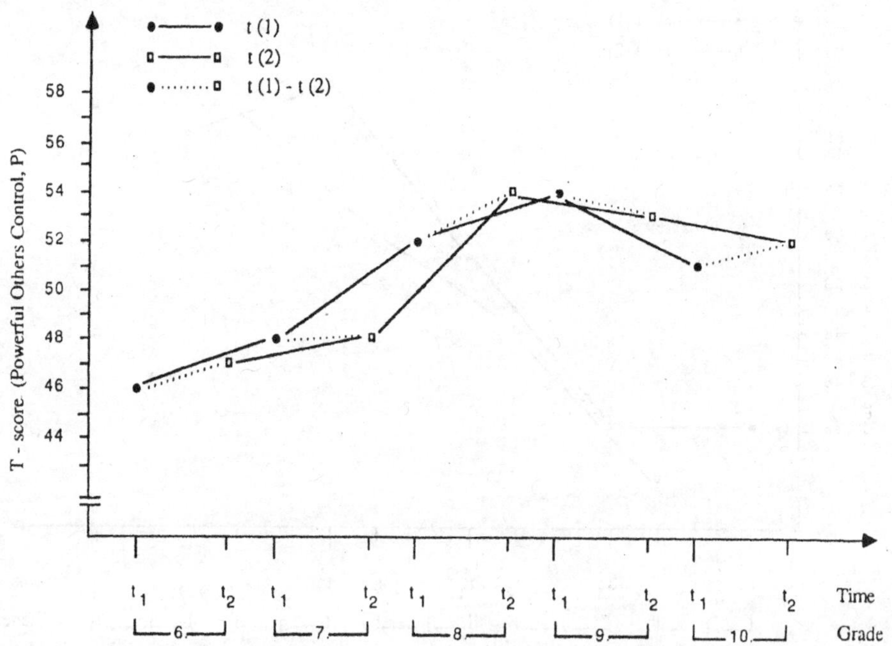

Figure 4 Cross-sequential Findings for Powerful Others Control in Locus of Control for Problem-solving.

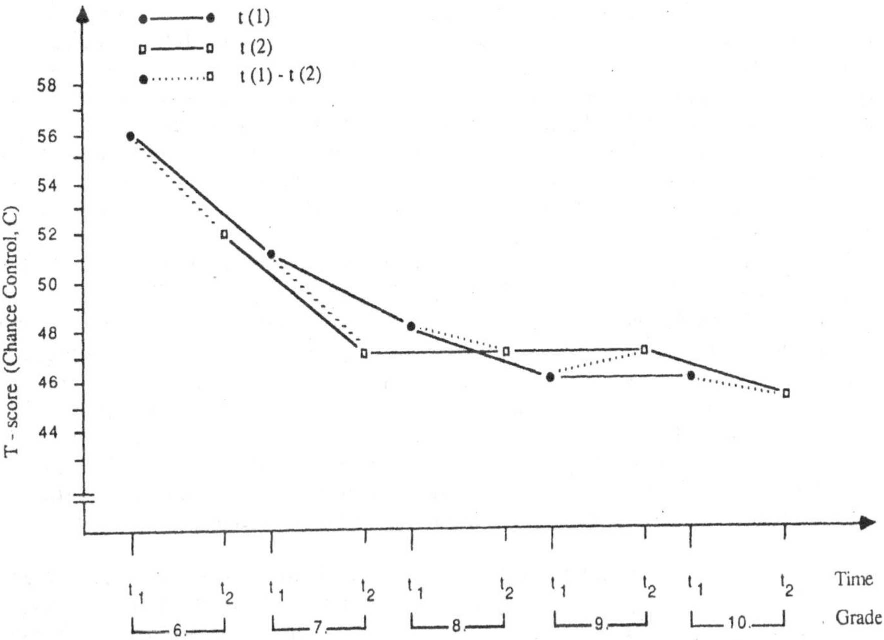

Figure 5 Cross-sequential Findings for Chance Control in Locus of Control for Problem-solving.

test anxiety; this effect disappears during the last year and does not stop the general trend of a decrease in test anxiety with age.

Likewise the longitudinal, $F(1,341) = 3.89, p < .05$ (explained variance: 10.5%), and cross-sectional findings, $F(4,341) = 3.78, p < .01$ (explained variance: 24.6%), for the development of the self-concept of own mathematical competence are in agreement. Besides statistically not assured weak decreases at grade six and nine there is a well-marked increase in this subject-specific self-perception. This differentiates the results of Larned and Muller (1979), who failed to find relevant differences in self-concept between grade six and nine cross-sectionally, and extends the longitudinal findings of Jerusalem (1984) for German secondary school students. Already, the symmetry of the developmental gradients for test anxiety and self-concept of own competence should be pointed out, which becomes obvious in comparing Figure 1 and Figure 2.

Internality in locus of control for problem-solving increases in longitudinal comparisons, $F(1,341) = 7.31, p < .01$ (explained variance: 18.2%), as well as in cross-sectional grade comparisons, $F(4,341) = 2.47, p < .05$ (explained variance: 12.4%; see Figure 3). For powerful others control (see Figure 4) only cross-sectionally a significant increase is confirmed, $F(4,341) = 2.66, p < .05$ (explained variance: 15.7%), whereas the longitudinal main effect does not reach significance, $F(1,341) = 2.77$. But it is worth noting that both gradients point toward an increase in domain-specific powerful others externality. Well-marked decreases in chance control for problem-solving behavior are documented with the longitudinal, $F(1,341) = 8.56, p < .01$ (explained variance: 19.0%), as well as with the cross-sectional data, $F(4,341) = 4.01,$

$p < .01$ (explained variance: 24.3%; see Figure 5). These results concerning the development of different aspects of domain-specific locus of control in adolescence confirm that different dimensions of control orientations show different developmental patterns—a result, which has been observed in recent studies in adulthood and old age (see Krampen, 1987b; Lachman, 1986) and cross-sectionally in adolescence (Connell, 1985). Such results have not been demonstrated longitudinally in adolescence, where research up to now has included only one-dimensional measures of locus of control (Prawatt, Jones & Hampton, 1979; Zerenga, Tseng & Greever, 1976).

General anxiety (MA) and generalized locus of control (LOC-K) do not show consistent developmental patterns. Whereas a cross-sectional main effect, $F(4,341) = 2.53$, $p < .05$ (explained variance: 11.0%), can be observed for unidimensional generalized locus of control (pointing toward an increase in internality with grade level), there is neither a corresponding main effect of Grade Level for general anxiety, $F(4,341) = 1.22$, nor longitudinal effects for both of the generalized personality variables measured, $F(1,341) \leq 3.17$. Thus, the developmental patterns of these two generalized variables do not fit into the developmental results for the domain-specific variables, which is a first hint to the adequacy of the hypothesis that domain-specific measurements are more useful in analyses of (domain-specific) test anxiety than generalized ones.

In the present frame of reference comparisons of Figure 1 (developmental gradient of test anxiety) with Figures 2 to 5 (gradients of self-related cognitions) are of special interest. These comparisons indicate a very high symmetry in the developmental patterns of test anxiety on the one hand and of the four domain-specific, self-related cognitions on the other. This symmetry includes even the statistically only partially confirmed developmental specifics at grade levels six and nine. But symmetries in developmental gradients point only toward covariations of the variables under consideration, not yet toward causal relationships between them. The results of corresponding analyses will be reported in the following.

Self-Related Cognition and Test Anxiety

The intercorrelations of all measured variables are presented in Table 1 separately for the first and second time of measurement. These synchronous correlations essentially confirm results of cross-sectional studies: generalized externality in locus of control is correlated with test and general anxiety, a low self-concept is correlated with test anxiety, general anxiety is correlated with test anxiety, etc. (see, e.g., Jopt, 1978; Krohne *et al.*, 1986; Wieczerkowski *et al.*, 1975). Noteworthy is only the remarkably high stability of these correlative relations: the coefficients of the second time of measurement rarely differ from those at the first time of measurement.

The autocorrelations of all variables (see the main diagonal in Table 2) show a medium developmental stability. In particular, they illustrate the plasticity of test anxiety and domain-specific self-related cognitions in adolescence and point out the need of (longitudinal) studies that search for the developmental determinants of such age-related changes. However, autocorrelations of the variables are only somewhat lower than their reliabilities (see Table 1). This impedes unequivocal interpretations of their developmental plasticity.

Table 2 also includes the cross-lagged correlations of all variables, whose numerical values drop markedly in comparison with the synchronous correlations. The relationships between all variables were analyzed bidirectionally by the *quasi-experimental* technique of cross-lagged correlation analysis (see, e.g., Kenny, 1979),

Table 1. Internal consistency as well as time-synchronous correlations of all variables at the first (above main diagonal) and second time of measurement (below main diagonal)[a]

Variable	SK	LOC-K	I	P	C	PA	MA	r_{tt}
Self-Concept (SK)	1·00	−0·43	0·58	−0·42	−0·59	−0·47	−0·39	0·81
Generalized Locus of Control (LOC-K)	−0·47	1·00	−0·21	0·27	0·24	0·35	0·45	0·59
Internality (I)	0·61	−0·27	1·00	−0·35	−0·23	−0·23	−0·13	0·64
Powerful Others Control (P)	−0·40	0·31	−0·31	1·00	0·57	0·38	0·35	0·67
Chance Control (C)	−0·51	0·27	−0·20	0·48	1·00	0·30	0·34	0·59
Test Anxiety (PA)	−0·50	0·41	−0·27	0·36	0·29	1·00	0·71	0·79
Manifest Anxiety (MA)	−0·32	0·40	−0·11	0·43	0·40	0·71	1·00	0·77
Int. Consistency (r_{tt})	0·77	0·58	0·71	0·69	0·65	0·77	0·75	—

[a] $r > 0·11$, $p < 0·05$

Table 2. Autocorrelations and cross-lagged correlations of all variables[a]

First time of measurement	Second time of measurement						
	SK	LOC-K	I	P	C	PA	MA
Self-Concept (SK)	0·69	−0·29	0·39	−0·37	−0·43	−0·27	−0·17
Generalized Locus of Control (LOC-K)	−0·32	0·44	0·18	−0·22	−0·12	0·11	0·19
Internality (I)	0·53	0·16	0·59	−0·22	−0·17	−0·24	−0·13
Powerful Others Control (P)	−0·32	−0·25	−0·13	0·64	0·35	0·08	0·07
Chance Control (C)	−0·41	−0·17	−0·14	0·30	0·58	0·23	0·12
Test Anxiety (PA)	−0·12	0·08	−0·08	0·04	0·07	0·71	0·64
General Anxiety (MA)	−0·15	0·13	−0·08	0·06	0·14	0·61	0·74

[a] Interval of ten months, $r > 0·11$, $p < 0·05$

which gives at least some clues for possible causal relations. The null hypothesis that there are no causal relations between variable pairs can be rejected with reference to a significant z-value in the Pearson-Filon test for the following pairs of variables:

(1) A low self-concept of own mathematical competence precedes (high) test anxiety ($z = 3.002$, $p < .01$). Figure 6 illustrates this finding exemplarily for the results presented in the following.

(2) Low internality in locus of control for problem-solving precedes (high) test anxiety ($z = 2.833$, $p < .01$).

(3) High chance control in locus of control for problem-solving precedes (high) test anxiety ($z = 2.836$, $p < .01$).

(4) High internality in locus of control for problem-solving precedes a high self-concept of own mathematical competence ($z = 2.913$, $p < .01$).

Differences between all the other cross-lagged correlations (see Table 2) are not significant in the Pearson-Filon test, $z \leq 1.557$. Therefore, the null hypothesis that there are no causal relations between these variable pairs and that other variables must

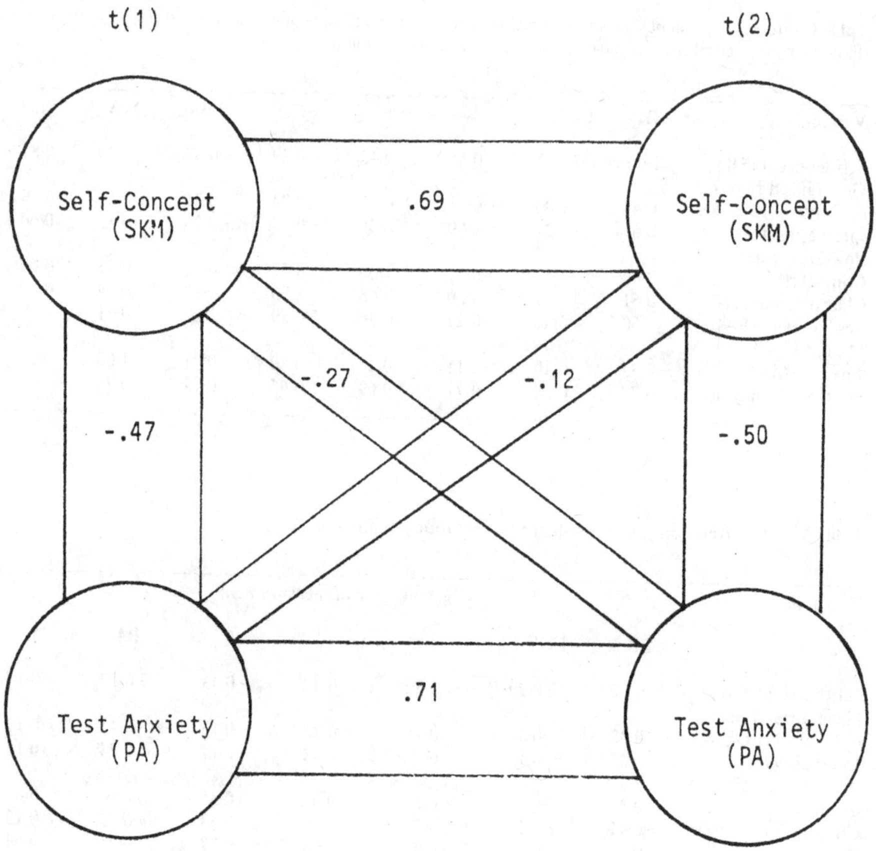

Figure 6 Cross-lagged Correlations for "Self-Concept of own competence" and "Test Anxiety" (Time Interval: Ten Months).

be responsible for their variability must be accepted. Thus, exclusively the domain-specific self-related cognitions (self-concept of own competence, internality and chance control) are quasi-experimentally confirmed to be antecedents of test anxiety. But it is worth noting that these quasi-experimental results may only be interpreted as hints for causal relations, which need experimental confirmation. To complete the picture, the probability of obtaining the presented number of significant differences (Pearson-Filon test) by chance in this group of cross-lagged analyses is $p < .001$.

Finally time-synchronous and cross-lagged multiple regression analyses were computed (1) to evaluate the relative prognostic value of the domain-specific self-related cognitions for test anxiety and (2) to compare the quantitative and qualitative stability of time-synchronous and cross-lagged results in a multivariate analysis. The results (see Table 3) show that the multiple correlations reach significance in all three analyses, but that cross-lagged prediction distinctly explains less variance of test anxiety than the two time-synchronous "predictions" (which are—of course—no predictions in the real sense of the word). Besides this quantitative difference there is also a qualitative one: structure coefficients of the cross-lagged multiple correlation point toward the (relative) high prognostic value of (low) self-concept, (low) internality

Table 3. Time-synchronous and cross-lagged multiple regression of domain-specific self-related cognitions for test anxiety[a]

Predictor Variable	First measurement (t_1)		Second measurement (t_2)		Cross-lagged (t_1-t_2)	
	r_c	st.	r_c	st.	r_c	st.
Self-Concept	−0·47	−0·89	−0·50	−0·94	−0·27	−0·82
Internality	−0·23	−0·44	−0·27	−0·51	−0·24	−0·73
Powerful Others Control	0·38	0·72	0·36	0·67	0·08	0·24
Chance Control	0·30	0·57	0·29	0·54	0·23	0·70
Multiple Correlation (R)	0·53*		0·53*		0·33*	
Multiple Determination (R^2)	0·28		0·28		0·11	
Rho	0·52		0·53		0·31	

*$p<0·01$.
[a] r_c = predictor-criterion correlation; st. = structure coefficients; $r_c \geq |0·11|$, $p<0·05$.

and (high) chance control; in contrast to these cross-lagged findings, chance control plays a minor role in the time-synchronous analyses. Instead, powerful others control, whose predictive value in the cross-lagged analysis is lowest, is the second best "predictor" of test anxiety in the two time-synchronous analyses (see Table 3).

DISCUSSION

By means of cross-sequential data the relevance of domain-specific self-related cognitions for the development of test anxiety in German secondary school students has been confirmed empirically. Already the inspection of the developmental gradients, which are in accordance with other results (see, e.g., Jerusalem, 1984; Krampen, 1987b), leads to the cross-sectionally as well as longitudinally confirmed impression of strong interdependencies between test anxiety on the one hand and self-concept of own competence, internality, powerful others control and chance control in domain-specific self-related cognitions on the other. The results of cross-lagged correlation analyses (involving a time interval of ten months) confirm this impression inference-statistically. Most findings support the hypothesis of social cognitive theories that self-related cognitions precede test anxiety and are causal for its development (e.g. Bandura, 1986a, 1986b; Schwarzer, 1986). Of course, the quasi-experimental design of the present study must be considered. The results only intimate possible unidirectional causations, which must be confirmed with experimental data.

At the same time comparisons between the results of time-synchronous (cross-sectional) and cross-lagged (longitudinal) analyses suggest that cross-sectional data tend to overestimate developmental relations quantitatively. The relationship between self-related cognitions and anxiety is better represented by current cognitions than by past cognitions. The demand for longitudinal studies within a developmental and etiological perspective is accentuated by the finding of a qualitative difference between cross-sectional and longitudinal results: whereas powerful others control orientations of students have a very high prognostic value for test anxiety in the time-synchronous analyses, they turned out to be of lowest importance in the cross-lagged, longitudinal predictions. Instead, fatalistic (chance) control orientations have a relatively high prognostic value for test anxiety.

In the present study the heuristic value of a hierarchical model of personality could be confirmed again (see Krampen, 1987a, 1988). The action-theoretical model of personality distinguishes between different levels of generalization in personality description and relates them by the transmission of the subjective perception of an action or life situation to statements about the optimal level of measurement. Consistent with our hypothesis, general anxiety and generalized locus of control play minor parts in the development of test anxiety in students. If one is interested in domain-specific variable (like test anxiety in school), it is best to apply domain-specific measurements of all variables (see also Bandura, 1986a). This is especially true when action or life situations are under consideration, which are more or less new and/or ambiguous for the individual.

Future research should consider additional aspects of domain specificity (like subject-matter related cognitions and anxieties; see, e.g., Lukesch, 1982) and construct differentiation (like worry and emotionality; see, e.g., Jerusalem, 1984; Lukesch & Kandlbinder, 1986; Schwarzer, 1986) which have been neglected in the present study. The same is true for situational, environmental and contextual determinants of test anxiety in students. The recent propagation of social cognitive approaches in anxiety research (and — in part — that of psychophysiological approaches) and the resulting concentration on person variables should not result in the neglect of such structural and contextual variables which have proved to be highly relevant correlates and determinants of test anxiety (see, e.g., Schwarzer, 1975, 1981). Besides methods which focus on the self-related cognitions of students and which are confirmed as essential by the presented results (see also Bandura, 1986a, 1986b), psychological prevention and modification of test anxiety must apply techniques which focus on the modification of achievement situations in school (e.g., optimizing their transparency and clearness; see, e.g., Gifford & Marston, 1966) and must consider the social and contextual determinants of test anxiety as well (see already Schreiber, 1899).

References

Bandura, A. (1986a). *Social foundations of thought and action: A social cognitive theory*. Englewood Cliffs, NJ: Prentice-Hall.

Bandura, A. (1986b). Fearful expectations and avoidant actions as coeffects of perceived self-inefficacy. *American Psychologist*, **41**, 1389–1391.

Brandtstädter, J. (1983). Emotion, Kognition, Handlungen: Konzeptuelle Beziehungen. In L.H. Eckensberger & E. Lantermann (Ed.), *Emotion und Reflexivität* (pp. 252–266). Munich, FRG: Urban & Schwarzenberg.

Connell, J.P. (1985). A new multidimensional measure of children's perceptions of control. *Child Development*, **56**, 1018–1041.

Feild, H.S. & Armanakis, A.A. (1974). On use of multiple tests of significance in psychological research. *Psychological Reports*, **35**, 427–431.

Gifford, E.M. & Marston, A.R. (1966). Test anxiety, reading ratio, and task experience. *Journal of Educational Psychology*, **59**, 303–306.

Hodapp, V. (1979). Angst und Schulleistung: Zur Frage der Richtung des Einflusses. In L.H. Eckensberger (Ed.), *Bericht über den 31. Kongreß der DGfPs in Mannheim 1978. Band 2* (pp. 17–21). Göttingen, FRG: Hogrefe.

Jacobs, B. & Strittmatter, P. (1979). *Der schulängstliche Schüler*. Munich, FRG: Urban & Schwarzenberg.

Jerusalem, M. (1984). *Selbstbezogene Kognitionen in schulischen Bezugsgruppen. Band 1*. Berlin: Free University of Berlin, Institute of Psychology.

Jopt, U.-J. (1978). *Selbstkonzept und Ursachenerklärung in der Schule*. Bochum, FRG: Kamp.

Kenny, D.A. (1979). *Correlation and causation*. New York: Wiley.

Kirsch, I. (1985). Response expectancy as a determinant of experience and behavior. *American Psychologist*, **40**, 1189–1202.

Kirsch, I. (1986). Response expectancy and phobic anxiety: A reply to Wilkins and Bandura. *American Psychologist*, **41**, 1391–1393.

Krampen, G. (1984). *Feldexperimentelle Prüfung der Effekte von Lehrerkommentaren zu Zensuren in Prüfungsarbeiten auf Schüler* (Trierer Psychologische Berichte 11, Heft 2). Trier, FRG: University of Trier, Department of Psychology.

Krampen, G. (1987a). *Handlungstheoretische Persönlichkeitspsychologie*. Göttingen, FRG: Hogrefe.

Krampen, G. (1987b). Entwicklung von Kontrollüberzeugungen: Thesen zu Forschungsstand und Perspektiven. *Zeitschrift für Entwicklungspsychologie und Pädagogische Psychologie*, **19**, 195–227.

Krampen, G. (1988). Toward an action-theoretical model of personality. *European Journal of Personality*, **2**, 39–55.

Krohne, H.W., Kohlmann, C.-W. & Leidig, S. (1986). Erziehungsstildeterminanten kindlicher Ängstlichkeit, Kompetenzerwartungen und Kompetenzen. *Zeitschrift für Entwicklungspsychologie und Pädagogische Psychologie*, **18**, 70–88.

Lachman, M.E. (1986). Locus of control in aging research. *Journal of Psychology and Aging*, **1**, 34–40.

Larned, D.T. & Muller, D. (1979). Development of self-concept in grades one through nine. *Journal of Psychology*, **102**, 143–155.

Lazarus, R.S. & Launier, R. (1978). Stress-related transactions between person and environment. In L. Pervin & M. Lewis (Eds.), *Perspectives in interactional psychology* (pp. 287–327). New York: Academic Press.

Lukesch, H. (1982). Fachspezifische Prüfungsängste. *Psychologie in Erziehung und Unterricht*, **29**, 257–267.

Lukesch, H. & Kandlbinder, R. (1986). Zeitlicher Verlauf und Bedingungsfaktoren der Prüfungsangstkomponenten Besorgtheit und Aufgeregtheit. *Zeitschrift für Entwicklungspsychologie und Pädagogische Psychologie*, **18**, 56–69.

Nicholls, J.G. (1979). Development of perception of own attainment and causal attributions for success and failure in reading. *Journal of Educational Psychology*, **71**, 94–99.

Nowicki, S. & Strickland, B.R. (1973). A locus of control scale for children. *Journal of Consulting and Clinical Psychology*, **40**, 148–154.

Pekrun, R. (1984). An expectancy-value model of anxiety. In H.M. van der Ploeg, R. Schwarzer & C.D. Spielberger (Eds.), *Advances in test anxiety research. Vol. 3.* Lisse/Hillsdale, NJ: Swets/Erlbaum.

Peterson, C. & Seligman, M.E.P. (1984). Causal explanations as a risk factor for depression: Theory and evidence. *Psychological Review*, **91**, 347–374.

Prawatt, R.S., Jones, H. & Hampton, J. (1979). Longitudinal study of attitude development in pre-, early-, and later adolescent samples. *Journal of Educational Psychology*, **71**, 363–369.

Rinke, R. & Schneewind, K.A. (1978). *LOC-E und LOC-K* (Arbeitsbericht 26 aus dem EKB-Projekt). Munich, FRG: University of Munich, Department of Psychology.

Rotter, J.B. (1982). *The development and application of a social learning theory. Selected papers*. New York: Praeger.

Schreiber, H. (1899). Gegen Prüfungen und Noten. *Zeitschrift für Philosophie und Pädagogik*, **6**, 31–38.

Schwarzer, R. (1975). *Schulangst und Lernerfolg*. Düsseldorf, FRG: Schwann.

Schwarzer, R. (1981). *Streß, Angst und Hilflosigkeit*. Stuttgart, FRG: Kohlhammer.

Schwarzer, R. (Ed.) (1986). *Self-related cognitions in anxiety and motivation*. Hillsdale, NJ: Erlbaum.

Smedslund, J. (1978). Bandura's theory of self-efficacy: A set of common sense theorems. *Scandinavian Journal of Psychology*, **19**, 1–14.

Van der Ploeg, H.M., Schwarzer, R. & Spielberger, C.D. (Eds.) (1984). *Advances in test anxiety research. Vol. 3.* Lisse/Hillsdale, NJ: Swets/Erlbaum

Wieczerkowski, W., Nickel, H., Janowski, A., Fittkau, B & Rauer, W. (1975). *Angstfragebogen für Schüler (AFS)*. Braunschweig, FRG: Westermann

Wilkins, W. (1986). Invalid evidence for expectancies as causes: Comment on Kirsch. *American Psychologist*, **41**, 1387–1389

Zerenga, W.D., Tseng, M.S. & Greever, K.B. (1976). Stability and congruent validity of the Rotter internal-external locus of control scale. *Educational & Psychological Measurement*, **36**, 473–475.

ANXIETY AND ATTENTION

MICHAEL W. EYSENCK*

Royal Holloway and Bedford New College, University of London, UK

Normal individuals high and low in anxiety differ from each other in their attentional functioning in various ways. More specifically, they differ with respect to the content, capacity, distractibility and selectivity of attention. Any complete theoretical account of anxiety and attention will have to account for all four differences, although it is likely that these various aspects of attentional functioning are dynamically interrelated. Anxious patients with generalized anxiety disorder appear to differ from normal controls in similar ways, and there is evidence that some aspects at least of non-normal attentional functioning in anxious patients may reflect a vulnerability factor rather than merely an anxious mood state.

KEY WORDS: Trait anxiety, clinical anxiety, attention, distractibility, working memory.

The term "attention" is one of the most notoriously vague theoretical constructs in psychology. Several theorists, including Allport (1980), have argued that the construct should be abandoned altogether. According to him, "attention" is frequently used as a synonym for the less acceptable term "consciousness", but without an adequate specification of its mode of functioning. In addition, the theoretical construct of "attention" has tended to be associated with the view that there is a single general pool of processing resources, whereas the evidence increasingly points to the existence of several different processing mechanisms or resources.

While there is some substance in these criticisms, they suggest caution in the use of the term "attention" rather than total abandonment. A reasonable attempt to solve the definitional problem was made by William James (1890), who stated: "It (i.e. attention) is the taking possession by the mind, in clear and vivid form, of one out of what seem several simultaneously possible objects or trains of thought. Focalisation, concentration, of consciousness are of its essence. It implies withdrawal from some things in order to deal effectively with others" (pp. 403–404).

The issue of whether there is a single global processing resource ("attention", "consciousness", or whatever) or numerous specific processing resources can most appropriately be resolved by assuming that there is a hierarchical processing system. The attentional system is at the top of the hierarchy, and the more specific processing systems are at the bottom. The working memory model proposed by Baddeley and Hitch (e.g. Baddeley, 1986) illustrates this theoretical approach.

In summary, it is perfectly possible to incorporate the "attention" construct within a reasonably adequate theoretical model of the information-processing system. From the perspective of individual differences, there are various aspects of attentional functioning that need to be considered. First, there is the issue of the *content* of the information to which attention is directed. Individuals high and low in anxiety may well differ in their tendency to process threat-related information. Secondly, there is

* Address correspondence to: Professor Michael W. Eysenck, Department of Psychology, Royal Holloway and Bedford New College, University of London, Egham Hill, Egham, Surrey TW20 0EX, UK.

the issue of the *capacity* of the attentional system as a function of the level of anxiety. Thirdly, there is the question of *distractibility*. Those high and low in anxiety may differ in their ability to maintain attentional focus on a particular stimulus object or experimental task in the presence of extraneous stimuli. Fourthly, there is the issue of attentional *selectivity*, i.e. the extent to which attention is directed to one set of stimuli rather than being spread among a number of sets of stimuli.

Thus, there are at least four different ways in which individual differences in anxiety might relate to attentional functioning. There are two main ways in which groups high and low in anxiety level have been obtained in order to test theoretical predictions. First, normal individuals who are extreme scorers on questionnaire measures of anxiety (e.g. the trait anxiety score from Spielberger's State-Trait Anxiety Inventory) have been compared on a number of attentional measures. Secondly, anxious patients (e.g. with a diagnosis of generalized anxiety disorder) have been compared with normal controls. It has been assumed by Eysenck and Mathews (1987) that normals scoring high on trait anxiety are more vulnerable to clinical anxiety than those scoring low, although unfortunately there is very little relevant evidence available. If the assumption is correct, it might be expected that those attentional differences between normals high and low in trait anxiety would tend to be found also when comparing anxious patients with normal controls. However, since anxious patients are in a highly anxious mood state as well as generally being high in trait anxiety, the converse would not necessarily apply.

Whatever the precise relationship between high trait anxiety in normals and anxiety disorders in patients, it seems unfortunate that there is so little experimental evidence concerned with attentional processes in anxious patients. In fact, clinical observations of anxious patients (e.g. Beck and Emery, 1985) often accord with experimental data obtained from normals high in trait anxiety, but such observations are obviously not an adequate substitute for proper experimental evidence.

ATTENTIONAL CONTENT

A theoretical assumption used in research by Mathews and myself is that there are individual differences in a selective mechanism that determines how processing resources are allocated among stimuli differing in their threat value. More specifically, if one threatening and one neutral stimulus are presented concurrently, then one might anticipate that those high in anxiety would tend to allocate more processing resources to the threatening than to the neutral stimulus, whereas those low in anxiety would do the opposite. This selective hypothesis can be contrasted with the theoretical formulation of Byrne (1964). He proposed that repressors avoid threatening stimuli, whereas sensitizers approach threatening stimuli, and he devised the Repression-Sensitization Scale to permit individuals to be classified as repressors or sensitizers. Since scores on the Repression-Sensitization Scale correlate approximately +0·85 with scores on the major measures of trait anxiety (Watson and Clark, 1984), repressors are basically individuals who are low in trait anxiety, whereas sensitizers are those who are high in trait anxiety.

The evidence has been reviewed elsewhere (e.g. Eysenck and Mathews, 1987), and will only be mentioned very briefly here. Most experiments to test Byrne's (1964) hypothesis have involved paradigms in which only one stimulus at a time is presented, and the results of such experiments have been "overwhelmingly negative" (Watson and Clark, 1984, p. 481). In contrast, several studies have provided convincing evidence in favour of the selective hypothesis. This hypothesis has been supported in studies of normals (Broadbent, personal communication; Eysenck, MacLeod and Mathews, 1987) and in studies using patients with generalized anxiety disorder (MacLeod, Mathews and Tata, 1986). In most of these studies, some of the threatening stimuli referred to physical health concerns (e.g. injury, agony), whereas others referred to social threat (e.g. criticized, ashamed). The typical finding is that allocation of processing resources is not affected by the nature of the threatening stimuli.

There is some evidence that the selective biases are influenced both by trait anxiety and by current mood state. The tendencies of normals high in trait anxiety to allocate processing resources to threatening stimuli and of normals low in trait anxiety to do the opposite were enhanced shortly before an important examination in unpublished data obtained by Mathews and MacLeod.

The general notion that anxious individuals selectively allocate processing resources to threatening rather than to non-threatening stimuli corresponds well with the theoretical views of Beck and Emery (1985). They made numerous clinical observations on patients with anxiety disorder, and concluded as follows: "An anxious patient will be hypersensitive to any aspects of a situation that are potentially harmful, but will not respond to its benign or positive aspects" (p. 33).

The issue of the stage of processing at which the selective biases are operating has been addressed by Eysenck (in press). In essence, the evidence suggests that the biases can occur at the pre-attentive level. However, since pre-attentive processes play an important part in determining attentional processes, these biases form an important part of the relationship between anxiety and attention.

The focus so far has been on selective biases as they relate to external stimuli. It is an interesting issue whether similar biases exist with respect to attention to information stored in long-term memory. The fact that individuals high in trait anxiety tend to worry much more than those low in trait anxiety (Borkovec, Robinson, Pruzinsky and DePree, 1983) is consistent with the notion of selective biases for stored information. However, it is extremely difficult to decide whether anxious individuals worry more because of their processing strategies or because they have more worry-related information stored in long-term memory (cf. Eysenck, 1984).

ATTENTIONAL CAPACITY

Eysenck (1979) proposed that individuals high in trait anxiety, especially when also high in state anxiety, have less working memory capacity available for task performance than those low in trait anxiety. He suggested that the reason for this was that worry, self-concern and other task-irrelevant cognitive activities pre-empt some of the limited capacity of working memory in individuals high in anxiety, a notion that is in line with several previous theoretical formulations (e.g. Wine, 1971). The working memory system itself (Baddeley, 1986) consists of a central executive resembling attention and two more specific components (the articulatory loop and the visuo-spatial sketch pad). The system as a whole is involved in active processing and in the temporary storage of information.

The most straightforward prediction from Eysenck's (1979) hypothesis is that adverse effects of anxiety on task performance should be greater with tasks making substantial demands on the capacity of working memory. Some of the earlier experimental evidence supporting this prediction was discussed by Eysenck (1982). However, stronger evidence indicating that high anxiety is associated with lower available working memory capacity has been obtained since then by Eysenck (1985) and by Darke (1986).

In summary, it seems reasonably clear that anxiety affects the amount of working memory capacity available for task performance, but the precise mechanisms involved remain somewhat obscure. However, it is an interesting speculation that the selective biases discussed in the previous section play a part. More specifically, the tendency of those high in anxiety to allocate processing resources selectively to threat-related information implies that there would be reduced allocation of processing resources to neutral information such as that incorporated within most cognitive tasks. As a consequence, there would be reduced working memory capacity available for the processing of the cognitive task.

A very similar theoretical position was adopted by Beck and Emery (1985) on the basis of therapeutic sessions with patients having anxiety disorders. According to them, "Because the patient 'uses up' a large part of his cognitive capacity by scanning for threatening stimuli, the amount available for attending to other demands is severely restricted" (p. 31).

DISTRACTIBILITY

Theorists differ in their views concerning the relationship between anxiety on the one hand, and distractibility and concentration on the other hand. According to Easterbrook (1959), anxiety augments attention to task stimuli, and so presumably increases the ability to resist distraction. In contrast, Wachtel (1967) proposed that anxiety leads to increased attentional lability, which implies that anxiety increases susceptibility to distraction. A similar theoretical position was adopted by Korchin (1964). His clinical observations led him to the following conclusion. "The anxious patient is unable to concentrate, hyper-responsive, and hyper-distractible."

Anxiety was found to reduce distractibility in a few experiments, but the more common finding is that those high in trait anxiety are more distractible than those low in trait anxiety (Dornic, 1977; Dornic and Fernäeus, 1981; Graydon, personal communication; Pallak, Pittman, Heller and Munson, 1975). Mathews, Eysenck and Richards (in work discussed by Eysenck, in press) discovered that patients with generalized anxiety disorder were less able than normal controls to ignore an unwanted stimulus on a modified version of the Tipper paradigm (Tipper, 1985). However, it should be noted that there is increasing evidence (Tipper, personal communication) that an inability to ignore unwanted stimuli is not specific to anxiety, but is also found with other dimensions of individual differences.

We have seen that susceptibility to distraction from *external* stimuli and events is affected by an individual's anxiety level. It is probable that anxious individuals are more likely than non-anxious ones to be distracted from an ongoing task by *internal* worries and preoccupations, a view that has been proposed by several theorists. For example, Wine (1971) argued as follows: "The highly test-anxious person responds to evaluative testing conditions with ruminative, self-evaluative worry, and, thus, cannot direct adequate attention to task-relevant variables" (p. 99).

Why should anxious individuals tend to be more distractible than non-anxious ones? The pre-attentive selective bias towards threatening stimuli shown by anxious individuals may be relevant. The tendency to allocate extra processing resources to threatening stimuli implies the withdrawal of resources from the ongoing task and subsequent disruption of task performance, i.e. distraction. However, this cannot be the whole story, because anxious individuals are characteristically more distractible than non-anxious ones even when the distracting stimuli are neutral in content. A more important factor may be the tendency of anxious individuals to scan the environment in order to detect threat, which could produce extra processing of distracting stimuli.

ATTENTIONAL SELECTIVITY

Easterbrook (1959) argued that states of high emotionality, arousal and anxiety all produce similar effects on cue utilization. The range of cues used (i.e. breadth of attention) reduces as anxiety or arousal increases, which "will reduce the proportion of irrelevant cues employed, and so improve performance. When all irrelevant cues have been excluded, however, . . . further reduction in the number of cues employed can only affect relevant cues, and proficiency will fall" (p. 193).

Easterbrook's (1959) hypothesis has been tested by using a paradigm in which a primary and a secondary task are performed concurrently. The general prediction is that heightened anxiety should have a more adverse effect on performance of the secondary than of the primary task. However, as Eysenck (1982) pointed out, "There are nine possible combinations of main-task and subsidiary-task performance, only three of which are clearly incompatible with Easterbrook's hypothesis; in those cases, arousal either has a less detrimental effect or a greater enhancing effect on the subsidiary task than on the main task" (pp. 50–51).

Eysenck (1982) reviewed 10 experimental tests of Easterbrook's (1959) hypothesis based on selecting extreme groups on anxiety from questionnaire assessment. The modal findings are that the high and low anxiety groups do not differ on performance of the primary task, but that the high anxiety group is significantly inferior to the low anxiety group on secondary task performance. These findings are consistent with Easterbrook's hypothesis, but there is some dispute about the appropriate interpretation. Easterbrook argued that attentional narrowing under high anxiety reflected the operation of a relatively passive and automatic process, but an alternative theoretical view is preferable. Given the reduced available capacity of working memory in anxious individuals, it is entirely reasonable for them actively to restrict the limited available attentional and other processing resources to those environment stimuli associated with the primary task.

CONCLUSIONS

The main thrust of this article is to argue that theoretical discussions of differences in attentional functioning between individuals high and low in anxiety have typically been over-simplified. Several such differences can be identified.

1. Those high in anxiety have a pre-attentive selective bias favoring the processing of threatening rather than neutral stimuli, whereas those low in anxiety have the opposite bias. There is as a consequence a difference in the content of the information to which attention is directed.
2. Those high in anxiety have less available working memory capacity to handle cognitive tasks than those low in anxiety. Thus, there is a difference in available capacity.
3. Those high in anxiety are typically more distractible than those low in anxiety.

4. Those high in anxiety exhibit greater attentional selectivity than those low in anxiety.

Although the content, capacity, distractibility and selectivity of attention are all conceptually distinct aspects of attentional functioning, it is entirely possible that in practice they are dynamically related to each other. For example, if an anxious person has a pre-attentive bias in favor of threat-related stimuli, then this could produce enhanced distractibility, and distractibility could in turn produce reduced available working memory capacity. More research is needed to investigate the interrelationships among these various aspects of attentional functioning.

In terms of practical relevance, it is especially important to consider possible attentional malfunctioning in anxious patients. The scattered evidence suggests that attentional functioning in anxious patients with generalized anxious disorder resembles that in normals high in trait anxiety, but no firm conclusions can be drawn as yet. A crucial issue here is that of causality: is attentional malfunctioning in anxious patients one of the factors involved in the aetiology of clinical anxiety, or is it merely a consequence of being in a clinically anxious state? Of course, this dichotomous view of attentional functioning may be over-simplified, and it is entirely possible that some aspects of attentional functioning do not correspond precisely to either category. The issue of causality may be addressed by considering individuals who have recovered from clinical anxiety. If they fail to exhibit the attentional malfunctioning of anxious patients, then presumably attentional malfunctioning is simply a reflection of anxious mood state. However, if recovered anxious individuals exhibit the same attentional malfunctioning as anxious patients, then the implication is that attentional malfunctioning reflects a long-term vulnerability factor that does not depend on the presence of a clinically anxious mood state.

The limited relevant evidence is discussed by Eysenck (in press). It was found by Mathews, Eysenck and Richards that both currently anxious patients and recovered anxious patients are less able than normal controls to ignore unwanted stimuli in the Tipper paradigm described earlier. The implication of these findings is that an inability to ignore unwanted stimuli reflects a vulnerability factor rather than anxious mood state. In more general terms, it might be expected that heavily over-learned, relatively automatic processes would tend to be associated with vulnerability to clinical anxiety, whereas more controlled processes would tend to reflect current anxious mood state.

In essence, what is required is a two-stage approach. The first stage involves accumulating sufficient evidence to permit an accurate *description* of the differences in attentional functioning between individuals varying in their anxiety levels. This stage has been accomplished reasonably successfully. The second stage involves assessing the *functional significance* of those differences. That stage, which includes a consideration of the causality issue, has hardly begun.

Acknowledgement

Many thanks are due to the Wellcome Foundation for their general research funding to Professor Andrew Mathews and myself, which enabled some of the research discussed here to be carried out.

References

Allport, D.A. (1980) Attention and performance. In *Cognitive Psychology: New Directions*, edited by G. Claxton. London: Routledge and Kegan Paul

Baddeley, A.D. (1986) *Working Memory*. Oxford: Oxford University Press

Beck, A.T. and Emery, G (1985) *Anxiety Disorders and Phobias A Cognitive Perspective* New York basic Books

Borkovec, T.D., Robinson, E., Pruzinsky, T. and DePree, J.A. (1983) Preliminary exploration of worry: some characteristics and processes. *Behaviour Research and Therapy*, **21**, 9–16

Byrne, D. (1964) Repression-sensitization as a dimension of personality. In *Progress in Experimental Personality Research*, edited by B.A. Mather. New York: Academic Press

Darke, S.G. (1986) The relationship between test anxiety and cognitive task performance. PhD thesis, unpublished, University of Sydney, Australia

Dornic, S. (1977) Mental load, effort, and individual differences. *Reports from the Department of Psychology, University of Stockholm*, No. 509

Dornic, S. and Fernaeus, S-E. (1981) Individual differences in high-load tasks: the effect of verbal distraction. *Reports from the Department of Psychology, University of Stockholm*, No. 568

Easterbrook, J.A. (1959) The effect of emotion on cue utilisation and the organization of behavior. *Psychological Review*, **66**, 183–201

Eysenck, M.W. (1979) Anxiety, learning, and memory: a reconceptualization. *Journal of Research in Personality*, **13**, 363–385

Eysenck, M.W. (1982) *Attention and Arousal: Cognition and Performance*. Berlin: Springer

Eysenck, M.W. (1984) Anxiety and the worry process. *Bulletin of the Psychonomic Society*, **22**, 545–548

Eysenck, M.W. (1985) Anxiety and cognitive-task performance. *Personality and Individual Differences*, **6**, 579–586

Eysenck, M.W. (in press) Anxiety and cognition: theory and research. In *Perspectives on Adversively Motivated Behavior*, edited by L.-G. Nilsson and T. Archer. Hillsdale, NJ: Erlbaum

Eysenck, M.W. and Mathews, A. (1987) Trait anxiety and cognition. In *Theoretical Foundations of Behaviour Therapy*, edited by H.J. Eysenck and I. Martin. New York: Plenum Press

Eysenck, M.W., MacLeod, C. and Mathews, A. (1987). Cognitive functioning and anxiety. *Psychological Research*, **49**, 189–195

James, W. (1890) *Principles of Psychology*. New York: Holt

Korchin, S. (1964) Anxiety and cognition. In *Cognition: Theory, Research, Promise*, edited by C. Scheeser. New York: Harper and Row

MacLeod, C., Mathews, A. and Tata, P. (1986) Attentional bias in emotional disorders. *Journal of Abnormal Psychology*, **95**, 15–20

Pallak, M.S., Pittman, T.S., Heller, J.F. and Munson, P. (1975) The effect of arousal on Stroop color-word task performance. *Bulletin of the Psychonomic Society*, **6**, 248–250

Tipper, S.P. (1985) The negative priming effect: inhibitory priming by ignored objects. *Quarterly Journal of Experimental Psychology*, **37A**, 571–590

Wachtel, P.L. (1967) Conceptions of broad and narrow attention. *Psychological Bulletin*, **68**, 417–429

Watson, D. and Clark, L.A. (1984) Negative affectivity: the disposition to experience aversive emotional states. *Psychological Bulletin*, **96**, 465–490

Wine, J. (1971) Test anxiety and direction of attention. *Psychological Bulletin*, **76**, 92–104

THOUGHT LISTING AND ENDORSEMENT MEASURES OF SELF-REFERENTIAL THINKING IN TEST ANXIETY

KIRK R. BLANKSTEIN *

Erindale College, University of Toronto, Canada

GORDON L. FLETT

York University, Canada

PAUL BOASE

Ontario Ministry of Transportation, Canada

BRENDA B. TONER

Clarke Institute of Psychiatry, Canada

The primary purpose of the present study was to examine cognitive reactions of high and low test-anxious subjects while performing a task of extreme difficulty. A sample of 44 subjects (28 females, 16 males) attempted a difficult analogies task and then reported their thoughts during the task. Subjects also completed the Sarason Test Anxiety Scale and several other self- report measures of their cognitive reactions to the task. Thought listings were classified according to their referent (self, task, or unrelated) and their valence (positive, negative, or neutral). Correlational analyses were then performed with the various measures and revealed an association between test anxiety and reports of negative thoughts involving the self. Test anxiety was not related significantly to the number of thoughts involving the task nor to actual performance on the task. However, test-anxious subjects did report more negative expectancies for their performance and greater cognitive interference during the task. Negative self-expectancies were also related to more negative self thoughts, fewer positive self thoughts, and fewer positive task-related thoughts. The results are interpreted as further evidence for both the role of negative self-related cognitions in the experience of test anxiety and the usefulness of unstructured measures in anxiety research.

KEY WORDS: Test anxiety, unstructured assessments, self-related cognitions, task performance, task expectations

* Address correspondence to: Kirk R. Blankstein, Erindale College, University of Toronto, Mississauga, Ontario, Canada, L5L 1C6.

Cognitive-attentional theories of test anxiety (e.g., Meichenbaum & Butler, 1980; Sarason, 1972, 1988; Wine, 1980) hypothesize that the test- anxious person becomes self-focused when confronted with the threat of evaluation and emits self-critical, ruminative self-statements that distract attention from the task. The heightened physiological arousal frequently reported by the test-anxious person is also interpreted cognitively within these theories. In contrast, the less test-anxious person is assumed to engage in task-relevant cognitions that facilitate efficient task completion. These cognitions are accompanied by a reduced level of physiological arousal in the low test-anxious individual.

At present, many studies have provided evidence that supports general cognitive-attentional theories of test anxiety (e.g., Brown & Nelson, 1983; Flett, Blankstein, & Boase, 1987; Galassi, Frierson, & Sharer, 1981; Minor & Gold, 1986; Sarason, Sarason, Keefe, Hayes, & Shearin, 1986; Zatz & Chassin, 1985). However, most existing findings are based on structured self-reports which have inherent limitations (see Blankstein, Toner, & Flett, in press). One alternative means of assessment is the use of unstructured methods. There is an increasing trend in the personality literature toward the use of unstructured methods for a variety of reasons (see Singer & Kolligian, 1987). Unstructured self-reports are particularly useful when studying test anxiety, for example, because they provide a more direct measure of the actual thoughts experienced by students during a test without imposing the experimenter's preconceptions on respondents. Moreover, they do not require that participants decide whether their actual thoughts approximate the thoughts listed by the experimenter.

One such unstructured self-report assessment method is the thought-listing technique developed by Brock (1967) and used extensively by Cacioppo and Petty (1981). Participants are simply instructed to list as many thoughts as they can recall experiencing throughout a task. The thoughts are then coded on relevant dimensions. Unfortunately, initial attempts to apply this more open- ended, respondent oriented strategy to the study of test anxiety met with little success. Separate studies by Glass and Arnkoff (1983) and by Galassi, Frierson, and Siegel (1984) both failed to detect a relation between test anxiety and coded thoughts. There are several possible explanations for these findings, however. For instance, Glass and Arnkoff (1983) examined imagined responses to an examination situation and did not actually assess thought listings following performance on an actual task. Galassi et al. (1984) failed to make the important distinction between thoughts involving the self versus thoughts involving the task. Moreover, both the Glass and Arnkoff (1983) and Galassi et al. (1984) studies may be criticized because coded thoughts were analyzed on the basis of frequency data. It has been recommended elsewhere (Cacioppo & Petty, 1981) that ratio scores or a related technique should be used to control for individual differences in total thought production.

More recently, Blankstein et al. (in press) demonstrated that differences in the listed thought of high test-anxious and low test-anxious students do indeed exist if a coding system that taps directly into negative, self-focused cognitions is employed and thought categories are analyzed on the basis of ratio scores rather than frequency scores. Specifically, Blankstein et al. had high test-anxious and low test-anxious subjects attempt an anagram task of moderate difficulty and then report their thoughts experienced during the task. It was found that high test-anxious students, relative to moderate and low, reported a higher ratio of negative thoughts about themselves and a lower ratio of positive thoughts about the task while attempting to solve anagrams. Since these differences were present despite the absence of group differences in performance, Blankstein et al. (in press) concluded that high test-anxious students are differentiated from their less test-anxious counterparts more by "... their negative self-deprecatory cognitions and a failure to engage in task facilitative thoughts than by actual test performance."

These data have several practical and theoretical implications and they are particularly interesting in light of recent observations by Kendall and Ingram (1987). Kendall and Ingram (1987) hypothesized that anxious individuals may be characterized by chronic ruminations about themselves until they experience a stressful situation. Once this stressful situation is encountered, anxious individuals shift their attention away from themselves at this point and become preoccupied with the demands of the situation. These processes should be reflected in the thoughts experienced during this stressful situation; anxious subjects, relative to less anxious subjects, should report a greater proportion of thoughts related to the stressful situation itself. It is clear that these predictions are not consistent with the results of the Blankstein et al. (in press) study. In fact, an opposite set of findings emerged. Test-anxious individuals reported a *greater* number of negative thoughts about themselves during the task and *fewer* positive thoughts about the task.

One possible explanation for this finding is that the subjects in the Blankstein et al. study were asked to list their thoughts while attempting anagrams that were either easy or moderate in degree of difficulty. Perhaps a different pattern of results would have been obtained if subjects had been attempting a more difficult task. If anything, however, being asked to perform a difficult task should exacerbate the tendency of the test-anxious individual to focus on negative aspects of the self. In their self-regulation model of test anxiety, Carver and Scheier (1984) postulated that test-anxious subjects should respond with task disengagement and greater self-focus when confronted with a difficult task.

Given these conflicting predictions, we felt that another study was in order. Consequently, the primary purpose of the present study was to assess thought listings of high text-anxious and low test-anxious subjects during a more difficult task. Consistent with the model of Carver and Scheier (1984) as well as with our original findings (Blankstein et al., in press), we expected that test anxiety would be associated with a greater number of negative self- related thoughts and a lesser number of positive task-related thoughts, irrespective of the increased difficulty level of the task itself.

A second goal of the present study was to more closely examine the role of outcome expectancies in the responses of high test-anxious and low test- anxious individuals. The self-regulation model (Carver & Scheier, 1984, 1986, 1988) predicts different responses depending on whether the test-anxious person anticipates a successful or unsuccessful performance. Carver and Scheier hypothesized that the test-anxious individual with negative outcome expectancies will indeed focus on negative aspects of the self and his or her performance will deteriorate as a result. In contrast, the test-anxious individual with positive outcome expectancies will remain task-focused and manifest enhanced performance. Recently, Rich and Woolever (1988) have provided experimental evidence that corroborates these claims.

At present, there have been few attempts to examine the link between outcome expectancies and reported thoughts in a testing situation. Based on the self- regulation model, it would be expected that individuals with negative outcome expectancies would report a greater number of negative thoughts about themselves and a smaller number of positive thoughts about themselves. In our previous paper (Blankstein et al., in press), we did find that a more positive expectation was associated with more task-facilitative thoughts. However, there was no significant relation between pretask expectancies and the number of positive or negative self-referential thoughts. Once again, the lack of expected associations may have been due, in part, to the fact that the test administered to subjects in the Blankstein et al. study was medium to low in level of difficulty. In light of this possibility, we re-examined the link between self-expectancy and cognitive reactions in the present study. We anticipated that the lower self-confidence inherent in negative performance expectations would result in more negative thoughts about the self and fewer positive thoughts about the self when confronted with a very difficult task.

A final goal of the present study was to compare the findings with unstructured thought-listing assessments with the findings obtained using more commonly employed structured assessments, including the Cognitive Interference Questionnaire (CIQ; Sarason & Stoops, 1978), and a measure modeled on the CIQ, the Perceived Physiological Interference Questionnaire (PPIQ; Blankstein et al., in press). These measures were included to obtain a broader assessment of the cognitive reactions experienced during a difficult task. We also re- examined possible test anxiety effects on task performance, performance expectancy, and performance evaluation.

METHOD

Participants

The subjects were 44 undergraduates (28 females and 16 males) enrolled in a second year Personality course at the University of Toronto. Subjects volunteered to participate. The average age of the subjects was 25.1 years.

Instruments and Procedure

The procedure was similar to that employed by Blankstein et al. (in press). As mentioned above, the main exception was that a difficult analogies test was substituted for a moderately easy anagram task. Subjects took the test during their regularly scheduled class in the usual testing room. Subjects were given ten minutes to complete ten analogies following written instructions designed to elicit evaluative stress. Pre-test ratings of both self and other expectations of the level of success on the analogies test and post-test evaluations of actual performance were recorded (1 to 7 scale). Subjects then completed a thought listing protocol, with instructions modified from Petty and Cacioppo (1977), which provided for the production of 24 listed thoughts. Specifically, subjects were told the following:

> Please list as many thoughts and feelings as you can recall having during this test. Every thought and feeling that went through your mind during that time is important (i.e., thoughts and feelings about yourself, the situation, or unrelated to the experiment). Be spontaneous. Ignore spelling, grammar and punctuation. It is important that you list all thoughts and feelings *as you experienced them.* Therefore do not choose your words as though you are writing an essay. Do not put the

thoughts and feelings into well-structured sentences, if they were not experienced in that form. Please be completely honest. Your responses will be confidential. Do not feel that you have to use all the space that has been provided. Please put only one thought or feeling per number.

Following Cacioppo and Petty (1981), listed thoughts were scored on a *polarity* dimension (positive, negative, and neutral thoughts) and a *referent* dimension (self-referential, task-related, and thoughts unrelated to one's self or the task). Although this coding system produces nine categories of thought classification, only four categories were considered to be critical based on test anxiety theory (positive and negative self-referential, and positive and negative task-referential). Each thought was rated by a judge who was blind as to students' test anxiety levels. A subsample of thought-listing reports was selected randomly and scored independently; inter-judge reliability exceeded 90%. Ratios of each category over the total number of thoughts were calculated for each subject to control for individual differences in the number of thoughts reported.*

Subjects also completed the CIQ as an endorsement measure of negative internal dialogue. It consists of 11 negative self-referential, task irrelevant thoughts that can be experienced by individuals during the performance of a task (scored on a five-point frequency of occurrence scale). The 11-item PPIQ, constructed to assess specific thoughts about physiological arousal (also scored on a five-point scale) was incorporated with the CIQ.

The 37-item true-false Test Anxiety Scale (TAS; Sarason, 1978) served as the measure of test anxiety and was completed by students two weeks later. Scores on the TAS ranged from 3 to 33 ($M = 16.7$; $SD = 7.8$).

RESULTS

Intercorrelations among test anxiety and the measures of expectation/evaluation, the critical categories of listed thoughts produced by the respondents, the endorsement measures of cognitive and physiological interference, and test performance were computed using the Pearson product-moment method.

Test anxiety was found to correlate significantly with two ratio scores of the unstructured production measure: negative self-referential listed thoughts, $r = .35$, $p < .01$, and positive self-referential listed thoughts, $r = -.28$, $p < .05$. Test-anxious students made more unfavourable statements about themselves, and fewer favourable statements about themselves relative to less test-anxious students. Additional analyses revealed that correlations between TAS scores and task referential thoughts (both positive and negative) were non-significant.

Consistent with these thought list results, test anxiety was associated with cognitive interference as assessed by the CIQ endorsement measure ($r = .28$, $p < .05$). Test

* Although only the results with the ratio scores are reported, it should be noted that analyses were also conducted using the raw frequency of thought listing responses rather than the ratio scores. Consistent with the findings of our previous study (Blankstein et al., in press), there was no relation between level of test anxiety and total number of listed thoughts. In addition, similar correlation results were obtained with the raw frequency and proportional thought listing data.

anxiety was not significantly related to scores on the PPIQ. In fact, although subjects listed 315 thoughts, not one suggested that perception of physiological arousal was salient.

Correlations Between Performance Expectations and Thought Listing Measures

One of the strongest correlations was obtained between test anxiety and self-expectations of performance, $r = -.45$, $p < .001$. Test-anxious subjects expected to perform poorly on the analogies. However, test anxiety was not correlated with expectations of others' performance. Thus, the negative self-expectancy in test anxiety is confined to the self. Test anxiety was unrelated to post-task evaluation. Furthermore, test anxiety did not predict actual task performance. However, the average level of performance on the task ($M = 3.9$, $SD = 1.6$) confirmed that the task was indeed difficult.

As expected, the pattern of correlations suggested that self-expectations prior to the test may be important predictors of cognitive reactions during the test itself. For example, the pre-test self-expectancy of success rating, although not predictive of actual task success, was correlated significantly with the ratios of both negative self-referential thoughts, $r = -.32$, $p < .05$, and positive self-referential thoughts, $r = .27$, $p < .05$. Moreover, pre-task self-expectancies were also correlated significantly with the number of positive task-related thoughts, $r = .28$, $p < .05$, and with scores on the CIQ, $r = -.30$, $p < .05$.

The role of individual differences in expectancy level was clearly demonstrated when we computed partial correlations that removed variance due to performance expectations. Many of the correlations reported above no longer attained significance. For instance, there were no significant first-order correlations between test anxiety and the proportion of positive self-referential thoughts, $r = -.19$, *ns*, nor was there a significant first-order correlation between test anxiety and the proportion of negative self-referential thoughts, $r = .24$, *ns*.

Correlations Between Remaining Thought Listing and Endorsement Measures

Several other significant associations should be noted. Scores on the CIQ were correlated significantly with the ratios of negative self-referential thoughts, $r = .27$, $p < .05$, and with positive task-related thoughts, $r = -.32$, $p < .05$. Finally, the post-test self-evaluation ratings were also related to the unstructured measures of thoughts during the task: there were significant correlations with the ratios of negative self-referential thoughts, $r = -.32$, $p < .05$, negative task-related thoughts, $r = -.48$, $p < .001$, and positive task-related thoughts, $r = .35$, $p < .01$.

Finally, neither the structured nor the unstructured measures of thoughts predicted analogies outcome.

DISCUSSION

The primary purpose of the present study was to examine the cognitive reactions of high test-anxious and low test-anxious subjects during a difficult task. In general, the findings of this study were consistent with the self-focusing emphasis of cognitive-attentional theories of test anxiety (e.g., Sarason, 1972). Consistent with the findings of Blankstein et al. (in press), analyses of the thought-list protocols showed clearly that relatively more test-anxious subjects listed a higher ratio of negative ideation directed at themselves during the test. In contrast to our original work, test anxiety did not predict the ratio of positive task referential thinking. However, test anxiety was correlated with the ratio of positive self-referential thinking: test-anxious persons engaged in fewer positive thoughts about themselves. Thus, the most robutst thought-list finding across the two studies is the negative self-focus that is characteristic of the internal dialogue of relatively test-anxious individuals during an evaluative task. The test-anxious student is negatively preoccupied with a preponderance of self-derogatory thoughts, thoughts about failure, and statements of negative mood (see Blankstein et al., in press) and there is little evidence to suggest that these self-related concerns lessen or disappear during a stressful experience such as performing a difficult task.

A second goal of the present study was to more closely examine the association between performance expectations and cognitive reactions during the task. The results involving our pre-task measure of self-expectancy demonstrated the pervasive role of self-judgments in test anxiety. Not only was it the case that negative self-expectancies of performance were associated with increased test anxiety, it was also found that self-expectancies of performance were associated with a number of the thought-listing measures. Subjects with more negative performance expectancies also reported experiencing more negative self-referential thoughts, fewer positive self-referential thoughts, and fewer positive task-related thoughts. Moreover, the association between test anxiety and degree of self-referential thinking, either positive or negative in content, was no longer significant once variance due to performance expectations was removed. These findings are noteworthy in that they support predictions from the self-regulation model (Carver & Scheier, 1984, 1986, 1988) concerning the importance of expectancy as a mediator of the effects of self-focused attention. Although these findings suggest that negative self-expectations are indeed a major contributor to the experience of test anxiety, our findings must be interpreted cautiously because they are based on responses to a single global rating of performance expectancy. Consistent with the recent focus on the extent to which stable individual differences in optimism-pessimism mediate affective and cognitive reactions (Carver & Gaines, 1987; Scheier & Carver, 1985; Scheier, Weintraub, & Carver, 1986), a logical extension of research in this area is an investigation of the thoughts reported by test-anxious individuals who are characterologically optimistic or pessimistic about their performance. We are currently conducting such a study.

Although it was not our major focus of interest, it should be noted that test anxiety did not predict endorsement of perceived physiological arousal, as assessed by our PPIQ. Furthermore, no subject produced even a single thought about physiological activity on the thought listing. This finding contrasts with some past research (e.g., Deffenbacher & Hazaleus, 1985), but it is consistent with the results of Blankstein et al. (in press) and supports their conclusion that thoughts related to physiological arousal are not always a strong component of the test-anxious person's internal dialogue during a task. Rather, thoughts involving self-evaluation and the characteristics of the task itself appear to predominate.

Additional results showed that test anxiety was not associated with deficits in task performance, despite the fact that negative expectations of performance outcome were correlated with test anxiety. Nor did the listed thoughts and endoresement measures predict analogies outcome in the present study. Nonetheless, it is clear from our subjects' retrospective self-reports that taking tests is an extremely unpleasant experience for many test-anxious students. They expect to do poorly and engage in a maladaptive, self- defeating, internal dialogue with a specific focus on negative self- referential thinking. They apparently can perform adequately at times, relative to their group, *despite* their efforts to undermine their performance. Would their performance be enhanced if they engaged in more positive self-referential and task-specific thinking? Although improved performances is a commendable goal of test anxiety intervention programmes (e.g., Dendato & Diener, 1986), it may be more appropriate to focus on reducing the negative expectancies and negative self-referential thoughts of the test-anxious person in order to enable the test-anxious person to feel more in control of the test situation.

Some limitations of the current research should be mentioned. First, our results were based on cognitive reactions during an analogies task. Although an attempt was made to simulate a test situation, it is important that future research assesses thought listings of high test-anxious and low test-anxious students during an actual test. Second, a related concern is that the current study focused on thought listings during a difficult task and it is likely that certain findings will not generalize to reactions in situations with less evaluative stress. Future research must examine directly the possible mediating role of this factor by manipulating various task parameters such as difficulty level and then measuring the thoughts and affective states of high test-anxious and low test-anxious subjects. Third, the present study has viewed test anxiety as a unidimensional construct but recent investigations have demonstrated that test anxiety is indeed multidimensional (Sarason, 1984). Thus, studies examining the relations between thought listings and specific components of test anxiety (i.e., tension, worry, test- irrelevant thinking, and bodly reactions) should provide a more complete understanding of the role of cognitive processes in test anxiety. Finally, the current study has identified a positive correlation between test anxiety and negative self-thoughts. However, it remains to be determined whether negative thoughts about the self have a causative role in the experience of test anxiety.

In summary, the present results further demonstrate the importance of using unstructured self-reports such as the thought listing technique for differentiating among the test-taking cognitions of high test-anxious and low test-anxious students. Test anxiety was clearly associated with reports of more negative thoughts involving the self and fewer positive thoughts involving the self. Overall, these findings suggest that future attempts to treat test anxiety should focus directly on boosting the test-anxious student's self-confidence and self-evaluative tendencies in performance situations.

References

Blankstein, K.R., Toner, B.B., & Flett, G.L. (in press). Test anxiety and the contents of consciousness: Thought listing and endorsement measures. *Journal of Research in Personality*

Brock, T.C. (1967). Communication discrepancy and intent to persuade as determinants of counterargument production. *Journal of Experimental Social Psychology*, **3**.

Brown, S.D., & Nelson, T.L. (1983). Beyond the uniformity myth: A comparison of academically successful and unsuccessful test-anxious college students. *Journal of Counseling Psychology*, **30**, 367–374

Cacioppo, J.T., & Petty, r.e. (1981). Social psychological procedures for cognitive response assessment: The thought-listing technique. In T.V. Merluzzi, C.R. Glass, & M. Genest, (Eds.), *Cognitive Assessment* (pp. 309–342 . New York: The Guilford Press

Carver, C.S., & Gaines, J.G. (1987). Optimism, pessimism, and postpartum depression. *Cognitive Therapy and Research*, **11**, 449–462

Carver, C.S., & Scheier, M.F. (1984). Self-focused attention in test anxiety: A general theory applied to a specific phenomenon. In H.M. van der Ploeg, R. Schwarzer, & C.D Spielberger, (Eds.) *Advances in test anxiety research* (Vol. 3, pp. 3–20). Hillsdale, NJ: Erlbaum

Carver, C.S., & Scheier, M.F. (1986). Self and the control of behavior. In L.M. Hartman & K.R. Blankstein, (Eds.) *Perception of self in emotional disorder and psychotherapy* (Vol. 11, pp. 5–35). New York: Plenum Press

Carver, C.S., & Scheier, M.F. (1988). A control-process perspective on anxiety. *Anxiety Research*, **1**, 17–22

Deffenbacher, J.L., & Hazaleus, S.L. (1985). Cognitive, emotional, and physiological components of test anxiety. *Cognitive Therapy and Research*, **9**, 169–180

Dendato, K.M., & Diener, D. (1986). Effectiveness of cognitive/relaxation therapy and study-skills training in reducing self-reported anxiety and improving the academic performance of test-anxious students. *Journal of Counseling Psychology*, **33**, 131–135

Flett, G.L., Blankstein, K.R. & Boase, P. (1987). Self-directed attention in test anxiety and depression. *Journal of Social Behavior and Personality*, **2**, 259–266

Galassi, J.P., Frierson, H.T. Jr., & Sharer, R. (1981). Behavior of high, moderate, and low test anxious students during an actual test situation. *Journal of Consulting and Clinical Psychology*, **49**, 51–62

Galassi, J.P., Frierson, H.T. Jr, & Siegel, R.G. (1984). Cognitions, test anxiety and test performance: A closer look. *Journal of Consulting and Clinical Psychology*, **52**, 319–320

Glass, C.R., & Arnkoff, D.B. (1983). Cognitive set and level of test anxiety: Effects on thinking processes in problematic situations. *Cognitive Therapy and Research*, **7**, 529–542

Kendall, P.C., & Ingram, R.E. (1987). The future for cognitive assessments of anxiety: Let's get specific. In L. Michelson & M. Ascher, (Eds.), *Cognitive-behavioral assessment and treatment of anxiety disorders* (pp. 84–104). New York: Guilford Press

Meichenbaum, D., & Butler, L. (1980). Toward a conceptual model for the treatment of test anxiety: Implications for research and treatment. In I.G. Sarason, (Ed.), *Test anxiety: Theory, research and applications* (pp. 187–208). Hillsdale, NJ: Lawrence Erlbaum

Minor, S.W. & Gold, S.r. (1986). Behavior of test-anxious students across time. *Personality and Individual Differences*, **7**, 241–242

Petty, R.E., & Cacioppo, J.J. (1977). Forewarning, cognitive responding, and resistance to persuasion. *Journal of Personality and Social Psychology*, **35**, 645–655

Rich, A.E., & Woolever, D.K. (1988). Expectancy and self-focused attention: Experimental support for the self-regulation model of test anxiety. *Journal of Social and Clinical Psychology*, **7**, 246–259

Sarason, I.G. (1972). Experimental approaches to test anxiety: Attention and the uses of information. In C.D. Spielberger, (Ed.), *Anxiety: Current trends in theory and research* (Vol. 2, pp. 381–402). New York: Academic Press

Sarason, I.G. (1978). The Test Anxiety Scale: Concept and research. In C.D. Spielberger & I.G. Sarason, (Eds.), *Stress and anxiety* (Vol. 5, pp. 193–216). Washington, DC: Hemisphere

Sarason, I.G. (1984). Stress, anxiety and cognitive interference: Reactions to tests. *Journal of Personality and Social Psychology*, **46**, 929–938

Sarason, I.G. (1988). Anxiety, self-preoccupation and attention. *Anxiety Research*, **1**, 3–7

Sarason, I.G., Sarason, B.R., Keefe, D.E., Hayes, B.E., & Shearin, E.N. (1986). Cognitive interference: Situational determinants and traitlike characteristics. *Journal of Personality and Social Psychology*, **31**, 215–226

Sarason, I.G., & Stoops, R. (1978). Test anxiety and the passage of time. *Journal of Consulting and Clinical Psychology*, **46**, 102–109

Scheier, M.F., & Carver, C.S. (1985). Optimism, coping, and health: Assessment and implications of generalized outcome expectancies. *Health Psychology*, **4**, 219–247

Scheier, M.F., Weintraub, J.K., & Carver, C.S. (1986). Coping with stress: Divergent strategies of optimists and pessimists. *Journal of Personality and Social Psychology*, **51**, 1257–1264

Singer, J.L., & Kolligian, J. Jr. (1987). Personality: Developments in the study of private experience. *Annual Review of Psychology*, **38**, 533–574

Wine, J.D. (1980). Cognitive-attentional theory of test anxiety. In I.G. Sarason, (Ed.), *Test anxiety: Theory, research and applications* (pp. 349–385). Hillsdale, NJ: Lawrence Erlbaum
Zatz, S. & Chassin, L. (1985). Cognitions of test-anxious children under naturalistic test-taking conditions. *Journal of Consulting and Clinical Psychology*, **53**, 393–401

PERFORMANCE DEFICITS FOLLOWING FAILURE: INTEGRATING MOTIVATIONAL AND FUNCTIONAL ASPECTS OF LEARNED HELPLESSNESS

JOACHIM STIENSMEIER-PELSTER* AND MARTIN SCHÜRMANN

Universität Bielefeld, Abteilung für Psychologie

(Received 1 August 1989)

This paper deals with the psychological processes that mediate between repeated, uncontrollable failure on one task and performance deficits on subsequent tasks. A model is presented that integrates Seligman's (1975) motivational and Kuhl's (1981) functional interpretation of performance deficits following failure. The central assumptions of this model were tested in a laboratory study with college students. In accordance with our model, repeated failure (1) increasingly led to task- and solution-irrelevant cognitive activities (state orientation, according to Kuhl) the more it was attributed to internal, stable, and global causes, and (2) led to an increment in effort the more it was attributed to unstable and specific causes. Furthermore, results indicated that the influence of failure on state orientation was partly mediated by the importance subjects attached to the failure, and that the performance on subsequent tasks was influenced by both the motivational (effort) and functional (state orientation) consequences of failure.

KEYWORDS: Performance, learned helplessness, action-control, task-irrelevant cognitions, attribution

A striking feature of the Olympic Games in 1984 at Los Angeles was the contest between the decathlon competitors Daley Thompson and Jürgen Hingsen in which Hingsen, although world record holder, lost. In as early as the first event, the 100-meter sprint, Hingsen lagged behind Thompson. The following events (shot put, high jump, 400-meter sprint, hurdles) all took a similar course. Whenever Hingsen achieved an extremely good result and could hope to equal or surpass Thompson, the latter always surpassed the former. At last, the seventh event, in which Hingsen threw the discus to a new personal record, appeared to be the reward for his efforts. Thompson, for all appearances defeated, also succeeded in achieving a new personal record and the old order, first Thompson, second Hingsen, was reestablished. The odds seemed to be against Hingsen in this contest. No matter how hard he tried to equal or surpass Thompson, his efforts were of no avail. In the eighth event, the pole-vault, Hingsen failed miserably. Instead of jumping 5.10 m or at least 5.0 m, which has been nothing special for him on former occasions, he mastered only 4.50 m.

Performance deficits following repeated uncontrollable failure, like the one shown by Hingsen, have been amply demonstrated in learned helplessness experiments (Hiroto, 1974; Hiroto & Seligman, 1975; Roth & Kubal, 1975; Mikulincer & Nizan, 1988; see Stiensmeier-Pelster, 1988, for a summary). In the study by Hiroto and Seligman, for example, the performance of students was tested on different tasks. Preceding the performance test, some students were exposed to repeated failure, while other students were exposed to success or no pre-treatment. Results indicated that

*Address correspondence to: Joachim Stiensmeier-Pelster, Universität Bielefeld, Abteilung für Psychologie, Postfach: 8640, 4800 Bielefeld 1.

students exposed to repeated failure, in comparison to students in the other two groups, displayed marked performance deficits, independent of whether the preceding failure-task was similar or dissimilar to the test-tasks. Thus, repeated uncontrollable failure on one task was followed by performance deficits on subsequent tasks even when they were dissimilar.

For a long time, Seligman's (1975) and Abramson, Seligman, and Teasdale's (1978) theory of learned helplessness was used to analyse such performance deficits in terms of insufficient motivation, that is, a motivational deficit. Recently, some authors (e.g., Kuhl, 1981, 1984) have suggested an alternative interpretation that emphasizes the mediating role of task-irrelevant cognitive activities, that is, a functional deficit. After briefly discussing these two positions, we present our own explanatory model integrating these two seemingly conflicting viewpoints. Finally, we present an experiment supporting the validity of the proposed integrative model.

ATTRIBUTING PERFORMANCE DEFICITS TO A MOTIVATIONAL DEFICIT: THE LEARNED HELPLESSNESS THEORY

According to learned helplessness theory (Seligman, 1975; Abramson, Seligman, & Teasdale, 1978), individuals who are exposed to uncontrollable failure develop the expectation that none of their activities will produce success in the future (i.e., an expectation of uncontrollability). Given certain circumstances (see below), this expectation should generalize to subsequent tasks. Whenever the expectation of uncontrollability is transferred to a subsequent task, it undermines the motivation to make any effort to solve these tasks (motivational deficit), and, as a consequence, causes a performance deficit. Thus, according to both Seligman and Abramson et al., performance deficits following repeated uncontrollable failure are due to *expectancy-mediated motivational deficits*.

The attributions a person makes following failure determine whether an expectation of uncontrollability is generalized to only similar or also to dissimilar tasks, and also whether this expectation holds only for the near future or also for longer periods of time. Abramson and coworkers, in line with Weiner's (1979; cf. also Weiner, Nierenberg, & Goldstein, 1976) attributional theory of achievement motivation, proposed that an expectation of uncontrollability will be generalized to a broad range of tasks and over an expanded time period when repeated, uncontrollable failure is attributed to global and stable causes. To the contrary, if the failure is attributed to specific and unstable causes, expectations are generalized to a limited range of tasks and over a restricted time period. Attribution along the locus of control dimension (internality-attributions), however, has no influence on the generalization of expectations, but rather on whether or not self-esteem deficits will occur following failure.

ATTRIBUTING PERFORMANCE DEFICITS TO A FUNCTIONAL DEFICIT: THE MEDIATING ROLE OF TASK-IRRELEVANT, COGNITIVE ACTIVITIES

During the last decade, the learned helplessness interpretation of performance deficits, especially the assumed mediating role of uncontrollability expectations and motivational deficits, has often been criticized for at least two reasons. First, some experiments demonstrated that uncontrollable failure causes performance deficits in subsequent tasks without the mediation of uncontrollability expectations (Kuhl, 1981; Mikulincer & Nizan, 1988). Second, according to the theory of achievement motivation, failure under certain circumstances leads to increased motivation (cf. Atkinson & Birch, 1974). Furthermore, Follette and Jacobson (1987) recently collected data showing that students who fail on an examination are willing to increase the effort (hours of learning) invested in preparing for a subsequent examination.

Because the expectancy-mediated, motivational deficit seems insufficient to explain performance deficits following repeated failure, Kuhl (1981, 1984) as well as others (Labelle, Metalsky, & Coyne, 1979; Coyne, Metalsky, & Lavelle, 1980; Carver, 1979; Carver, Blaney, & Scheier, 1979; Diener & Dweck, 1978) have favored an alternative interpretation. This emphasizes the mediating role of task-irrelevant, cognitive activities. All of these approaches consider a cognitive interference to be the crucial mediating variable between failure on one task and performance deficits on subsequent tasks. Such interfering cognitions are conceptualized as self-preoccupation (Sarason, 1975), worry (Liebert & Morris, 1967), cognitive withdrawal (Carver, 1979), or state orientation (Kuhl, 1981, 1984). In our opinion, Kuhl's concept of functional helplessness or state orientation is the best elaborated approach: In Kuhl's (1981) theory, repeated failure (besides the expectation of uncontrollability) causes a so-called functional helplessness or state orientation. State orientation is defined as cognitive activities that are preoccupied with the failure, its causes and consequences, as well as with the emotional state created by the failure. Such cognitive activities are irrelevant to the task and its solution and interfere with task-oriented attention and information processing. They therefore hinder effective problem solving.

The intensity of state-orientation following failure is particularly influenced by two variables: (1) the strength or certainty of the perceived uncontrollability/unavoidability, and (2) the importance of the failure. As Stiensmeier-Pelster has shown in various learned helplessness experiments, failure causes an increasing intensity of state orientation, the more people are certain that it is uncontrollable or unavoidable (Stiensmeier-Pelster, 1988; Stiensmeier-Pelster & Schürmann, in press), and the more importance they attach to the failure (Stiensmeier, 1985, 1986).

The most striking feature of Kuhl's theory is his set of assumptions regarding the generalization of uncontrollability expectations, motivational deficits, and state orientation. According to Kuhl, the task-irrelevant, state-oriented, cognitive activities developed during the exposure to repeated failure on one task generalize to subsequent tasks independent of whether they are similar or dissimilar to the failure task. They also generalize to subsequent situations, even to situations that are not related to an achievement domain. In contrast, the expectation of uncontrollability should only generalize to the subsequent task when it is similar to the failure task, that is, when subjects perceive it as involving the same abilities. As a consequence, Kuhl maintains that failure does not lead to decreased motivation in solving subsequent tasks given that these tasks are dissimilar to the failure task. Furthermore, in line with the theory of achievement motivation (Atkinson & Birch, 1974), Kuhl assumes that, in some circumstances, failure can even cause an increment in the motivation to solve subsequent tasks.

According to Abramson et al. (1978), the kind of attribution a person makes responsible for his/her failure influences whether or not the expectation of uncontrollability and its accompanying motivational and performance deficit generalize across different tasks and over time. But the Kuhl (1981) position states that the kind of attribution makes no difference. Attributions are regarded as a kind of state-oriented cognitive activity. "Examples of state-oriented activities may be . . .

examining the cause for not having reached a goal, . . ." (p. 159). They are considered as task-and solution irrelevant and as interfering with optimal cognitive functioning. Therefore, they should hinder effective performance. Furthermore, persons showing performance deficits following exposure to repeated failure should not differ from persons without performance deficits in the kind of attributions they make, but in the overall frequency of the attributional activity in which they engage.

Summarizing Kuhl's position, one can state the following: Whenever failure on one task is followed by performance deficits on subsequent tasks that are dissimilar to the failure task, the observed performance deficits are due to generalized, task-irrelevant, state-oriented, cognitive activities, that is, to a *functional* deficit, but not to a generalized, expectancy-mediated *motivational* deficit.

Recently the assumed mediating role of task-irrelevant, state-oriented, cognitive activities has been demonstrated in several studies (Kuhl, 1981; Kuhl & Weiss, in press; Stiensmeier-Pelster, 1988; Stiensmeier-Pelster & Schürmann, in press: Mikulincer & Nizan, 1988). However, none of these studies found any indication that uncontrollability expectations have a mediating role.

AN INTEGRATIVE MODEL

In our opinion, neither Seligman's nor Kuhl's assumptions tell us the whole story regarding performance deficits following repeated, uncontrollable failure. We therefore have proposed our own model (see Stiensmeier-Pelster, 1988, for a detailed description of this model) that describes some psychological processes (motivational as well as functional) mediating between failure in one task and performance deficits in subsequent tasks. This model (depicted in Figure 1) integrates the essential aspects of the above-mentioned motivational (Seligman; Abramson et al.) and functional (Kuhl, and others) interpretations of performance deficits following repeated failure.

The key assumptions of our model (a chronological description of the processes summarized in the model is given in Figure 1) are: (1) Failure has motivational (effort) as well as functional (state orientation) consequences, (2) the effect of repeated failure on performance on subsequent tasks is mediated by both of these consequences, and (3) the kind of attribution made responsible for the failure is one of the essential variables mediating the amount of state orientation that develops as a consequence of failure as well as the amount of effort spent on solving subsequent tasks. Note that this is completely in contrast to Kuhl's conceptualization of attributional activity (see above). Let us give some reasons for the above assumptions.

As discussed earlier, failure causes an increasing amount of state orientation the more it is considered to be uncontrollable or unavoidable and the more it is considered personally relevant or important (see Stiensmeier-Pelster & Schürmann, in press; Stiensmeier, 1985, 1986 for an empirical validation of these assumptions). As shown in Figure 1, we assume that the perceived cause of the outcome influences both: (a) whether or not failure is considered as uncontrollable/unavoidable, and (b) the importance that will be attached to the failure. In this context, we propose that failure will be experienced as uncontrollable/unavoidable only if it is attributed to uncontrollable causes, such as lack of ability, bad luck, or task difficulty, but not if it is attributed to controllable causes, such as lack of effort (cf. Weiner, 1979, 1986). Thus, state orientation following failure will increase in intensity, the more subjects tend to attribute failure to uncontrollable causes. Regarding the importance attached to the failure, we maintain that failure will be considered to be increasingly important the

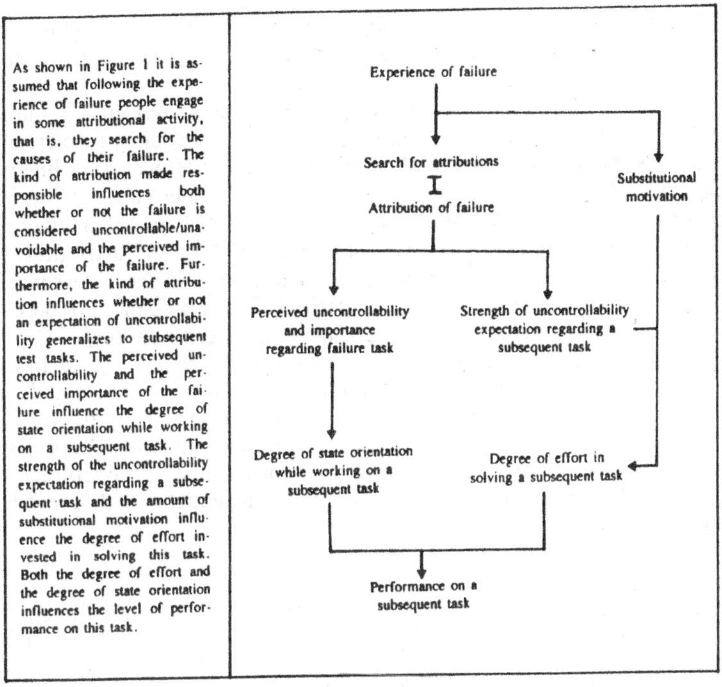

As shown in Figure 1 it is assumed that following the experience of failure people engage in some attributional activity, that is, they search for the causes of their failure. The kind of attribution made responsible influences both whether or not the failure is considered uncontrollable/unavoidable and the perceived importance of the failure. Furthermore, the kind of attribution influences whether or not an expectation of uncontrollability generalizes to subsequent test tasks. The perceived uncontrollability and the perceived importance of the failure influence the degree of state orientation while working on a subsequent task. The strength of the uncontrollability expectation regarding a subsequent task and the amount of substitutional motivation influence the degree of effort invested in solving this task. Both the degree of effort and the degree of state orientation influences the level of performance on this task.
Experience of failure
Search for attributions
Attribution of failure
Substitutional motivation
Perceived uncontrollability and importance regarding failure task
Strength of uncontrollability expectation regarding a subsequent task
Degree of state orientation while working on a subsequent task
Degree of effort in solving a subsequent task
Performance on a subsequent task

Figure 1 Effects of failure on performance on a subsequent task: Psychological processes involved and their chronological course.

more it is attributed to internal causes. In the case of extrinsically motivated activities, failure is also increasingly important the more it is attributed to stable and global causes.

There are several reasons for the plausibility of the last two assumptions. Success and failure that are caused by internal factors are more relevant for one's self-esteem than success and failure brought about by external factors. Furthermore, in an achievement-related context, failure that is absolutely due to the task difficulty (an external factor) often does not have such important consequences (e.g., often does not lead to bad grades because it is not diagnostic for ability) as failure that is due to lack of effort or ability (internal factors). In the case of extrinsically motivated activities, the importance of failure is, among other things, a function of the importance of the goal pursued and of the probability of achieving this goal in the future. The more one perceives the causes of one's failure as stable and global, the lower one perceives this probability to be (a more detailed discussion of the effect of attribution on importance is given in Stiensmeier-Pelster, 1988, Chapter 4).

In summary, we assume that failure attributions influence the amount of state orientation developing as a consequence of failure, and that this influence is mediated through the perception of uncontrollability/unavoidability and the personal importance of the failure. To conceptionalize attribution as one important mediating variable, it has to be assumed that failure will initiate an attribution process. As Weiner (1985, 1986) states, an attribution process is initiated whenever an outcome is negative, unexpected, or important. Thus, the first step on the path from repeated failure on one task to performance on subsequent tasks is regarded to be a "spontaneous causal thinking" (Weiner, 1985), that is, looking for the causes responsible for the failure (cf. Figure 1).

Concerning the motivational consequences of failure, we assume in accordance with Kuhl (1981, 1984) that failure will cause a spontaneous tendency to increase one's efforts to solve subsequent (functionally equivalent) tasks. However, in line with the considerations of Abramson et al. (1978) and Weiner (Weiner et al., 1976), it is also assumed that the expectation of success in a subsequent task as well as the degree to which motivation will increase is influenced by the kind of attributions made responsible for the failure. Both the expectation to succeed and the increment in effort should be stronger, the more that failure is attributed to causes that are perceived as irrelevant to the subsequent tasks (i.e., to unstable and specific causes).

Whereas increased motivation should enhance performance, state orientation should hinder it. Thus, whether or not failure will cause performance deficits on subsequent tasks depends on the amount of state orientation and the amount of effort expended. The relative influence of state orientation and effort also depends on the nature of the task, that is, whether performance on the task is susceptible to task-irrelevant, state-oriented cognitions as well as being dependent on different levels of motivation.

AN EMPIRICAL TEST OF THE VALIDITY OF THE INTEGRATIVE MODEL

Overview, Experimental Design, and Hypothesis

Some of the central ideas of our mode were tested within the framework of a learned helplessness experiment. In the first part (training phase), subjects were confronted with randomly manipulated success or failure when solving Raven Matrices (Raven, 1974). The attributions that subjects regarded as responsible for their success or failure on the Raven Matrices were recorded. In the second part (test phase), subjects had to work on Brickenkamp's (1962) d2-Concentration Test (d2 Test). The training and test phases were presented as two completely different experiments by: (1) reporting different purposes for each experiment; (2) carrying out the first experiment in groups and the second in individual sessions; and (3) having different experimenters perform each experiment in different rooms and in different areas of the university.

The importance subjects attached to their success or failure was recorded as a dependent variable after the induction of success or failure. Following both the Raven Matrices and the d2 Test, subjects were asked to indicate the effort they had expended on solving these tasks. The performance on the d2 Test and the amount of state orientation subjects showed while working on this test was also recorded.

In line with our model, we anticipated the following: (1) Failure in comparison to success will cause an increased amount of state orientation to the extent that subjects attribute their failure to internal, stable, and global causes. (2) Failure will be regarded as increasingly important the more subjects attribute it to internal, stable, and global causes. (3) The impact of the failure attribution on state orientation will be mediated by the importance subjects attach to their failure. (4) Failure in comparison to success will lead to increased effort in solving the d2 Test. However, the increment in effort is less, the more the failure is attributed to stable and global causes. (5) The induction of failure in comparison to success will result in improved performance on the d2 Test provided that subjects attribute their failure to external, unstable, and specific causes.

Subjects

Subjects were 46 female students studying different subjects at the University of Bielefeld who were paid for their participation. A female psychology student participated as the confederate of the experimenter.

Procedure

Training phase. One subject and an ostensible second subject (i.e., the confederate) took part in each session of the training phase. After entering the laboratory they were told that the aim of the experiment was to investigate performance on intelligence test tasks under competitive conditions. Therefore, it was explained, they had to work on six tasks taken from the Advanced Progressive Matrices, a culture-free intelligence test developed by Raven (1974/75). Two examples were used, explaining how the tasks had to be solved. Then subjects were informed that they had to compete in solving the tasks, and that the first subject to offer the correct solution would receive DM 1 (about 50 American cents) as a financial reward, and that offering incorrect solutions would result in a deduction of DM 0.50 from the reward. Penalizing incorrect solutions was introduced to prevent random guessing.

Working on the tasks proceeded as follows: Each task was projected separately onto a screen. Whenever one of the participants wished to offer a solution, the experimenter interrupted the projection. If the solution was correct, the subject was rewarded and the next task was projected. If the solution was incorrect, the previously fixed amount of reward was deducted, and the projection of the task was resumed.

Failure and success were induced by arranging the outcomes so that subjects managed to outperform the confederate on either five (success) or only one (failure) of six trials. Two facets of the procedure made this arrangement possible: (1) the behavior of the confederate, and (2) the compilation of the tasks. Without the knowledge of the subjects five very difficult and one easy task were used in the failure condition and one very difficult and five easy tasks in the success condition. Three intended failure subjects, who solved more than one task prior to the confederate, did not participate any further in the experiment. In order to test the effectiveness of the manipulation, subjects were asked, "Do you consider your performance to be a success or a failure?" This question was answered on a 7-point scale with the poles *total success* and *total failure*. Subsequently, subjects were asked to give an attribution for their performance. Analogous to the procedure used in the Attributional Style Questionnaire (cf. Peterson, Semmel, von Baeyer, Abramson, Metalsky, & Seligman, 1982; German adaption by Stiensmeier, Kammer, Pelster, & Niketta, 1985), subjects first had to state what they considered to be the main cause for their outcome. Then they had to rate this cause regarding its internality ("Is the cause for your performance to be found more in yourself or more in other persons or circumstances?"), stability ("Will the cause for your performance also be important if you have to work on Raven-Intelligence-Test tasks in the future?"), and globality ("Does the cause only influence your performance when working on Raven-Intelligence-Test tasks, or does it also influence your performance when working on other tasks or when coping with problems?"). All responses were given on 7-point scales.

The assessment of the attributions marked the end of the alleged first experiment. The subjects were thanked for their cooperation and, since the second experiment would be conducted in individual sessions, they were asked to decide among themselves who would begin first and who would wait for about 10 minutes. The confederate was always prepared to wait.

Test phase. The second experimenter met the subject at the first laboratory and took her to the second. After arriving at the second laboratory the experimenter told the subject that the purpose of his experiment was to study power of concentration. Subjects were given the d2 Test, a concentration test developed by Brickenkamp. The experimenter read aloud the instructions recommended by Brickenkamp (1962), and the subject worked out the examples given on the test paper. Just at the moment when the subjects were supposed to start working on the test items, the procedure was interrupted. The subjects were asked to concentrate on the cognitions and feelings they were experiencing at this moment. They were then asked to indicate how much they were thinking about the Raven Matrices, their performance on the Raven Matrices, and the causes for and possible consequences of their performance on the Raven Matrices. All answers were given on 7-point scales with the poles *no such cognitions at all* and *extremely distracted by such cognitions.* Subsequently they had to work on the d2 Test. After finishing the test, they were asked to indicate how much effort they had expended on the d2 Test on a 7-point scale with the poles *no effort at all,* and *very much effort.*

At the end of the experiment, the subjects were thoroughly debriefed regarding the manipulation and the real purpose of the study.

Results

Effectiveness of the manipulation. Two failure and four success subjects did not label their performance as being either more of a failure or more of a success in line with the intended manipulation. The data from these subjects were dropped from the analysis. From the remaining 37 subjects, 18 were in the failure and 19 in the success condition. The attributions subjects ascribed for their outcome did not differ with regard to their internality, stability, and globality as a function of either success or failure (all Fs $<$ 1.5).

Amount of state orientation. Figure 2 shows the amount of the subjects' state orientation (composite score of all four items) while working on the d2 Test as a function of the induced outcome and the attribution made. Subjects were differentiated across the median of their composite attribution scores (composite score = internal + stable + global).

An analysis of variance showed a main effect for the outcome manipulation ($F(1,33) = 5.2, p < .05$) and the expected interaction between the outcome manipulation and the attributions made ($F(1,33) = 4.4, p < .05$). In line with our predictions, failure caused an increment in state orientation only when it was attributed to internal-stable-global causes. A further analysis indicated that the influence of attribution on state orientation following failure was especially due to the attribution-generality scores (i.e., stability + globality). Although internality also correlated with state orientation in the predicted direction, this correlation failed to reach significance (cf. Table 1).

The mediating role of importance. As can be seen from Table 1, attribution-generality scores correlated in the predicted direction with the importance attached to the failure. However, in contrast to our predictions, there was no correlation between the perceived importance of the failure and the internality of the perceived importance of the failure and the internality of the attributions. In line with the assumption that perceived importance has a mediating role in the development of state orientation following failure, students were increasingly state-oriented the more they perceived the failure to be personally important ($r = .63, p < .01$). Furthermore, the correlation between state orientation and the attribution-generality scores decreased to $r = .28$

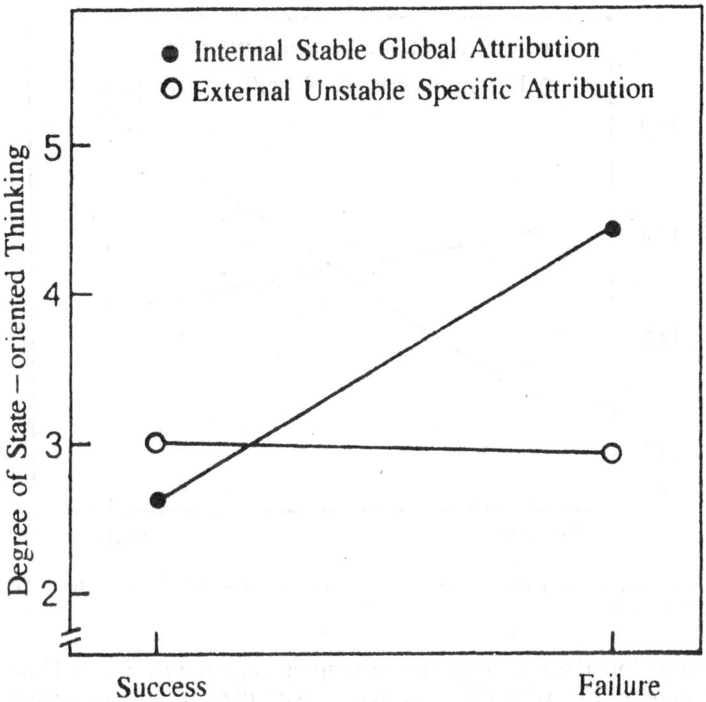

Figure 2 Degree of state-oriented thinking while working on the d2 Test dependent on success vs. failure on the Raven-Matrices and kind of outcome-attribution.

(nonsignificant) when the importance ratings were treated as a concomitant variable. Although the correlation between attribution-internality scores and state orientation increased to $r = .36$ after controlling importance ratings, it still failed to reach significance.

Changes in effort. In line with our hypotheses, subjects increased their efforts on the d2 Test in comparison to the Raven Matrices following failure on the latter ($M = +.7$) and slightly decreased their efforts following success ($M = .1$; $F(1,33) = 9.3, p < .01$).

Table 1 Pearson Correlations Between Attribution-Internality and Attribution-Generality Scores and State Orientation, Importance, Increment in Effort, and Performance Following Failure on the Raven Matrices

	Attribution of Internality	Attribution of Generality[1]
State Orientation	.28	.45*
Importance	.00	.40*
Increment in Effort	−.13	−.44*
Performance	−.20	−.50*

* $p < .05$
[1] Attribution-Generality Scores = Stability + Globality

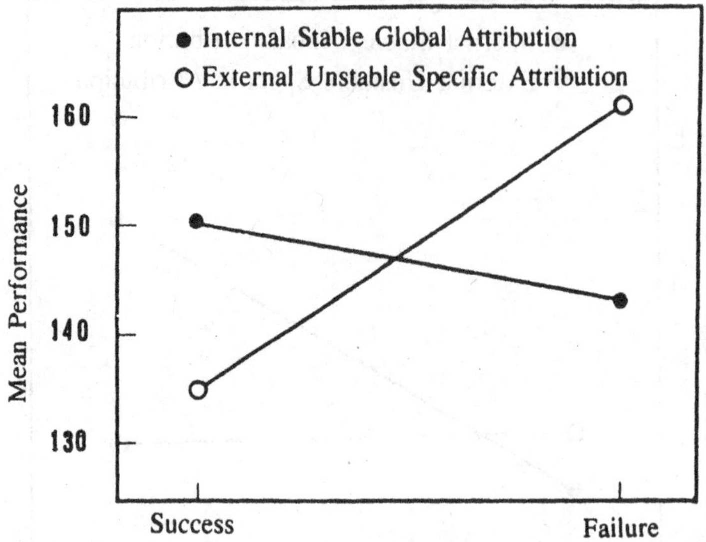

Figure 3 Mean performance on the d2 Test dependent on success vs. failure on the Raven-Matrices and kind of outcome attribution.

No effects were found using composite attribution scores (all *F*s < 1.9). However, the increment in effort following failure correlated with the attribution-generality scores (cf. Table 1). In agreement with our hypothesis, subjects showed a lower increase in effort, the more they attributed their failure to stable and global causes.

Performance. Figure 3 shows the number of correctly checked d's in the d2 Test as a function of the outcome on the Raven Matrices and the attribution-composite scores. An analysis of variance showed only one significant effect, the expected interaction between the independent variables *outcome* and *attribution* ($F(1,33) = 4.6, p < .05$). In line with our assumptions, subjects showed the best performance when they failed on the Raven Matrices and attributed their failure to internal-stable-global causes. Further correlational analysis indicated that the effect of attributions on performance following failure on previous tasks was especially due to the attribution-generality scores (cf. Table 1). Although attribution-internality scores correlated with performance in the same direction, this correlation did not reach significance.

Discussion

The results support some of the central ideas of our model. Individuals who are exposed to repeated failure show differing amounts of state orientation and effort while working on a subsequent, dissimilar task, depending on the kind of attributions they consider responsible for the failure. Following failure, people (1) tend to become increasingly state-oriented the more they prefer internal, and in particular, stable and global attributions; and (2) increase their effort the more they attribute the failure to unstable and specific causes. Furthermore, our results indicate that the link between failure attributions and state orientation is partly mediated by the importance people attach to the failure. Concerning performance-related consequences of failure, we were able to show that, following failure, the subjects who make external, unstable, and specific attributions demonstrate the best performance. Remember that as a consequence of failure these subjects showed a performance-boosting increment in effort without any performance-hindering state orientation.

Of course, there may be some interpretative ambiguities. One could argue that increased state orientation following failure causes internal-stable-global attributions instead of the other way round. However, if increased state orientation causes internal-stable-global attributions, there would be a greater tendency to such attributions following failure rather than following success. As the results indicate, such differences do not exist. Moreover, attribution and importance ratings were assessed simultaneously, so that perceived importance may have caused a tendency toward stable and global attribution instead of the other way round.

References

Abramson, L. Y., Seligman, M. E. P., & Teasdale, J. D. (1978). Learned helplessness in humans: Critique and reformulation. *Journal of Abnormal Psychology*, **87**, 49–74.

Atkinson, J. W., & Birch, D. A. (1974). The dynamics of achievement-oriented activity. In J. W. Atkinson & J. O. Raynor (Eds.), *Motivation and achievement*. Washington, D. C.: Winston.

Brickenkamp, R. (1962). *Test d2: Aufmerksamkeits-Belastungs-Test* (The d2 Test: A concentration test). Göttingen: Hogrefe.

Carver, C. S. (1979). A cybernetic model of self-attention processes. *Journal of Personality and Social Psychology*, **37**, 1251–1281.

Carver, C. S., Blaney, P. H., & Scheier, M. F. (1979). Reassertion and giving up: The interactive role of self-directed attention and outcome expectancy. *Journal of Personality and Social Psychology*, **37**, 1859–1870.

Coyne, J. C., Metalsky, G. I., & Lavelle, T. L. (1980). Learned helplessness as experimenter-induced failure and its alleviation with attentional redeployment. *Journal of Abnormal Psychology*, **89**, 350–357.

Diener, C. I., & Dweck, C. S. (1978). An analysis of learned helplessness: Continuous changes in performance, strategy, and achievement cognitions following failure. *Journal of Personality and Social Psychology*, **36**, 451–462.

Follette, V. M., & Jacobson, N. S. (1987). Importance of attributions as a predictor of how people cope with failure. *Journal of Personality and Social Pschology*, **52**, 1205–1211.

Hiroto, D. S. (1974). Locus of control and learned helplessness. *Journal of Experimental Psychology*, **102**, 187–193.

Hiroto, D. S., & Seligman, M. E. P. (1975). Generality of learned helplessness in man. *Journal of Personality and Social Psychology*, **31**, 311–327.

Kuhl, J. (1981). Motivational and functional helplessness: The moderating effect of action versus state orientation. *Journal of Personality and Social Pscyhology*, **40**, 155–170.

Kuhl, J. (1984). Volitional aspects of achievement motivation and learned helplessness: Toward a comprehensive theory of action-control. In B. A. Maher (Ed.), *Progress in experimental personality research* (Vol 13). New York: Academic Press.

Kuhl, J., & Weiss, M. (in press). Performance deficits following uncontrollable failure: Impaired action control or generalized expectancy deficits. In J. Kuhl & J. Beckmann (Eds.), *Volition and personality: Action- and state-oriented modes of control*. Göttingen: Hogrefe.

Lavelle, T. L., Metalsky, G. I., & Coyne, J. C. (1979). Learned helplessness, test anxiety, and acknowledgement of contingencies. *Journal of Abnormal Psychology*, **88**, 381–387.

Liebert, R. M., & Morris, L. W. (1967). Cognitive and emotional components of test anxiety: A distinction and some initial data. *Psychological Reports*, **20**, 975–978.

Mikulincer, M., & Nizan, B. (1978). Causal attribution, cognitive interference, and the generalization of learned helplessness. *Journal of Personality and Social Psychology*, **55**, 470–478.

Peterson, C., Semmel, A., von Baeyer, C., Abramson, L. Y., Metalsky, G. I., & Seligman, M. E. P. (1982). The Attributional Style Questionnaire. *Cognitive Therapy and Research*, **6**, 287–299.

Raven, J. C. (1974/1975). *Advanced progressive matrices*. London: Lewis.

Roth, S., & Kubal, L. (1975). Effects of noncontingent reinforcement on tasks of differing importance: Facilitation and learned helplessness. *Journal of Personality and Social Psychology*, **32**, 680–691.

Sarason, I. G. (1975). Anxiety and self-preoccupation. In C. D. Spielberger & I. G. Sarason (Eds.), *Stress and anxiety* (Vol. 2). Washington: Hemisphere.

Seligman, M. E. P. (1975). *Helplessness: On depression, development, and death*. San Francisco: Freeman.

Stiensmeier, J. (1985). Wichtigkeit als Bedingung von Lageorientierung (Importance as a determinant of state orientation). *Archiv für Psychology*, **137**, 1–11.
Stiensmeier, J. (1986). Wichtigkeit und Kontrollerleben als Bedingungen von Lageorientierung (Importance and perceived controllability as determinants of state orientation). *Archiv für Psychologie*, **138**, 127–138.
Stiensmeier, J., Kammer, D., Pelster, A., & Niketta, R. (1985). Attributionsstil und Bewertung als Risikofaktoren der Depressiven Reaktion (Attributional and commitment style as risk factors for depression). *Diagnostica*, **31**, 300–311.
Stiensmeier-Pelster, J. (1988). *Erlernte Hilflosigkeit, Handlungskontrolle und Leistung* (Learned helplessness, action control, and performance). Heidelberg, New York: Springer.
Stiensmeier-Pelster, J., & Schürmann, M. (in press). Theoretical and empirical considerations on the antecedents and consequences of action versus state orientation. In J. Kuhl & J. Beckmann (Eds.), *Volition and personality: Action- and state-oriented modes of control*. Göttingen: Hogrefe.
Weiner, B. (1979). A theory of motivation for some classroom experiences. *Journal of Educational Psychology*, **71**, 3–25.
Weiner, B. (1985). "Spontaneous" causal thinking. *Psychological Bulletin*, **97**, 74–84.
Weiner, B. (1986). *An attributional theory of motivation and emotion*. New York: Springer.
Weiner, B., Nierenberg, R., & Goldstein, M. (1976). Social learning (locus of control) versus attributional (causal stability) interpretations of expectancy of success. *Journal of Personality*, **44**, 52–68.

TEST ANXIETY AND CAUSAL ATTRIBUTIONS: SOME EVIDENCE TOWARD REPLICATION

JOHN J. HEDL, Jr.
The University of Texas, Southwestern Medical Center at Dallas

(Received 6 March 1990)

The purpose of the present study was to examine the nature of causal attributions and their relationship to measures of trait and state test anxiety, and perceptions of success. Eighty-four female undergraduates completed a sentence memory task after which they rated their level of perceived success, generated reasons for their performance, and rated these reasons for their performance along three causal attribution dimensions (internality, stability, globality). Perception of success was related to the three explanatory style dimensions, with internality as the weakest of the three relationships. Although the expected test anxiety-outcome interactions were not found, test anxiety relationships were noted indirectly from both the attribution rating scale analyses and directly from the content analyses. For the former results indicated that the strongest relationships were between test anxiety (trait and state) with perception of success. Content analyses supported the importance of the internality dimension, and supplemented the rating scale analyses. The pattern of findings was interpreted to suggest the importance of task and/or situational variables in the attribution process, a point of recent interest.

KEY WORDS: Test anxiety, causal attributions, internality, stability, globality, success perception

The interest of test anxiety researchers in the attribution process is relatively recent. An early study by Doris and Sarason (1955) suggested that high test-anxious students blamed themselves for programmed failure more than lows. But it wasn't until the late 1970s that another test anxiety study appeared in this area (Arkin & Maruyama, 1979). In a relatively short period of time, however, "People's beliefs about the causes of their success and failures are (sic) ... the crucial intervening cognitions mediating the effects of anxiety on performance" (Arkin, Detchon, & Maruyama, 1982, p. 1111). These attributional inferences are viewed as important since they have been linked to future behavior such as persistence and intensity of effort, approach and avoidance of tasks, and the like (Dweck & Wortman, 1982).

Two different research paradigms have been adopted to study test anxiety and the attributional process. One line of research has used forced-choice techniques adapted from the general attribution literature (see Weiner et al., 1971). These studies involved asking high and low test-anxious students to rate the presence and/or contribution of ability, effort, task difficulty, or luck to their performance. In several studies, Arkin and his colleagues, using this Weiner-type methodology, found a weak relationship between performance anxiety and specific attributions in a college course (Arkin & Maruyama, 1979), and a tendency for attributions to change overt the course of a semester (Arkin, Detchon, & Maruyama, 1981). In a later study Arkin et al. (1982) showed that test anxiety was related to attributional accounts of the factors influencing performance in an anagram task. Recently, Leppin, Schwarzer, Belz, Jerusalem, and Quast (1987) used this methodology in an

Address correspondence to: John J. Hedl, Jr., Ph.D., The University of Texas, Southwestern Medical Center at Dallas, 5323 Harry Hines Blvd., Dallas, Texas 75235–9089, USA.

anagram task and found test anxiety relationships. Although this forced-choice methodology has yielded variations in attributional processes related to ability, task difficulty, effort and luck, it does not permit students to cite other idiosyncratic causal attributions which might provide additional insight about test anxiety cognitions.

Several more recent test anxiety studies have adopted a paradigm used in the learned helplessness area (see Seligman, Abramson, Semmel, & von Baeyer, 1979) in which students were asked to generate spontaneously their own attribution judgment and then rate their judgment on three dimensions central to the theory of learned helplessness and attribution theory (internality, stability, globality). For example, Arkin, Kolditz and Kolditz (1983) in a classroom test situation noted significant relationships (albeit modest) between test anxiety and internality and stability, but not globality for students who perceived their performance to be a failure. In contrast, Hedl (1987), in a laboratory-based memory experiment, used this methodology and found globality to differentiate high and low test-anxious students, given a low perception of success, and not internality nor stability. Thus, we have inconsistent evidence in these two experiments about the relative importance of the internality, stability, and globality dimensions for understanding test anxiety and attribution processes.

The purpose of the present study was to replicate the findings of Hedl (1987), using the second type of open-ended attribution rating methodology. Measures of trait and state test anxiety (worry, emotionality) were related to perceptions of success and explanatory style (internality, stability, globality) in a sentence memory experiment. The sentence memory task used in Hedl (1987), which will not be discussed in this paper, was modified and designed to explore the relationship of test anxiety to sentence encoding strategies (imagery, semantic) and effort-toward-comprehension processes (see Hedl & Bartlett, 1985; in press). Content analyses of the students' self-generated attributions were completed as before and related to test anxiety and perceived success.

METHOD

Subjects

Subjects were 84 female volunteers from introductory psychology classes at a local metropolitan university who received course credit for their participation.

Instrumentation

The Test Anxiety Inventory (TAI: Spielberger, 1980) was used to assess level of trait test anxiety. The Worry-Emotionality Questionnaire was used to measure state test anxiety (WEQ: Morris, Davis & Hutchings, 1981). Both scales yield total scores as well as subscale scores for worry and emotionality.

Self-ratings of success were used since prior research has shown large individual differences in individuals' subjective definition of success and failure (see Arkin & Maruyama, 1979) and this methodology was used in Hedl (1987). Perceived success is not isomorphic with actual success, but significant correlations ($ps < .01$) with the two memory measures were noted with the success perception measure in this study (.50 with free recall; .57 with cued recall). This perception of success measure was derived by summing the three self ratings for encoding, free recall and cued recall. The endpoints of this 11-point probability of success scale were "definitely didn't do well" and "definitely did well."

Procedures

The present experiment used procedures similar to our previous memory experiments (see Hedl & Bartlett, 1981, 1982, 1985, 1989, in press, for descriptions of the sentence materials and experimental protocols). After an introduction to the experiment students completed the TAI followed by the presentation of the sentence materials and then the memory test procedures (free recall, cued recall). Students then completed the WEQ with retrospective state instructions. They then responded, using an eleven-point probability scale, to indicate how well they thought they performed during the comprehension, free recall, and cued recall phases of the experiment.

Students then wrote down the "main cause" of their performance today with one line provided for the response. Following Seligman et al. (1979) and our previous study (Hedl, 1987), students rated their "cause" along three dimensions using a 7-point scale defined as follows:

Dimension	*Attribution Question*
Internality/Externality	Is the cause of your performance today due to something about you or something about other people or circumstances? (*Totally due to circumstances* = 1; *Totally due to me* = 7).
Stability/Instability	Will the cause of your performance today be present again in the future? (*Will never again be present* = 1; *Will always be present* = 7).
Globality/Specificity	Is the cause something that just influences your performance in this experiment or does it also influence other areas of your life? (*Influences just this particular situation* = 1; *Influences all situations in my life* = 7).

High scores are thus indicative of attributions that are internal, stable, and global with low scores indicative of attributions that are external, unstable, and specific.

Finally, students rated the percentage of time they spent "concentrating" on the sentences from 0% to 100% (11-point scale). Students were then debriefed and given the opportunity to ask questions about the experiment.

RESULTS

Multiple regression methodology was used to examine the relationship of test anxiety, perceptions of success, and their interaction to the observed attribution ratings of internality, stability, and globality. Content analyses related the types of self-generated causes to levels of test anxiety (trait and state) and perceived success. The means, standard deviations, and intercorrelations of the test anxiety and attribution measures are given in Table 1. The intercorrelations of the trait and

Table 1 Means, Standard Deviations, and Intercorrelations of the Test Anxiety and Attribution Variables ($N = 84$)

		Attribution Ratings			
	Mean (SD)	Total	I	S	G
Trait Test Anxiety (TAI)					
Total Score	42.0 (10.9)	−13	−07	−11	−10
TAI Worry	15.1 (5.0)	−17	−06	−19	−12
TAI Emotionality	18.0 (5.0)	−10	−08	−04	−08
State Test Anxiety					
Total Score	15.7 (4.8)	−05	00	−07	−04
WEQ Worry	9.1 (3.2)	−13	−08	−14	−05
WEQ Emotionality	6.6 (2.4)	07	10	05	−01
Success Perception	1.7 (.46)	40**	19	32**	33**
Attribution Ratings					
Total Score	15.6 (3.2)	—	70**	72**	70**
Internality	5.5 (1.5)	—	—	28*	20
Stability	5.0 (1.4)	—	—	—	26*
Globality	5.1 (1.6)	—	—	—	—
Concentration	.5 (.25)	20	00	17	26*

Note. I = Internality; S = Stability; G = Globality.
Decimals are omitted from the correlations.
*$p < .05$ **$p < .01$

state test anxiety measures are given in Table 2. The data have been collapsed across two encoding conditions (imagery, semantic) as preliminary analyses showed the same general pattern (see Hedl & Bartlett, 1985). The structure of the results section is similar to Hedl (1987).

Trait Test Anxiety, Perceived Success, and Attributions

Multiple regression methodology was used to examine the effects of trait test anxiety (TAI total score)[1], perceived success (summated rating), and their interaction on the attribution ratings. To reduce problems of multicollinearity among the three predictors, the deviation score approach was used (see Cohen, 1975, p. 227); that is, TAI and perceived success scores were expressed as the deviation from their respective means while the interaction term was the product of the two deviation scores (see also Cronbach, 1987). All analyses used the regression approach with simultaneous testing of effects.

Following Hedl (1987), an initial analysis focused on the total attribution scores derived by summing the three ratings for internality, stability, and globality for each student (see Peterson, Villanova, & Raps, 1985). This analysis yielded a significant overall model ($F(3,80) = 5.51, p < .002$), and a significant effect for perception of success ($t = 3.36, p < .002$). The effects for test anxiety and the interaction were not significant.

The individual analyses of the stability ($F(3,80) = 3.13, p < .03$) and globality ($F(3,80) = 3.29, p < .03$) ratings yielded the same pattern of a significant overall model. Additionally, level of perceived success was significantly related (positively)

1. The total score was used given the significant correlation between the two subscales ($r = .59, p < .01$) in this experiment, and the robust correlation between total to TAI worry and TAI emotionality subscales ($rs = .89, p < .001$).

Table 2 Intercorrelations of the Test Anxiety, Success, and Concentration Measures ($N = 84$)

	2	3	4	5	6	7	8
Trait Test Anxiety							
1. TAI Total	85**	89**	35**	40**	18	−09	−33**
2. TAI Worry	—	59**	34**	47**	06	−11	−31**
3. TAI Emotionality	—	—	32**	28**	26**	−06	−24*
State Test Anxiety							
4. WEQ Total	—	—	—	89**	81**	21	−25*
5. WEQ Worry	—	—	—	—	46**	16	−37**
6. WEQ Emotionality	—	—	—	—	—	21	−01
7. Concentration	—	—	—	—	—	—	13
8. Success (see right-most column)							

Note. Decimals are omitted.
*$p < .05$ **$p < .01$

to both stability ($t = 2.64$, $p < .01$) and globality ratings ($t = 2.89$, $p < .005$). Neither level of test anxiety nor the interaction were significant for either analysis. In contrast, the analysis of the internality ratings did not yield any significant effects.

State Test Anxiety and Attribution Ratings

An initial model examined the total attribution score as a function of state test worry, level of perceived success, and their interaction. The overall model reached significance ($F(3,80) = 5.92$, $p < .002$) as did the individual effect for success perception ($t = 3.25$, $p < .002$). The state test worry and interaction effects were not significant for the total score.

Similar to the TAI findings, the individual analyses yielded significant overall models for the stability ($F(3,80) = 3.49$, $p < .02$) and globality ratings ($F(3,80) = 3.52$, $p < .02$). Level of perceived success was again predictive of the stability ratings ($t = 2.36$, $p < .03$) and globality ratings ($t = 3.01$, $p < .004$). And, state test worry was unrelated to the stability and globality dimensions. Neither level of state test anxiety nor perception of success were predictive of internality ratings. Further, none of the three analyses yielded a significant interaction term.

Trait Test Anxiety, State Anxiety, and Perceived Success

To examine the independent effects of trait test anxiety and state test anxiety (worry and emotionality) with perceived success, a model with TAI total scores and WEQ worry and WEQ emotionality scores as predictors was tested. Here the overall model was significant ($F(3,80) = 7.02$, $p < .0003$). Both level of test anxiety ($t = -1.95$, $p < .05$) and level of state worry yielded significant negative relationships ($t = -3.16$, $p < .003$) with perceived success. Level of state emotionality was only marginally related to perceived success when the effects of trait test anxiety and state worry were taken into account ($t = -1.75$, $p < .09$).

Content Analyses of Self-Generated Attribution Causes

To supplement the attribution rating analyses, a content analysis of subjects' written responses was conducted using the categorical scheme used in Hedl (1987) which was derived from one reported by Peterson, Schwartz, and Seligman (1981), and used by Arkin et al. (1983) (see also Janoff-Bulman, 1979). Each attributional statement generated by the students was coded as external, behavioral, or characterological. The external category included attributions referring to situations or circumstances, other people, luck, fate, God, etc. The behavioral category included attributions to some action by the subject, such as preparation, effort (or lack of it), etc. Responses in this category were further coded as positive ("tried hard") or negative ("didn't try hard"). The characterological category included references to personality characteristics such as ability, intelligence, etc. As with the prior study the distinction between behavioral and characterological attributions concerned whether the attribution referred to something the student *did* or something the student *has*.

A mixed category (where several attributions were used by the student) and uncodeable category were also included in the analysis. Agreement of two raters, blind to any information about the subjects, was 95% for the written responses. In cases of disagreement, the two raters came to a mutual decision after discussion. Two subjects did not write down a "cause" and were excluded from the content analysis.

Table 3 presents the frequency of attributions coded according to this attribution scheme, presented separately by level of test anxiety (trait and state) and level of perceived success. For comparisons to Arkin et al. (1983), a tripartite split was used for the anxiety distributions, a median split for the success perception measure.

Table 3 Frequency of Self-Generated Causal Attributions as a Function of Test Anxiety and Perceived Success ($N = 82$)

	Nature of the Causal Attribution				
	Char	Behavioral	External	Mixed	Un
High Trait Test Anxiety					
Success	1+	6 (4+, 2−)	3	0	0
Failure	2−	10 (1+, 9−)	4	0	0
Low/Mid Trait Test Anxiety					
Success	5+	13 (11+, 2−)	6	4	3
Failure	0	12 (4+, 8−)	10	2	0
High State Worry					
Success	0	4 (1+, 3−)	3	2	1
Failure	2−	7 (1+, 6−)	12	1	1
Low/Mid State Worry					
Success	5+	17 (15+, 2−)	5	2	1
Failure	1+	14 (3+, 11−)	3	1	0
Totals %	8 (9.7%)	42 (51.2%)	23 (28%)	6 (7.3%)	3 (3.6%)

Note. Char = Characterological, Un = Uncodeable. Success and failure categories determined by a median split.

Overall (bottom row of Table 3), the predominant self-generated cause was rated as behavioral (51%), with 43% of these coded as positive in nature and 57% negative. Twenty-three percent of the causes were coded as external, and approximately 10% were characterological. Only seven percent involved two or more causes and four percent were uncodeable (e.g., "No special cause").

Given the similarity of the mid and low TAI groups across the self-generated causal categories, they were combined for the analyses. The mixed and uncodeable categories were excluded from consideration given the small expected frequencies. For the high TAI group, a 2 × 3 chi square was not significant, nor was a 2 × 3 analysis for the combined low/mid TAI group. Several subanalyses were nevertheless suggestive. For the characterological category and the two TAI groups, a Fisher's exact probability was marginal ($p = .10$), suggesting that positive characterological attributions are more likely to be given by the low/mid TAI group under conditions of perceived success. And negative characterological attributions were more likely by the high TAI students under failure perception. Inspection of the characterological responses for low TAI students showed that they generally related to positive, enduring characteristics, mostly related to memory ability ("I have a good memory"). The two negative characterological attributions given by the high TAI students were to lack of memory ability ("When free recalling, I usually have difficulty remembering").

Analyses of the frequency of positive and negative behavioral attributions were suggestive as well. For the high TAI students, the chi square was 3.27 ($1, N = 16, p < .07$); for the combined mid/low TAI group it was 4.86 ($1, N = 25, p < .03$). This reflected the tendency for all students to cite more positive behavioral attributions given a success perception, and more negative behavioral attributions given a failure perception. The analyses of the external category were not significant for the high TAI group, but the combined low/mid TAI group showed the highest frequency of external attributions under a failure perception.

The cross-classification by level of state worry yielded a similar pattern for the characterological and behavioral attributions across success and failure perceptions. In addition, the external category emerged and suggested that high state worried students (i.e., those who reacted most to the task) tended to externalize failure more than the other three groups (Fisher's Exact = .058).

Anxiety and Performance

For consistency of presentation with the prior study, the correlations between the test anxiety measures and memory performance (free and cued recall) are presented in Table 4. These data have been reported elsewhere in more detail (Hedl & Bartlett, 1985, in press). For the TAI, all three subscale scores were signific[illegible] related to free and cued recall memory performance.

For state test anxiety, a different pattern emerged. Bo[illegible] the total WEQ score and WEQ worry score were significantly related to free and cued recall memory performance. The WEQ emotionality score was not related to either memory measure. Only state test anxiety (total, worry) yielded significant relationships with the self ratings of sentence comprehension by the students (column 1).

Concentration

The regression model examining trait test anxiety and perceived success for the self-ratings of "concentration" was not significant ($F(3,80) = 1.22$). For the state

Table 4 Intercorrelations of the Test Anxiety and Memory Performance Measures ($N = 84$)

	Comprehension	Free Recall	Cued Recall
Test Anxiety Inventory			
TAI Total	−.10	−.39**	−.32**
TAI Worry	−.05	−.24**	−.24**
TAI Emotionality	−.11	−.40**	−.32**
WEQ Questionnaire			
WEQ Total	−.23*	−.28**	−.35**
WEQ Worry	−.31**	−.29**	−.44**
WEQ Emotionality	−.05	−.17	−.12

Note. Memory performance has been collapsed across two encoding conditions (imagery, semantic).
$^{*}p < .05$ $^{**}p < .01$

test anxiety analyses, however, the overall regression model was significant ($F(3,80) = 3.91, p < .02$ and significant effects ($ps < .02$) were noted for worry ($t = 2.28$), level of perceived success ($t = 2.49$), and their interaction ($t = 2.38$).

To explore the conditional relationship between worry and perceived success on reported concentration, three representative regression equations (see Cohen, 1977, p. 312) were developed, one for a low worry score (−3), one for an average worry score (Mean), and one for a high worry score (+3). The resulting representative equations are:

Low Worry: Concentration = .02 (Success) + .49
Average Worry: Concentration = .16 (Success) + .55
High Worry: Concentration = .30 (Success) + .60

From inspection of these equations, given a low worry score there is little or no linear regression of concentration on success perception. In contrast, for average and high worry scores a positive linear regression is noted with the slope of concentration on success perception becoming steeper as worry increases. Thus, a poor perceived outcome combined with high worry affected concentration most strongly.

DISCUSSION

The results were generally consistent with those reported by Hedl (1987) in terms of the nature and direction of the relationships between trait and state test anxiety, and perceived success within this experimental memory paradigm. The findings for test anxiety-performance and self-reported concentration were in accord with prior research, and will not be discussed per se. Of more primary interest, with minor exceptions, the attribution measures generally varied as expected from the literature in relation to outcome perception, a point covered first. Test anxiety and attribution comparisons with Hedl (1987) and Arkin et al. (1983) are then addressed.

In this study, both the stability and globality dimensions were significantly correlated to level of perceived success, while the internality correlation was marginally significant ($r(82) = .19, p < .10$). The results of the self-generated attribution analyses to be discussed subsequently suggests the prevalence of internal attributions in this situation, however. Further, internality had the highest mean score (5.50 on a 7-point scale) of the three attribution dimensions in this study (see Table 1, column 1) and we might have a ceiling effect which served to reduce the correlation somewhat. For Hedl (1987), main effects for internality and globality were significant while the main effect for stability was not. For Arkin et al. (1983), internality, stability, and globality were significant in relation to outcome perception.

Collectively, across all three studies with this attribution paradigm we have consistent evidence for the importance of the internality, stability, and globality dimensions to outcome perception. Of nine relationships examined, seven were significant, one was marginal (internality), and one was not significant (stability). The marginal internality effect in the present study might be partially attributed to a ceiling effect as mentioned previously. For stability, no reason is apparent for the lack of a main effect in Hedl (1987). There was, however, suggestive evidence ($p < .10$) of a relationship between test anxiety and stability ratings under ambiguous success perceptions (see Hedl, 1987, p. 59). These variations may also be related to more general reliability of measurement issues related to these one-item scales, a point offered in the depression literature (Coyne & Gottlieb, 1983; Peterson et al., 1982; Peterson et al., 1985). Thus, these three studies support the typical asymmetrical outcome-attribution covariation coined the "self-serving bias" (Arkin, Cooper, & Kolditz, 1980).

In reviewing the three studies from a test anxiety-causal attribution perspective, several points of comparison are informative. The first concerns the presence or absence of significant test anxiety by outcome perception interactions for the three attribution dimensions. The second concerns the consistency of the self-generated causal attribution patterns across studies. These will be addressed in turn.

In their major analyses Arkin et al. (1983) noted significant test anxiety - perceived outcome interactions for internality and stability, but not for globality. A significant test anxiety-outcome interaction was found for globality in Hedl (1987) while none of these interactions were significant in the present study.

The lack of consistent test anxiety-outcome interactions for the three attribution ratings in the two lab-based experiments was somewhat surprising. However, the interactions for the internal and stability dimensions (different measures) were nonsignificant in the laboratory anagram task reported by Arkin et al. (1982) as well. Most likely, it may point to the importance of task (classroom test vs. laboratory task) and situational characteristics (clarity of feedback, importance of grade, etc.) for the study of test anxiety and attributions. It may be that the use of an actual classroom examination where outcome is important to a course grade, coupled with feedback that is relatively explicit (i.e., a grade score, etc.) results in a greater threat, and therefore more effort to "explain" the result by the student (Arkin et al., 1981). As one student wrote in the present study "I feel I did personally well because the outcome isn't weighted in a grade."

The content analyses of the self-generated "causes," a second point of comparison between studies, is informative for several reasons. First, they supplement the information provided by the rating analyses. Second, they again direct our attention to the potential importance of task and situational characteristics for the study of attributions and test anxiety.

Although the variations were modest, the pattern of causal statements tended to vary as a function of level of trait (and state) test anxiety and level of perceived success in predictable ways. Low test-anxious students tended to attribute success to positive, characterological attributes (memory ability) and effort. In contrast, given a low success perception, there was some evidence that the external and behavioral attributions (primarily lack of effort) were more frequent for these low/mid test-anxious.

Comparatively, the effects for the high test-anxious students were not as dramatic across outcome conditions. For failure, the predominant cause was again behavioral (lack of effort). They did cite negative characterological attributions for failure. For success, the pattern was not as pronounced. External attributions appeared with similar frequency (25% vs. 30%) across the two outcome conditions. Analyses as a function of state worry reinforced the trait findings. For low/mid worried students success was attributed to positive effort and characterological traits, while failure was attributed to lack of effort. For the highly worried students, in order of priority, failure was predominately attributed to external influences, lack of effort, and to negative characterological traits.

Compared to Arkin et al. (1983), the low/mid test-anxious students responded similarly. That is, they were more internal following success, and more external following failure. The major difference between studies seemed to occur for the high test-anxious students for the failure conditions. The highs in the present study were less characterological than Arkin et al.'s (12% vs. 30%), more behavioral (62% vs. 39%) with external attributions being similar (23% vs. 25%). The suggestion is that the task (actual, artificial) may be an important determinant of observed causal attributions, particularly for the elicitation of characterological attributions.

In this experiment, there were few references to ability and few to task difficulty. This pattern was noted in Hedl (1987) as well. Thus, when students generate their own "causes," as compared to rating the presence or absence of ability, task difficulty, effort, luck and so forth, these ability and task difficulty attributions are infrequent. In the two Hedl studies the overall rate of characterological attributions across all students was approximately 10% while the rate was approximately 11% in Arkin et al. (1983). Methodologically, the study of causal content statements may require larger sample sizes.

The differences in self-generated causal content between these studies suggests that lab-based experiments may yield different patterns of attributions compared to more real-life situations such as classrooms (see Arkin et al., 1981). Presumably in this context the stakes for failure of a classroom test are higher, and causal explanations for failure more complex, and ego-defensive of self-serving (Arkin et al., 1981). As Frieze (1976) noted earlier, students work harder to explain failure than success. Arkin et al. (1983) also noted a number of multi-causal explanations, while few were noted in the two lab-based experiments. They also noted that anxiety reactions were cited as being causal by the students, while anxiety attributions were not found in the lab-based experiments.

While a task/situational interpretation is preferred to account for variation in the findings, differences in types of subjects cannot be discounted. Arkin et al. (1983) included both males and females while Hedl (1987) and the present experiment included females only. Gender differences in the attribution literature have been acknowledged, particularly if level of initial expectation varies by gender (Deaux, 1984). For the internality, stability, and globality measures specifically, measurement issues may be a consideration as well, a point suggested in the depression literature in reference to the variation in results across studies.

Lastly, in this study the pattern of relationships between trait and state test anxiety, perception of success, and attribution ratings were similar across Hedl (1987) and the present study. This consistency of findings suggests the viability of a model originally suggested by Hedl (1987). Outcome perception (success) exerts a direct influence on the attribution process, and that trait and state test anxiety exert a more indirect influence. Specifically, trait test anxiety is related to the attribution process through its direct link to success perception, and indirectly through its relationship with state worry. In turn, state worry (but not emotionality) is related through its relationship with success perception. While this interpretation appears supported by the findings of two studies, it remains for future research to address this interpretation using causal modeling techniques.

In summary, the present findings were generally consistent with prior research work, and suggest the viability of including attributional processes in a test anxiety transactional model (Spielberger & Vagg, 1987). Both trait and state test anxiety were found to have predictive roles, primarily in relation to the perception of task success. Task and situational variables appear to influence the attribution process in relation to test anxiety and need to be considered in comparing attributional outcomes across studies, a point made by Leppin et al. (1987) just recently. Future research delineating the salient characteristics of tasks and situations would seem to be in order.

Author Notes

Portions of these data were presented at the meeting of the Society for Test Anxiety Research, Amsterdam, The Netherlands, June 30 - July 2, 1989.
The author thanks several anonymous reviewers for suggestions to improve the manuscript.

References

Arkin, R. M., & Maruyama, G. M. (1979). Attribution, affect, and college exam performance. *Journal of Educational Psychology*, **71**, 85–93.

Arkin, R. M., Cooper, H., & Kolditz, T. (1980). A statistical review of the literature concerning the self-serving attribution bias in interpersonal influence situations. *Journal of Personality*, **48**, 435–448.

Arkin, R. M., Detchon, C. S., & Maruyama, G. M. (1981). Causal attributions of high and low achievement motivation college students. *Motivation and Emotion*, **5**, 139–152.

Arkin, R. M., Detchon, C. S., & Maruyama, G. M. (1982). Roles of attribution, affect, and cognitive interference in test anxiety. *Journal of Personality and Social Psychology*, **43**, 1111–1124.

Arkin, R. M., Kolditz, T. A., & Kolditz, K. K. (1983). Attributions of the test-anxious student: Self-assessment in the classroom. *Personality and Social Psychology Bulletin*, **9**, 271–280.

Cohen, J. (1975). *Applied multiple regression/Correlation analysis for the behavioral sciences*. Hillsdale, NJ. Erlbaum

Coyne, J. C. & Gotlieb, I. H. (1983). The role of cognition in depression: A critical appraisal. *Psychological Bulletin*, **94**, 472–505.

Cronbach, L. J. (1987). Statistical tests for moderator variables: Flaws in analyses recently proposed. *Psychological Bulletin*, **102**, 414–417.

Deaux, K. (1984). From individual differences to social categories. *American Psychologist*, **39**, 105–116.

Doris, J., & Sarason, S. B. (1955). Test anxiety and blame assignments in a failure situation. *Journal of Abnormal and Social Psychology*, **50**, 335–338.

Dweck, C. S., & Wortman, C. B. (1982). Learned helplessness, anxiety, and achievement motivation. In H. W. Krohne & L. Laux (Eds.), *Achievement, stress, and anxiety* (pp. 93–125). Washington, DC: Hemisphere.

Frieze, I. H. (1976). Causal attributions and information-seeking to explain success and failure. *Journal of Research in Personality*, **10**, 293–305.

Hedl, J. J., Jr. (1987). Explorations in test anxiety and attribution theory. In R. Schwarzer, H. M. van der Ploeg, & C. D. Spielberger (Eds.), *Advances in test anxiety research* (Vol. 5) (pp. 55–65). Lisse: Swets & Zeitlinger.
Hedl, J. J., Jr., & Bartlett, J. C. (1981, April). *Test anxiety and sentence memory*. Paper presented at the meeting of the American Educational Research Association, Los Angeles.
Hedl, J. J., Jr., & Bartlett, J. C. (1982), March). *Toward improving the magnitude of test anxiety and sentence memory experiments*. Paper presented at the meeting of the American Educational Research Association, New York.
Hedl, J. J., Jr., & Bartlett, J. C. (1985, March-April). *Test anxiety and effort-toward-comprehension in sentence memory*. Paper presented at the meeting of the American Educational Research Association, Chicago.
Hedl, J. J., Jr., & Bartlett, J. C. (1989). Test anxiety and recognition memory for sentences. *Anxiety Research: An International Journal*, **1**, 269–279.
Hedl, J. J., Jr., & Bartlett, J. C. (in press). Depression and test anxiety in comprehension and memory: Independent effects? In C. D. Spielberger & Diaz-Guerrero, R. (Eds.), *Cross-Cultural Anxiety* (Vol. 4). Washington, DC: Hemisphere.
Janoff-Bulman, R. (1979). Characterological versus behavioral self-blame: Inquiries into depression and rape. *Journal of Personality and Social Psychology*, **37**, 1978–1809.
Leppin, A., Schwarzer, R., Belz, D., Jerusalem, M., & Quast, H.-H. (1987). Causal attribution patterns of high and low test-anxious students. In R. Schwarzer, H. M. van der Ploeg, & C. D. Spielberger (Eds.), *Advances in test anxiety research* (Vol. 5) (pp. 67–86). Lisse: Swets & Zeitlinger.
Morris, L. W., Davis, M. A., & Hutchings, C. H. (1981). Cognitive and emotional components of anxiety: Literature review and a revised worry-emotionality scale. *Journal of Educational Psychology*, **73**, 541–555.
Peterson, C., Schwartz, S. M., & Seligman, M. E. P. (1981). Self-blame and depressive symptoms. *Journal of Personality and Social Psychology*, **41**, 253–259.
Peterson, C., Semmel, A., von Baeyer, C., Abramsom, L. Y., Metalsky, G. I., & Seligman, M. E. P. (1982). The Attributional Style Questionnaire. *Cognitive Therapy and Research*, **6**, 287–299.
Peterson, C., Villanova, P., & Raps, C. S. (1985). Depression and attributions: Factors responsible for inconsistent results in the published literature. *Journal of Abnormal Psychology*, **94**, 165–168.
Seligman, M. E. P., Abramson, L. Y., Semmel, A., & von Baeyer, C. (1979). Depressive attribution style. *Journal of Abnormal Psychology*, **88**, 242–247.
Spielberger, C. D. (1980). *Preliminary manual for the Test Anxiety Manual*. Palo Alto, CA: Consulting Psychologists Press.
Spielberger, C. D., & Vagg, P. R. (1987). The treatment of test anxiety: A transactional process model. In R. Schwarzer, H. M. van der Ploeg, & C. D. Spielberger (Eds.), *Advances in test anxiety research* (Vol. 5). (pp. 179-186). Lisse: Swets & Zeitlinger.
Weiner, B., Frieze, I. H., Kukla, A., Reed, L., Rest, S., & Rosenbaum, R. M. (1971). *Perceiving the causes of success and failure*. Morristown, NJ: General Learning Press.

SUBJECT INDEX

AUTHOR INDEX